Birds of passage

Birds of passage

Migrant labor and industrial societies

Michael J. Piore

Professor of Economics
Massachusetts Institute of Technology

Cambridge University Press

Cambridge
London   New York   Melbourne

Published by the Syndics of the Cambridge University Press
The Pitt Building, Trumpington Street, Cambridge CB2 1RP
Bentley House, 200 Euston Road, London NW1 2DB
32 East 57th Street, New York, NY 10022, USA
296 Beaconsfield Parade, Middle Park, Melbourne 3206, Australia

First published 1979

Printed in the United States of America
Typeset by David E. Seham Associates, Inc., Metuchen, New Jersey
Printed and bound by Hamilton Printing Company, Rensselear,
New York

Library of Congress Cataloging in Publication Data

Piore, Michael J.

Birds of passage

Bibliography: p.

Includes index.

1. Alien labor.   2. Alien labor–United States.
3. Emigration and immigration. I. Title.
HD6300.P56   331.6′2   78–12067
ISBN 0 521 22452 7

To Olga

Contents

Preface ix

1
Introduction *1*

2
The jobs *15*

3
The migrants *50*

4
Particular characteristics of
the migrant labor market *86*

5
The impact of migration on
the place of origin *115*

6
The historical evolution of long-distance
migration in the United States *141*

7
The dilemmas of current
U.S. immigration policy *167*

Notes 193

Bibliography 211

Index 218

Preface

This volume was originally prepared for the National Council on Employment Policy. It is based upon research sponsored by the U.S. Department of Labor, the Sloan Foundation, and the Ford Foundation.

The argument draws heavily upon interviews with migrants and with various people who work with migrants and migrant communities in an official or professional capacity. Without their cooperation, the book would not have been possible.

I am also indebted to a number of students and colleagues whose own research I have drawn upon and who have been helpful in the development of these ideas. The list of people who contributed in this way is too long to include here. Particularly important were my colleagues on the Ford Foundation dualism project, Suzanne Berger, Lisa Peattie, and Martin Rein. I am also grateful to Myron Weiner and the Migration and Development Study Group, which he organized, for creating an institutional framework supportive of work of this kind and to the Center for International Studies at MIT in which both the dualism project and the Study Group have been housed. I am especially indebted as well to Duncan Foley, Charles Myers, Charles Sabel, and Peter Temin, all of whom offered extensive critical comment and advice. This would no doubt be a better book if I had managed to respond more fully to their criticism and accepted more of their suggestions. Finally, I am grateful for the help and support of my wife, Nancy, and my children, Adam and Ana. In a certain sense, the book is really for them.

This book is dedicated to my grandmother. I do not believe it is the story of her own migration: That is a story I have never fully understood. But what I did come to understand through her was that migration to a country like the United States could be a painful, mysterious process, and that most academic accounts offered little to dispel the mystery or alleviate the pain. Understanding that, I came to hear, in conversation with contemporary migrants, a different story. That is the story this book tries to tell.

1
Introduction

In the last twenty years most industrialized Western countries have experienced extremely heavy in-migration of foreign workers. By 1975 foreign workers had come to constitute 10 percent of the labor force in Western Europe as a whole. They represented 11 percent of the labor force in France and 9 percent in West Germany.[1] In some countries the proportion of foreign workers is even higher. In Switzerland it surpasses 25 percent.[2] Since the middle 1960s the United States has also been experiencing a considerable influx of foreign workers: The bulk of our migrant labor force is clandestine and its exact size is consequently unknown. Estimates run from two to twelve million.[3]

In their origins these migrations often went unnoticed. Where they were officially recognized, as in Germany and Northern Europe, they were generally thought to benefit both the sending and the receiving nations. Both countries thought of the migrants as temporary. In the sending country the migration was supposed to relieve population pressure and overcome rural unemployment, to generate scarce foreign exchange, and to develop the skills requisite for an industrial labor force. In the receiving country, migrants were supposed to complement native labor, taking jobs that the latter did not want and in this way overcome critical labor shortages. Over time, however, the migration process has been the source of an increasing number of problems and a focal point of clashes between native and foreign populations.[4] The host countries have been forced to worry about whether to permit workers they initially thought of as temporary to bring their families, and how, when and if they do, to house those families, educate their children, and provide for their health and general social welfare. The migrants themselves, who were initially accepting of wages and working conditions that native workers would not tolerate, have begun to resist these jobs, to organize for improvements in the workplace, and to pressure for access to more attractive job opportunities that natives *do* want.[5] These pressures for better housing, jobs, and social services have brought foreigners into direct conflicts with natives. Such conflicts have been aggravated by latent racial and national prejudices, which the antagonisms between natives and migrants seem to have brought to the fore. The result has often been policy reversals and efforts by the recipient country to curtail the migration process, but that process has turned out to be extremely resistant to these efforts. Even when it originated in governmental efforts and institutions, the government seems unable to bring the population movement to a halt once it has begun. Authorities either lack the techniques for doing so or are unable to command through the political process resources comparable to the rhetoric of official policy; in response to efforts to stop it, the migration goes underground.

The migrations have also created problems for the donor country, which have aggravated its own internal politics and contributed to strained relationships between the receiving and sending nations. The return migrants have proved very resistant to the kinds of industrial jobs in their native lands that they were supposedly learning to fill. Instead, they have more often tended, on returning to their home villages, to use their earnings to buy land or foreign consumption goods. The foreign exchange they bring back thus often serves simply to increase the import of luxury consumer durables, and when it does not, it inflates land prices.[6] The return migrants are often also unwilling to perform traditional agricultural work, and their attitudes have served to degrade such work, even to make it unacceptable among those who have not migrated. In the extreme, return migration has killed traditional agriculture or forced these countries in turn to recruit migrants from still less-developed nations to perform the work. Finally, the migration has served to transmit the economic fluctuations in the industrialized world to the underdeveloped nations that send the manpower: When economic activity declines abroad, remittance falls off; workers are unemployed and sent home; youth, who had anticipated migration, are denied visas. These effects become stronger over time as the sending economy increasingly adjusts to and orients itself toward the migration process.

Characteristics of the migration process and its implications

The migration process out of which these policy problems grow has several distinct characteristics. Some of these characteristics are surprising to our conventional notions of industrial development and economic growth and of the way in which industrial economies operate. But the characteristics of migration seem to provide the clues to an alternative understanding, one which at least serves to resolve some of the paradoxes of the migration process. Perhaps it can resolve some of the dilemmas of policy as well. The first characteristic of the migration process is that it seems to respond to the attraction of the industrial countries. In Europe many governments have in fact organized programs that deliberately recruit migrants and manage their stay. In the United States the process is considerably less institutionalized, and because it is clandestine, its exact nature is somewhat obscure, but here also the strategic factor in initiating the migration and controlling its evolution appears to be the search of American employers for new sources of labor. Second, the migrants appear to be coming to take a distinct set of jobs, jobs that the native labor force refuses to accept. Third, the migrants initially see themselves as temporary workers and plan to return home; however, many of them fail to realize their plans and either never return or come back repeatedly to the industrial country, becoming more or less permanent members of the labor force. Fourth, the migrants themselves appear to be largely unskilled; typically they cannot speak the language of the host country; often they are unschooled and illiterate even in their own language; they sometimes come from backward rural areas with little contact with the kind of urban, industrial environment where they work and live.

The last characteristic is a real paradox, given conventional notions of industrial society. We are accustomed to thinking of industrialization and economic growth as a process that in some basic way involves increasingly sophisticated technologies and a progressively more highly educated and well-trained labor force. Indeed, just a few years ago we were beset by fears that the educational requirements of the economy were surpassing the preparation of the labor force and were leaving a growing residue of technologically unemployed. Why, if this is true, do industrial economies seem to generate these particular migration streams? What are these jobs that native workers do not want? How is it that industrial economies seem not only able to absorb, but in fact are actively seeking out uneducated, illiterate workers from the very types of societies to which they are, in the conventional view of what industrialization is all about, generally contrasted?

If the process of migration in the host country contradicts the conventional notions about industrialization and underdevelopment, then perhaps it is not so surprising that the return migrants should fail to play the role anticipated for them in the country of origin. Those roles after all are also derived from these same conventional notions. Moreover, if the developed nations need unskilled, illiterate workers to fill industrial jobs, perhaps the lack of a skilled labor force is not the obstacle to development it has been thought to be: Perhaps underdeveloped countries also tend to need for their internal development the kind of unskilled, illiterate workers they are sending abroad. And if there is something about industrial society that renders its own labor force ill-adapted to its productive requirements, it should not be surprising – though it is certainly paradoxical – that prolonged exposure to that society should render the migrants less suited, rather than more suited, to the needs of industrialization.

Further exploration of the migration process raises fundamental questions not simply about what the process of economic development and industrialization is about but about how developed economies seem to operate. It is generally supposed that the motivation of the migration process is an income differential between that of the sending region and the employment opportunities at the other end of the migration stream. Such a differential does indeed exist, but it does not seem to govern the migration process in any of the conventional senses of the term. The donor countries are not typically the countries with the lowest incomes, which would provide the widest income differential. There are large surpluses of labor in the home country, but the migration seems to be confined to the numbers of people who can get jobs. Unemployment among migrants in the receiving country seems to be relatively low. The surplus labor might be thought to create jobs in the receiving country, but it doesn't seem to have that effect. This could be attributed to institutional restraints, such as the minimum wage, minimal health and safety standards, and so on, but whenever these restraints operate to curtail labor for jobs that already exist, migration manages to persist by circumventing the law. The surplus labor might be thought to act as a drag upon wages, but relative wages at the bottom of the market do not seem to decline. This too might be the result of an institutional restraint imposed by the minimum wage, but there are sectors of the economy that exploit alien workers by paying them below the minimum. The existence of these sectors raises further questions: Why, if some sectors pay below the minimum, don't all sectors violate the law in this regard? If the minimum wage can be more or less effectively enforced, why can't similar restraints be imposed upon migration itself?

This book is an attempt to answer these questions about the long-distance migration to industrialized areas, to work out the puzzles and resolve the paradoxes out of which these questions arise. It seeks to do this in terms of a single, sustained argument, or theory, about the nature of the migrants and the roles they play within the industrial world. That theory grows out of a variety of research projects, spread over a number of years. In some of these, migration was only peripherally connected to what was being studied. In others, it was the focal point of concern. The most important pieces of research in the development of the argument were: a series of studies of the labor-market problems of black workers in the United States;[7] a study of the nature and origins of Puerto Rican migration to Boston;[8] a continuing investigation of clandestine migration and undocumented workers from the Caribbean basin and Mexico to industrial areas in the United States;[9] studies of the structure and characteristics of low-wage labor markets in Europe.[10] A last body of research material reflected in what follows concerns the historical development of the structure of the American labor market and the role of immigrant workers within it.[11]

Much of the material presented here has been covered elsewhere, in the articles, research reports, and policy papers that result from individual research projects. The principal reason for drawing them together in book form is to present the elements of the theory as parts of a single, unified argument and thereby to emphasize the coherence of the perspective upon the migration phenomenon that is being developed. This seems particularly important for the policy debates toward which much of the research has been directed and in terms of which this book is bound to be read. There has been a tendency for the participants in that debate to pick and choose from the various research reports separate pieces of evidence or distinct analytical points with which they happen to agree and to discard other components as unacceptable or irrelevant, or to combine them with views about migration drawn from a completely different analytical perspective. This is not necessarily wrong. But because the particular view of migration developed here grows out of the inadequacies and paradoxes of other, more traditional views and because a good deal of the plausibility of any one of the elements of the argument derives from the plausibility of the larger story of which it appears to be a part, the argument cannot be *arbitrarily* broken into a series of components.

What is true of the policy debate is true, in a somewhat different sense, of debates within the economic profession, and a second reason for this book is to clarify the relationship between the perspective developed in earlier work and that of conventional economic theory. The perspective upon migration developed here is concerned with the same set of analytical and policy issues that conventional economic theory addresses. It also shares with conventional theory a set of standards for logical consistency and coherence and is meant to be evaluated against those standards. But the argument itself is definitely unconventional. It derives from a perspective upon the nature of economic activity that is fundamentally different from that of conventional economic analysis. Because it is so different, it leads not only to an alternative view of the phenomenon of migration with which it starts but also to a range of issues apparently removed from migration, such as the minimum wage, unemployment, and ultimately the very nature of industrial society.

The contrast to conventional theory can be overdrawn. There is very little in the analytical structure of the argument that conventional theory explicitly rejects and, hence, very little that actually *conflicts* with orthodox analytical approaches. In this sense, the contention is simply that conventional theory is irrelevant to the problem being considered. On the other hand, the argument hinges upon aspects of socioeconomic behavior from which orthodox theory explicitly abstracts and deliberately neglects. It is the role and function of theory to simplify, to repress detail, and, in so doing, to call to the attention of the analyst, the researchers, and, in the case of economic theory, the policy maker, the essential elements of a process. If it fails in this role, by suppressing the details that are essential and bringing to the fore elements that are, in fact, irrelevant or incidental, then the theory itself must be counted a failure. It is basically the conviction that conventional theory fails in this sense and the desire to provide an alternative theory of economic behavior in at least that segment of the labor market that migrants occupy that motivates this book.

All of this can be exemplified by one of the principal theoretical issues raised below, that of how to *describe* jobs and workers. Conventional theory seeks to do this in terms of income. The principal difference among jobs that it recognizes are the differences in the incomes that they offer, and the principal differences among workers are the income opportunities available to them and their own income-generating capacities. Other job attributes and worker traits are suppressed or, more precisely, moved by the nature of the theoretical apparatus to the background of the analyst's perspective. In this, conventional theory treats the market for labor like the market for a shirt or any other commodity that is bought and sold freely and regularly. In so doing, it does not mean to imply that workers *are* shirts, only that by focusing upon those ways in which they resemble shirts and suppressing those ways in which they do not, one can better understand the phenomenon of migration.

This book starts from the proposition that income is not the critical analytical variable, but rather that it is the attempt to view income as such that leads to the paradoxes with which the problem was introduced at the beginning of the chapter. One can better understand migration by ignoring income differences and recognizing instead that people are rooted in a social context in ways that other commodities are not; migrant behavior can be better understood in terms of the specific attributes of the jobs available to migrants and the meaning attached to those attributes in the social context in which work is performed. Again, the contention is not that income makes no difference; nor will it never be an important variable in understanding population movements. The argument, in other words, is not that workers are in *no* way like shirts, nor that there is never any point in recognizing the similarities between workers and shirts. But there *is* a very strong contention that the phenomenon of migration cannot be understood by treating workers like shirts; that the critical factors governing the migration process are the social forces that differentiate the market for men from the market for shirts, and that it is those social forces that the analytical apparatus must bring to the fore.

Because much of the policy debate on immigration has been structured by conventional economic theory, the role accorded income differentials also illustrates misunderstandings that this book seeks to overcome in that area as well. In trying to cope with the flow of undocumented workers to the United States, for example, the emphasis upon income has led people to focus upon the underdeveloped state of the Mexican economy from which many of the migrants came and the population pressures in that country. The notion is that the migrants are coming from Mexico because of the higher wages in the States and that if Mexican per capita income could be raised, either through development or a reduced birthrate or both, the flow of workers would be halted. By the same token, the low-wage scale of the jobs that the migrants take in the United States is attributed to the plentiful supply of labor in Mexico, and it is believed that by reducing migrant flows from Mexico, the jobs would be forced to pay higher wages and be able to attract native workers. Thus, some of my colleagues have wanted to add to the list of policy proposals in the last chapter measures designed to raise the income and reduce the birthrate in Mexico.

The basic thrust of the argument in the book, however, is that job characteristics other than income operate both to make the society tremendously resistant to their elimination and to make native workers reluctant to accept them. This implies that if the income differential between the United States and Mexico were somehow to disappear, the American economy would simply seek elsewhere for other workers. The theory, therefore, deliberately ignores income in order to focus on an alternative set of attributes that will explain why the economy needs these jobs, why native workers reject them, how the society would seek other workers if Mexican labor became scarce, and where it would be likely to find them. The policy suggestions at the end of the book grow out of the answers developed to these questions. To add Mexican economic development to the list, however desirable it may be for other reasons, would thus do violence to the basic thrust of the undertaking.

Having attempted to distinguish the perspective developed here from that of conventional economic and policy analysis, something should be said about its relationship to the Marxian analytical perspective as well. This is required not only because Marx provides the principal alternative approach to conventional analysis but also because Marxian economics as an *analytical endeavor* is very similar to that of the present undertaking. Both seek to understand the behavior of workers and managers in terms of the larger social systems in which their lives are rooted. And both understand as well the structure of employment opportunities as governed by social and historical processes that dominate and overcome the kinds of forces upon which conventional theory focuses, that is, employers' interest in the relative prices of the different types of labor that alternative employment structures imply. It is in the identification of the social and historical processes that govern the evolution of the job structure that the following analysis departs from orthodox Marxian analysis.

In orthodox Marxian analysis the central historical process affecting the job structure is the *division of labor*. That process is envisaged as one in which productive operations are broken into increasingly specialized and more finely divided tasks, and all jobs in the economy tend toward those in Adam Smith's pin factory or on the modern automobile assembly line. Work under these circumstances comes to involve very little inherent skill; it also loses any intrinsic meaning that it might have as the creation of a product useful, or even recognizable, divorced from the larger social context in which it occurs. In and of itself, in other words, the output of one isolated task on an automobile assembly line is useless, and the task itself taken in isolation is meaningless. These characteristics of the process of division of labor play two critical roles in the historical trajectory of the capitalist system as envisaged by Marx. First, because the productive process is the ultimate determinate of human attitudes and behavior in the Marxian system, the progressive reduction of work through the division of labor into inherently simple, and very similar, single operations leads to the homogenization and eventual unity of the working class, and this, in turn, is a critical factor in the Marxian view of the inevitability of revolution. Second, because these single-task jobs have no intrinsic meaning and are defined only as parts of a broader productive process, their emergence implies the "socialization" of production. As constituent elements of production and work lose inherent, independent meaning, in other words, it is increasingly difficult for them to be coordinated and controlled through market mechanisms. And they come instead to be explicitly planned and coordinated either within the firm or through the social relationships that develop among firms doing business with each other. In this sense, the division of labor is a process that not only prepares the groundwork for socialism but also leads, itself, toward the socialization of productive operations.

The view of industrialization that underlies the subsequent

analysis in this volume explicitly rejects the notion of the division of labor as embodied in orthodox Marxian theory. It envisages instead a historical trajectory in which there continues to be significant differences among employment opportunities in terms of the degree of skill involved in the work and the extent to which the work leads directly to a recognizable product that can impart some intrinsic meaning to work tasks. It is not that the division of labor as foreseen by Marx fails to occur. But it occurs in a context in which there are other countervailing factors that operate to moderate and divert the impact upon the job structure. What is true of the job structure is also true of the process of production itself. While certain commodities tend over time to be produced in large firms with socially integrated production processes whose components have no independent meaning, there is a continuing role in the system for craftlike production, which Marx says belongs to an earlier historical epoch, whose output is intrinsically useful and meaningful and where the market continues to play a significant role in coordination and control.

To recognize the vitality of features of the productive system, which for Marx could only be vestigial, is not to offer a fully developed alternative to the division of labor as an account of the historical trajectory of the productive apparatus. In this sense, the analysis that follows has nothing like the breadth and coherence of the Marxian framework. Among the other things that result from that fact is an inability to say anything one way or the other about either the likelihood of revolution or the possibility of socialism. But because of the critical role that the division of labor plays in Marx's own views about these two things, the understandings about them that would be consistent with the analytical framework of this book would be very different from those of Marx, however close the ultimate conclusions might turn out to be. In any case, because it cannot assure the possibility of a socialist outcome, let alone the historical inevitability of such an outcome, the analysis that follows is a good deal more concerned about ameliorative policy measures within the current system than is analysis conducted within a Marxian framework.

While the book is deliberately ambitious in its scope and the theory it develops is meant to apply to a wide range of migrations, it is not intended to present a universal theory. A final task of this introductory chapter is thus to delimit its purview. This is a little difficult to do without anticipating the argument that follows, but the domain of the theory can be bracketed by identifying those specific migratory movements that are clearly included and those that are clearly not. Included are those migrations that were the subjects of the research projects out of which the theory was developed: the movement of black workers out of the American South, the migration of Southern and Eastern European peasants to the United States in the late nineteenth and early twentieth centuries, guest workers in contemporary Europe, undocumented workers from Mexico and the Caribbean in the industrial cities of the United States. All of these are long-distance migrants from underdeveloped rural areas. In addition, all of these migrations appear to have been induced by the industrial society in order to fill a particular set of needs, and the migrants themselves appear to have shared a common set of attributes that enabled them to meet those needs. A number of other migrations, which were not the subject of specific research for this book, appear to share these characteristics and thus fall within the purview of the theory. Among them, for example, are international migrations in Western Europe in the period leading up to World War I and in the interwar period. Certain internal migratory movements in the early industrial history of Western European nations and in a number of underdeveloped countries today also seem to meet this pattern. Migrations that do not fit this pattern, and which the theory does not attempt to cover, are short-distance movements within a single country, for example, frontier workers such as those who live in Mexico and work in the United States (green carders), or what in Europe are known as *frontalier,* and the migratory movement of agricultural workers, either temporary or permanent. This last exclusion is of particular importance for the policy conclusions of the last chapter because it specifically excludes from the purview of the analysis Mexican workers in agriculture in the southwestern United States and in the border cities on the frontier. There are also sources of migratory movement that must be excluded because, although they are similar to those that the theory is designed to cover and often substitute for the latter in terms of the social functions they perform, they have unique characteristics and particular motivations and are generated by factors originating outside the industrial country, so that they are functional to the latter only fortuitously and ex post. Among migrations of this type are the Jewish migration to the United States in the period preceding World War I and, more recently, the Cuban refugees; the migration from East Germany to the German Federal Republic; and the movement of Algerians to metropolitan France immediately after independence.

The book is developed as follows. Chapters 2 and 3 develop the basic analytical perspective. Chapter 2 focuses on the demand for migrants and explains why the characteristics of the migration process lead one to believe that it is demand, rather than supply, that is strategic in generating the population movement and how the work that migrants perform appears to be rooted in the productive system. Chapter 3 is concerned with the migrants themselves: It examines how their temporary commitment makes them initially accepting of a set of job characteristics that repel native workers, how that commitment, along with the motivation and attitudes of the migrants, changes as the migration stream ages, and finally what the problems precipitated by those changes pose for the socioeconomic system.

Chapter 4 focuses on certain implications of the understanding of migration, developed in the initial chapters, for various economic and political processes surrounding migration in the industrial country: the competition between migrants and native workers, wage determination, unemployment, and the organization of migrant communities.

Chapter 5 examines the impact of migration upon the place of origin in relation to the factors governing that process in the developed area and to the interpretation of industrialization and development toward which an understanding of those factors leads.

The sixth and seventh chapters constitute an attempt to apply the analytical framework to the American experience.

Chapter 6 examines the role of migration in American economic history. Chapter 7 examines the problems posed by the current migration of undocumented workers from Mexico and the Caribbean. These chapters are designed to elucidate the current policy debates in the United States. But they should also be of more general interest as an illustration of the underlying analytical perspective that the book seeks to develop.

2
The jobs

The Irish emigration into Britain is an example of a less civilized population spreading themselves, as a kind of substratum, beneath a more civilized community; and, without excelling in any branch of industry, obtaining possession of all the lowest departments of manual labor.[1]

Before 1880, "English-speaking" workmen had manned America's iron and steel plants. Then immigrants from South and East Europe began to arrive in increasing numbers. More than 30,000 were steel workers by 1900. The newcomers soon filled the unskilled jobs in Northern Mills . . . The recent arrivals dominated the bottom ranks of the steel industry.[2]

Most of the Negroes who came North went into lower paid work requiring little or no skill or experience. The bulk of them became unskilled or semi-skilled operatives in the steel mills, automobile plants, foundries and packing houses. Many went to work at road building and other construction jobs. Others, and this includes many women, went into commercial laundries, food industries, and the less skilled branches of the Needle trades. In some cities certain of the specialized sewing trades, for example, the making of lamp shades in Chicago, have come to depend very heavily upon the labor of Negro women.

The jobs into which the Negroes went were usually those which native Americans or Americanized foreign-born white labor did not want.[3]

Immigrant workers in France, Germany, Switzerland and Britain are usually employed in occupations rejected by indigenous workers . . . Typically such jobs offer low pay, poor working conditions, little security and inferior social status.[4]

Most of the respondents in our study group were employed in the secondary section of the U.S. labor market, i.e., most were employed in low-wage, low-skill, low status jobs . . . Respondents' concentration at the bottom of the U.S. labor market, with more than three-quarters employed in unskilled or semi-skilled jobs, contravened the heterogeneity of the study group. Despite the fact that the respondents from Mexico, other nations in the West, and in the East tended to have different characteristics as individuals and workers in their country of origin, their roles in the U.S. labor market were markedly similar.[5]

This chapter examines the sources of demand for migrant workers. It focuses upon the distinguishing characteristics of the jobs that migrants hold and explores the relationship between those characteristics and the structure of consumption and production in industrial societies. The underlying policy question, toward which the chapter is directed, is that of whether it is possible, and if so, at what cost, to deal with the policy problems that migration generates by eliminating the jobs that migrants fill.

The chapter is divided into three sections: The first section outlines the basic characteristics of the migration process for which a theory of the demand for migrant workers must account. The second section identifies alternative theories of the demand for migrants and examines them in the light of these characteristics. The final section is designed to summarize the material presented in the chapter and underscore the basic conclusions that emerge from it.

The salient characteristics of the migration process

A good theory of migration between developed and underdeveloped regions must recognize four basic characteristics of the process: (1) the jobs that migrants hold in different countries and at different historical time periods seem to be a piece; (2) the strategic factor in initiating the migrant streams to fill these jobs is active recruitment on the part of employers or their agents from the *developed* region; (3) the ease with which employers are able through recruitment to initiate a new stream of migration suggests that, for all practical purposes, the supply of potential migrants is completely elastic, or, in other words, inexhaustible; and (4) the migration process, once under way, has been extremely difficult to halt (legislation attempting to block migration has, in virtually all industrial countries, been consistently evaded). Together these characteristics imply that the critical factors in understanding the migration process and its evolution over time lie in the developed region.

The job characteristics

It is clear in every country that migrants are not spread evenly throughout the industrial structure. They are concentrated in certain industries and occupations. They seem also to be concentrated in certain types of firms and completely excluded in other types of firms, industries, and occupations.

As the introductory quotations suggest, there is a strong sense among people knowledgeable about the phenomenon that the jobs in which migrants are concentrated all have something in common, and that such jobs can in some way be sharply distinguished from jobs held by native workers. This sense is generally shared by the lay public. As one moves from one country to another and reads through historical descriptions, one even begins to believe that there is something in common among jobs held by migrants in widely diverse geographic areas and very different historical periods: The jobs tend to be unskilled, generally but not always low paying, and to carry or connote inferior social status; they often involve hard or unpleasant working conditions and considerable insecurity; they seldom offer chances of advancement toward better-paying, more attractive job opportunities; they are usually performed in an unstructured work environment and involve an informal, highly personalistic relationship between supervisor and subordinate.[6]

Industrial statistics, however, do not classify jobs according to these criteria, and the market eludes efforts to pin down the impression that one is dealing with a defined entity in terms of conventional industrial and occupational statistics. The difficulty can be seen in Tables 2-1 and 2-2, which compare industrial and occupational distributions of alien workers in France and Germany, the two largest employers of foreign workers in Europe, and a sample of undocumented workers apprehended in the United States. Certain common patterns are evident in these tables. In all three countries foreigners are overwhelmingly concentrated in manual-job categories (70 percent in France, 88 percent in Germany, 73 percent in the United States), and the figures are even higher if one includes service workers who are generally unskilled (77 percent in France, 90 percent in the Central States of the United States). They also tend to be systematically concentrated in certain industries (construction and manufacturing) and excluded from others (trade, transportation, communications, and government). But the patterns give way to considerable diversity as one drops below the highest levels of aggregation. In Europe, for example, assembly-line jobs, particularly in automobiles, are considered low status and generally unacceptable among the native population, and these jobs are heavy employers of immigrants. In the United States automobile assembly-line jobs have remained attractive to the native population. The difference may be accounted for in some small measure by differences in relative pay; but even in Europe automobile assembly is a relatively well-paying job. Another difference between the United States and Europe is construction: That industry is the most intensive employer of immigrants throughout Northern Europe. In a good part of the United States, however, construction crafts are the aristocracy of blue-collar work; positions are reserved for native workers, and the minorities, which make up the migrant populations, have been carefully excluded. Here one might attribute the difference to the strength of trade-union organization in the United States, which has maintained a much higher relative wage in construction and imposed an organization of work that makes it difficult to dilute skills and employ the much less-skilled immigrant labor force, but such an explanation begs the question of why the industry is organized differently abroad. When one works through the comparison in this way, the only immigrant jobs that seem common throughout the industrial world are menial jobs, particularly those involving personal services. The prototype, of course, is domestic work in private households and service workers in restaurants and hotels. Even here, however, there are differences. In France, for example, the immigrants are limited to the truly menial work in the service industries – chambermaids and dishwashers. They have never penetrated into higher level jobs as waiters, cooks, and even bellhops as they have in other countries. The declining industries, which were the original fountainhead of industrial development – textiles, garments, shoes and their subsidiaries, dyeing, tanning, and the like – also appear to be consistent employers of immigrants.

Although the attempt to characterize migrant jobs in a way that would explain, in and of itself, the dimensions of the migrant labor market has proved frustrating, the character of those jobs is only one source of clues about the determinants of the demand. A second source is the nature of the recruitment process.

Employer recruitment

The massive migrations from underdeveloped to developed areas seem to be initiated by active recruitment on the part of employers in the developed region for labor to fill a quite specific set of jobs. Thus, it is the employers, not the workers, and the jobs, not the incomes, that are strategic. Certain conditions in the donor country are required for the process to take place at all. But the active agent seems to be the evolution of the developed country and the forces emanating from it.

This is almost impossible to see once a migration flow has become well established because by then it is almost completely self-sustaining. It is difficult to distinguish recruitment efforts from the voluminous information that flows back and forth between people "here" and people "there." To a large extent, variations in the needs for labor are absorbed automatically by temporary visitors who stay if they happen to find a job and return home as planned when jobs are scarce. It is, moreover, not always possible to identify the origins of these self-

Table 2-1. *Employment of foreign workers by industry*

	Foreign workers as proportion of total employment		Distribution of foreign workers		Distribution of apprehended aliens U.S.			U.S. labor force, 1970
	Germany 1972	France 1968	Germany 1972	France 1968	Total U.S.	East Coast	North & Midwest	
Agriculture, forestry, and fishing	7.9	12.5	0.9	6.8	17.2	5.6	13.5	5.1
Mining[c]	11.5	14.4	1.3	2.9	0.1	—	—	0.6
Construction	19.5	20.9	16.3	31.2	16.3	10.7	4.8	5.3
Manufacturing	14.4	8.9	62.0	34.8	33.4	39.7	44.2	24.1
Trade[b]	4.9	5.0	5.5	7.6	17.7	25.6	26.0	17.9
Transportation[b,d]	3.8	3.5	2.3	2.3	1.6	2.1	1.0	6.0
Government[b]		1.8	1.9	2.8	—	—	—	5.1
Domestic services[c]		13.0		5.4	3.2	0.9	1.9	2.6
Services except domestic[a,b]					10.3	15.0	8.7	26.2
Self-employed					—	—	—	6.9
Total			100.0	100.0	100.0	100.0	100.0	100.0

[a] In the case of France and Germany, this category includes water, electricity, gas, telephone, radio, and TV.
[b] These categories are not strictly comparable across countries.
[c] In Germany, coal mining is excluded.
[d] In the United States, this includes public utilities.

Source: Data for France and Germany: Bundesansalt für Arbeith der Präsident, *Trends in the Use of External Sources of Labour in France, Germany and Great Britain: An Essay on Behalf of the European Communities*, Directorate-General for Social Affairs, Nuremberg, December 1974. Tables for Germany: D/3/1a and D/3/1b, pp. 51–2; tables for France: F/3/1a and F/3/1b, pp. 103–4.

For the United States: David S. North and Marion F. Houstoun, *The Characteristics and Role of Illegal Aliens in the U.S. Labor Market: An Exploratory Study* (Washington, D.C.: Linton, 1976), pp. 113, 122.

Table 2-2. *Employment of foreign workers by occupation (in percent). Part A: France and United States*

	France 1968		Distribution of apprehended aliens U.S. 1975		
	Distribution of foreign workers	Foreign workers as percent total	Total	East	North & West
Farmers	2.2	1.2	15.6	5.1	11.5
Farm workers	6.0	1.4			
Owners in industry and commerce	3.7	2.5	3.3	5.4	4.8
Liberal professions and higher management	2.0	2.8			
Middle management	2.4	1.6	3.1	5.1	2.9
Clerical and sales workers	4.2	1.8	} 17.5	28.2	26.9
Service workers	} 7.2	12.2	} 3.2	0.9	1.9
Private household workers			—		
Miscellaneous	1.9	8.3			
Manual workers	70.4	4.8	60.0	54.4	35.2
Total	100.0	100.0	100.0		
Distribution of manual workers					
Foremen	1.6	4.2			
Skilled	24.8	8.9	16.0	15.4	4.8
Semiskilled	31.1	10.8			
Miners	3.1	20.1			
Apprentices	1.1	3.8			
Unskilled	38.2	22.7	41.2	39.0	30.4

Table 2-2. *Employment of foreign workers by occupation (in percent). Part B: Germany*

	Distribution of foreign workers in manufacturing Germany 1972[a]
Manual workers	88
Skilled	16
Semiskilled	41
Unskilled	31
Employee	11
Apprentice	1
Total	100.0

[a] These figures are not for total employment and hence are not strictly comparable to Part A of table.
Source: France: Bundesansalt, op. cit., Table F/6/1a, p. 115. Germany: Ibid., Table D/3/3b, p. 66. United States: North, Houstoun, op. cit., p. 110.

sustained migration streams. But when the origins can be identified, it is invariably the employer who is the active agent.

This is clearest in some of the European countries in the 1960s where the migrations were organized by official government agencies, which acted as intermediaries between employers seeking workers and the underdeveloped countries where those workers were found.[7] But it is possible to identify such recruitment activities in the early stages of a number of other migrations. Employers, acting on their own or through steamship companies, were active in the recruitment of European immigrants to the United States prior to World War I.[8] The black migration from the rural South to northern industry was induced by similar recruitment activities on the part of employers and railroads, beginning with the war itself and continuing in the twenties.[9] My own studies of recent Puerto Rican migration into the Boston area suggest that the critical elements in that migration were large manufacturing employers who paid individual workers to return to their home villages and recruit their friends and relatives to follow them back to New England.[10] Similar, though necessarily more circumspect, recruitment activities on the part of employers appear to underlie the migration of undocumented workers to the same areas.[11]

These recruitment activities seem to explain both the timing of particular migration movements and the particular areas between which migrant flows develop. Recruitment is the key to the seeming paradoxes of migration processes; it explains why one region develops significant out-migration, and another, essentially comparable in terms of income, transportation costs, culture, and labor-force characteristics, never does so; how a low-income area can exist for years as an isolated, self-contained economy despite its relative proximity to an industrialized area and then suddenly begin to generate significant emigration flows. It is U.S. recruitment in Europe, for example, that explains why the black population remained in the South after the Civil War; it was recruitment in the South that explains why large numbers of blacks moved north beginning with World War I. Similarly, employer recruitment patterns explain why West Germany has relied upon Italian and Turkish immigration and avoided the peoples of North and black Africa. Of course, behind employer recruitment efforts lies a host of other factors. Some of these are tangential to the problems with which we are concerned: The French recruited in the postwar period in the colonies and in their former colonies apparently because they were familiar and convenient; the Germans are alleged to recruit in Eastern Europe and the Middle East because they are concerned about racial purity; large American employers apparently had a policy of mixing ethnic and racial groups in their labor force in order to forestall the cohesion of the working class. But, as noted above, recruitment efforts also appear to be systematically related to the requirements of labor for a particular set of jobs; consequently, the character of these jobs and their role in the structure of industrial countries must lie at the heart of the process we are investigating.

Inexhaustible supplies of labor

The third characteristic of the migration process is that, for all practical purposes, the supply of labor available to industrialized areas from underdeveloped regions or countries appears to be virtually unlimited. For those who subscribe to an explanation based upon income, the vast income differentials prevailing between developed and underdeveloped areas and the magnitude of the former relative to the latter suggest that this *must* be the case. But, whatever the explanation, unlimited supply is demonstrated by the ease with which new migration streams are initiated when older streams are cut off or exhausted. In postwar Western Europe, France and Germany, the dominant recruiters of foreign workers in terms of the size of their labor markets, illustrate this point perfectly. France drew heavily upon Eastern Europe, especially Poles, in the prewar period. These labor supplies were cut off, first by the war and then by the Iron Curtain. But France shifted easily to North Africa, Italy, and Spain. In the late sixties, as the internal development process in Italy and Spain choked off those streams, the French shifted again, this time to Portugal and Yugoslavia. The pattern of West Germany has been very similar: initial reliance on Eastern Europe prior to World War II, a shift to East German refugees in the 1950s, and further shifts to Italy and subsequently Turkey and Yugoslavia when the refugee flow was curtailed by the Berlin Wall.[12] The same pattern is evident in the United States: initial reliance upon European immigration; a rapid shift to southern black and Mexican labor when European immigration was cut off by World War I and after the war by legislative restrictions; another shift to Mexican and Caribbean migrants when domestic labor reserves were exhausted in the 1960s.[13] In each of these cases, what is notable is not only the fact that the employers were able to find labor quickly and easily when they needed it, but also that the labor, which responded so readily when actively recruited, exhibited so little tendency to move spontaneously on its own initiative before the initial recruitment efforts were made. The weakness of spontaneous migration flows is all the more sur-

prising in the face of the persistence of the flows once they
have begun. That persistence, even when governments have
acted emphatically to curtail population movements, provides
the final set of clues upon which a theory of the demand for
migrant labor can be built.

Persistence of migration processes

The most conspicuous example of the inability of authorities to
control an ongoing migration flow is the contemporary United
States, where, despite the rhetorical commitment to a policy of
limited immigration, at least 2 and possibly as much as 12 percent of the labor force is composed of undocumented workers.[14] But the European countries also present numerous, albeit less spectacular, examples of the difficulties in attempting
to close down or curtail established flows, and illegal immigration there has been a perpetual problem in the postwar period.
In Germany illegal immigrants have been estimated at 15 percent of all foreign workers.[15] In France in 1968 clandestine
immigration was estimated to comprise 82 percent of all new
entrants.[16] And the most recent efforts to curtail immigration
in the face of the 1974–5 recession have led to a resurgence of
illegal or quasi-legal adjustments, which some believe acted for
a time to completely cancel out the adjustments evident in official figures.

Explanations of the demand for migrants

What are the possible explanations for the demand for migrant
labor and how well do they account for the characteristics of
the migration process we have just outlined? The most prominent explanations suggest that migration: (1) is a response to
general labor shortages; (2) satisfies the need to fill the bottom
positions in the social hierarchy; and (3) meets the requirements of the secondary sector of a dual labor market.

Migration as a response to labor shortages

If the only aspect of the migration process that needed to be
explained was the character of the jobs that migrants hold,

migrations might simply be attributed to general labor shortages. The confusion of occupations and industries evident in
international comparison could then be read to imply that what
is really common to the industries that employ immigrants is
simply that they employ immigrants. That fact alone is enough
to impart to the work environment certain distinguishing
characteristics. It would, for example, explain the low social
status: The immigrants clearly carry low social status in most
industrial societies in and of themselves, and if that status does
not already adhere in the work that they perform, they quickly
confer it upon the work when they take it on. To the extent
that the immigrants are temporary workers, an immigrant
labor force will have a high turnover; this will forestall the development of strong social groupings in the workplace and
produce more individualistic, and possibly personalistic, relations between labor and management. To the extent that the
immigrants are target earners, they will have backward-
bending supply curves and this will affect compensation systems and the way in which they respond to economic pressures
and so on. The legal status of immigrants may also affect their
willingness and ability to join trade unions and that in turn will
produce differences between migrant and native jobs along the
various dimensions of work that union organizations seek to
change. All of this will give a distinguishing caste to the immigrant labor market; the caste, however, derives from the labor
force and not from the jobs.

One might, under this hypothesis, imagine the process
through which immigrants are attracted to industrial
economies as being one that is at root governed by the process
of economic expansion.[17] As economic expansion proceeds
from some relatively low level (the United States in the Great
Depression on the eve of World War II; Europe beginning its
recovery after the war came to an end), it absorbs the native
labor force. It then begins to experience labor shortages. Those
labor shortages naturally concentrate in the low-paying, low-
status jobs because natives gravitate toward better-paying,
more prestigious positions. The labor-short jobs must then
compete for workers. They might do so by offering higher
wages, better working conditions, and the like. Or they might

substitute capital for labor. But under these circumstances, the amount of employment would clearly have to be reduced; either the labor-short jobs would themselves be eliminated or the labor shortages would be transferred to other jobs, which would be eliminated. The alternative is to recruit foreign workers. In this view, it is not necessarily critical that immigrants are unskilled and come from underdeveloped regions. When the migration is an internal one, this could easily be explained by a theory in which jobs are allocated among workers on the basis of their productivity.[18] The rural workers are seemingly the least productive and, hence, are the last in line. They are absorbed only when the labor shortages begin to emerge. When the workers are foreign, however, one may also think of nationality as conferring a kind of monopoly power upon the native labor force. Nationality is, in other words, like union membership, but a national group is a much more powerful, cohesive unit than a union. Hence, national restrictions are used to reserve good jobs for natives and to exclude foreigners even when the foreigners are, in fact, more skilled and more productive.

This view of the demand for migrants does not provide a very clear idea of what might be involved in curtailing the migrant labor force. Presumably, it would involve a decline in the national standard of living, as one supposes the resort to migrants to be a kind of "least cost" alternative: If it was cheaper to substitute capital for labor or to raise wages to attract native workers, employers – one would normally suppose – would have chosen that course of action on their own. It would also affect certain economic indexes, which are of interest in the formulation of national policy independently of their impact upon the standard of living. The index most prominent in discussions of migration in Europe is the balance of payments. It is clear from even a cursory glance at the industries where migrants are concentrated that some of them are under very intense competitive pressure from abroad; that is why they cannot pay the wages required to attract native labor; and, if migration was curtailed, they could no longer survive domestically and the goods they produce would be imported. An attempt to curtail the demand for migrant workers would also presumably require the limitation of the rate of economic expansion to that which could be sustained by native labor and, in the short run, this would undoubtedly result in slower rates of economic growth and quite possibly higher rates of unemployment.[19]

Beyond these general remarks, one can only say that the elimination of migrants would involve certain structural adjustments in production in which some native workers would lose their jobs and have to find others. In general, immigrants are employed in businesses owned by natives and managed by native supervisors. The equipment is often built and repaired by native craftsmen, and the productive process is frequently integrated in such a way that the work of immigrants utilizes goods and services produced by native workers or serves as inputs into the productive activities of natives. All of these native workers would be affected by the elimination of the immigrants and the consequent increasing costs of the things they produce. This is perhaps obvious, but it is just such effects that are generally neglected by proposals to curtail immigration. Such effects must be in part responsible for resistance to immigration laws, and they would have to be dealt with if such laws are to be effective. The kinds of structural adjustments that would be required would depend precisely on which industries and occupations were affected and how the economy reacted to changes in costs. As we have seen, there is no general pattern among countries, and so one would have to look at the specific nations involved. Even then, it is probably very difficult to predict exactly what adjustments in the productive structure would follow.

There would also have to be corresponding adjustments in the structure of consumption, and it is no doubt more useful to try to envisage the effects of immigration in these terms than simply as an overall decline in native living standards. Again, however, the diversity of national patterns makes it difficult to generalize, except to say that in all countries there would be less household help; hotels and restaurants would either be more expensive or less sanitary; in France, the streets would be dirtier; in England, there would be less public transportation.

The limitations of the conventional view. The preceding discussion of the demand for migrant labor is built upon conventional economic reasoning. As an explanation of the characteristics of the migration process outlined earlier in this chapter, it has three principal failings. First, given the ease with which employers are able to generate new migrant streams, a theory that attributes the characteristics of migrant jobs to the characteristics of the migrants themselves is not very satisfactory. Employers clearly exercise some choice in terms of the workers they recruit for the jobs. Even if one were to grant the assumption that this explanation seems to require, that is, that job characteristics reflect the character of the labor force, one must suspect that employers in their selective recruitment policies have sought a labor force that fits a predetermined set of jobs. And the theory then loses its power as an explanation of the character of immigrant jobs. The basic assumption underlying the explanation, however, is itself suspect. There are certain immigrant groups who, in terms of motivation and background, deviate significantly from the dominant pattern: Although they seem to gravitate toward a particular set of jobs, the characteristics of those jobs, along dimensions such as skill, social status, wages, job security, subvisory-subordinate relations, and the like, which we have emphasized here, do not differ from the job characteristics of other migrants.[20]

Second, the conventional view does not explain why the size of the migration labor market is not much larger than it is. Given the existing income differential and the ease with which employers seem to be able to tap new sources of labor to sustain a given demand, it is impossible to understand in conventional terms why that demand is not much more extensive. The theoretical problem is, in most graphic form, that the conventional explanation implies that every American family should have a foreign maid.

Third, there is a corresponding problem in explaining why the market for migrants is not smaller than it is. Virtually all industrialized countries have tried in recent years to reduce the size of the market, and those efforts have invariably been frustrated. The conventional view will explain the politics of migration through which those efforts have been thwarted only by stressing something that conventional economic models almost never stress, that is, the *inertia* of the structure of economic activity, especially in the short run. It must assert that people do not like to change either their consumption patterns or their patterns of productive activity, and that when there is great pressure to make such changes, they seek ways, such as the recruitment of migrants, to avoid them.

The importance of inertia in governing the processes involved makes these particular hypotheses about the role of migration in the economy very unsatisfactory. It is precisely this "inertia" with which policy must deal if it is to moderate the demand for migrants successfully. But there is no theory of inertia in economics; nor, for that matter, is there much of a theory of inertia in other disciplines. This makes other hypotheses both more attractive and more plausible. Before turning to these alternatives, however, it is important to consider one extension of the inertia hypothesis: that inertia affects not only the structure of production and consumption but also the structure of relative wages.

The wage structure and structural inflation.[21] Conventional economic theory treats the wage structure as an instrument that varies so as to distribute labor to various different sectors of the economy. The wage, however, also plays a social function: It confers status and prestige. Since status and prestige are also generally assumed to adhere in the job to which the wage is attached, people have very distinct notions about what the appropriate wage relationships are among different kinds of work. They expect the wage structure and the hierarchy of status and prestige to coincide. The existence of these two distinct functions of the wage, the economic and the social, creates a variety of analytical problems.

Economists do not always recognize the social function of the wage as distinct from the economic; they generally *assume* that the economic function dominates. This, however, is by no means clear: The social function could be such that the economic function is not allowed to operate at all. But, even if the economic function dominates, one needs to specify how the relationship between these two functions is worked out. The

specification that is least troublesome from the point of view of
conventional economic theory is that the social wage follows the
economic: The status and prestige that adhere in the job are
determined by and reflect the wage that is attached to it. If this is
true, however, it is clearly true only in the long run. In the
short run, the two are distinct, and the distinction creates the
possibility that changes in wage relationships generated by
economic pressures, such, for example, as cutting off immigration, will be resisted by the native work force. The resistance
may at first take the form of social pressure directed at first-
line supervisors responsible for hiring and wage setting or at
fellow workers tempted to accept migrant work. But if not successful, it will eventually be translated into direct cost pressure
through job actions in the form of slowdowns, sabotage, and
strikes. If workers were always successful in their efforts, then
the possibility of adjusting to localized labor shortages through
wage changes would be completely foreclosed. The structure
of relative wages would be, in other words, completely *inert*. In
practice, such pressure in pursuit of the socially acceptable
wage is not always commanding. In the long run, curtailment
of the supply of migrants can thus probably compel the requisite changes in relative wages. But in the short run, labor shortages of this kind are likely to produce wage-wage inflationary
spirals in which the initial rise of migrant wages in response to
market pressures is partially offset by a dynamic in which
workers act to restore the original differentials through wage
increases on other jobs. This process is important for two
reasons: On the macro level, that is, for the economy as a
whole, this suggests that we must anticipate as a consequence of
curtailing migration not simply a decline in living standards,
adjustments in the balance of payments, slower growth, and
higher native unemployment. We probably must anticipate a
certain amount of additional inflationary pressure as well. On
the microeconomic level, that is, in enterprises and in specific
industries, it is clearly the fear of the leverage that wage increases at the bottom would impose on their own internal wage
structure that leads employers to seek out and encourage
foreign migration. It is simply inconceivable to a restaurateur
that he can raise the wage of the dishwasher and the busboy

without paying more to the waiter and the cook as well; the hospital administrator cannot envisage paying more to orderlies without paying more to nurses; if the warehouseman gets more in a shoe plant, the production workers will get more as well; and you cannot pay stitchers a higher wage than you pay cutters. Even if these traditional relationships will yield in the long run, the employer is unwilling or unable to absorb the short-run costs, and his resistance could be the genesis of both the initial migration streams and evasion of the law.

Hierarchy as a motivating force

It is in no sense clear, however, that these social forces, which conventional economic analysis generally ignores, can be integrated into the theory as easily as the foregoing suggests. A second explanation of the role of migration in the economic structure revolves around the notion of a hierarchy of jobs or of employment opportunities.[22] In conventional theory, the existence of such a hierarchy is viewed as simply an accidental result of differences in the productivity of individual workers or, possibly, of the nature of technology. It is possible, however, that such a hierarchy is critical to the motivation of the labor force, that is, that it is basically the accumulation and maintenance of social status, and not income, that induces people to work. People work, in other words, either to advance up the hierarchy of jobs (and, hence, of social status) *or* to maintain the position they have already achieved. Such a view implies that there will be acute motivational problems in two kinds of jobs: the jobs at the very bottom of the social hierarchy, because there is, in effect, no position to be maintained, and the jobs that, whatever their position in the hierarchy, are basically dead end and provide no opportunities for advancement. Recruitment for both types of jobs is a basic problem for the economy. The problem in the case of dead-end jobs is not fundamental. Such jobs could be placed high enough in the social hierarchy so that people would be motivated to work *toward* them and would fear losing them once the positions had been obtained. Or the society could simply dispense with the jobs through substitution, technological change, or other adjustments in its pattern of consumption and production. Positions at the bottom of the hierarchy, however, create a fundamental dilemma because, in a very real sense, the bottom of the hierarchy can never be eliminated. If the bottom jobs were somehow cut off, the jobs directly above them would be at the bottom. The locus of the problem would be changed, but the problem itself would remain. Migrants provide a solution to the problem essentially because they come from outside and remain apart from the social structure in which the jobs are located. The exact sense in which this is true, and the way in which it affects their motivation, will be discussed in some detail in the next chapter.

This view does not necessarily imply that all the jobs migrants hold are fundamental to basic motivational forces. But it does suggest that there is some core of such jobs that are. To reduce migration below the level required to maintain that core, given the present economic system, therefore, it is necessary to attack the problem not through the elimination of jobs but through the substitution of other kinds of workers. To go beyond this and dispense with migrants altogether we would have to devise a social system that relied upon a very different kind of motivation. The question of whether or not it would be possible to do so basically lies beyond the scope of this book, but we return to it briefly at the end of the chapter.

It may be noted that this view of the migration process does not necessarily exclude the more conventional view. The system may tend periodically to generate a demand for labor that exceeds the supply, and migrants may be recruited under these circumstances to fill vacancies, possibly vacancies fairly high up in the job structure. The hypothesis about hierarchy and motivation itself suggests no reason why many of these vacancies could not be eliminated without touching the underlying socioeconomic system. But the conception of man out of which that hypothesis grows suggests why efforts to eliminate even these jobs are likely to meet considerable resistance. Central to that conception is the notion that economic activity is embedded in a wider social system. It is only in the comparatively unique case of the temporary migrant that work is *simply* a means to an end, a situation in which most jobs can be reduced to the income that they offer and, in these terms, are fungible. For most of us, our roles in the productive structure and our patterns of consumption are much more fundamental to the way in which we conceive of ourselves and understand the world. Changes in the productive structure thus seem to threaten the core of what we think we are, and it is for this reason that they are resisted. The impact of changes in these things is not adequately measured by the income gained or lost. Compensation, even if assured, will not relieve our basic fears and, hence, cannot overcome the underlying resistance to change.[23]

The view of migration as necessitated by the problem of manning the lower rungs of the job hierarchy thus seems to overcome or at least to point toward a view of human motivation that promises to overcome several of the limitations of the more conventional economic view. It begins to provide an explanation of the characteristics of migrant jobs and an understanding of the kinds of inertia in patterns of consumption and production that overcome attempts to eliminate them. It fails, like the conventional view, however, to explain why the market for migrants is not larger than it is. What limits the attraction of the higher standard of living that a more extensive utilization of migrants from underdeveloped areas would seem to permit? It is in answering this question that a third perspective appears most promising. That perspective is provided by the dual labor-market hypothesis.

The dual labor-market hypothesis

The dual labor-market hypothesis is that the functioning of the labor markets is best understood in terms of a model in which the market is divided into a primary and a secondary sector. Migrants are found in the secondary sector. The jobs in the primary sector are largely reserved for natives. There is thus a fundamental dichotomy between the jobs of migrants and the jobs of natives, and the role of migrants in industrial economies can be traced to the factors that generate the distinction initially, to the role and function of the secondary sector in which migrants are found, and to the evolution of its labor require-

ments.[24] To analyze processes of this kind, a theory of
economic duality is required.

The most promising theory roots dualism in the flux and
uncertainty that inheres in all economic activity. Such variability is created by a whole host of factors, ranging from the
natural variations introduced by the seasons and the weather to
the social variability of trends in fashion and taste and including the economic fluctuations of boom and depression, the
human successes and failures that dominate the fate of individual enterprises, speculation, invention, and bankruptcy. All
of these fluctuations alternately absorb resources into a given
productive activity and then discharge them to find employment elsewhere. A fundamental problem in social organization
is how that process is to be handled and who precisely is to bear
its costs.

The organization of capitalist economies creates a basic distinction between capital and labor in this regard. Capital is the
fixed factor of production. It can be idled by fluctuations in
demand, but it cannot be laid off; the owners of capital are
always forced to bear the cost of its unemployment. Labor is
the variable factor: When demand declines, labor is simply re-
leased. In the sense that workers can be said to own their own
labor power, the owners of labor are like the owners of capital:
They each bear the cost of unemployment for the factor that
they own. But there is a basic difference between the owners of
capital and those of labor in that in a capitalist system it is the
former who organize and control the productive process. The
effect of this difference is that labor is forced to bear a dispro-
portionate share of the cost of economic flux and uncertainty.
Whenever possible, the capitalist will try to seek out the more
stable and certain portions of demand and reserve it for the
employment of his own equipment. The clearest case of this
distinction is one in which there are two distinct technologies of
production, one that is intensive in capital and employs relatively little labor, the other that is labor intensive and utilizes
less capital. When demand can be divided into stable and variable portions, as for example in any industry with a stable basic
demand and a high seasonal component, the capital-intensive
technique will be used to meet basic demand and the labor-

intensive method will be used for the seasonal portion. In this sense, the most basic dualism in the economy is between capital and labor.

The duality between capital and labor, however, inevitably creates certain distinctions among workers as well. In the case of seasonal industry, for example, it is clear that if the capital-intensive method of production utilizes a group of workers fundamentally different from the labor-intensive technique, one group of workers will per force have secure jobs and the other will not. But there are also cases in which the employer is forced to invest in labor in very much the same way he invests in capital, in order, for example, to have a skilled labor force when workers cannot or will not invest in training themselves or when laborers must be recruited and housed at an isolated and remote location. The nature of the system creates incentives to organize production so that these workers too have more stable, secure employment opportunities and, in this way, extends the dualism inherent in the distinction between capital and labor to a distinction within the labor market itself.

To some extent, the skill requirements of jobs tend to be positively correlated with the variability of demand for output, and where this is so, it mitigates pressures for a dual labor market. The correlation between skill and variability arises because production can be routinized when demand for output is stable and predictable. The production operation can be broken into a series of standardized, repetitive tasks, which are then assigned to individual workers or to specialized machinery set up to handle only those operations, more or less in the manner of Adam Smith's famous pin factory. When work is structured in this way, the worker is not required to know more than the few tasks he or she actually performs. The economies of mass production depend heavily upon this form of work organization, and in mass-production industries considerable effort has been devoted to organizing the market in order to create a reasonably stable demand for a standardized product.[25] Lately, this same form of work organization has been extended to service industries through a similar pattern of market organization, a development typified by the McDonalds hamburger. Mass production of this type contrasts with the "job shop," which responds to an extremely variable demand by producing short runs of a variety of different items. Because the product in a job shop is always changing, workers must be able to perform a variety of different tasks and to continually readjust and occasionally rebuild machinery and equipment as it is shifted from one item to another. All of this can entail considerable skill. To the extent that it does so, the jobs, however great the flux and uncertainty with which they are associated, cannot be shifted to the secondary sector of the labor market. On the other hand, it is possible to shift the unskilled jobs, for which the demand is relatively stable, into the secondary sector.

The practical significance of skill in defining the frontiers of the primary sector of the dual labor market has been greatly reduced in modern capitalist economies by organized pressures on the part of workers to escape the role that the logic of the system assigns to them. Through such pressures, the natural tendencies toward dualism inherent in the system have been greatly exaggerated, and numbers of relatively unskilled jobs have been forced, as it were, into the primary sector. The forms that such organized pressures have taken varies substantially from country to country, and within any given country it tends also to vary over time. In Italy and France, since the late 1960s, organized pressure has resulted in restrictions on the layoff or discharge of any workers for economic reasons. In Italy, those restrictions seem in fact to amount to an outright prohibition. In the United States, the restrictions are somewhat less severe; in particular firms and industries certain workers may have virtual job guarantees, and one can argue that the thrust of guaranteed-income demands in auto and steel is moving the whole economy in that direction. But in most of American industry, employers can discharge workers so long as they do so in accord with certain basic procedures guaranteeing due process. They are generally also able to lay off workers when production declines, although they must do so in order of seniority and, frequently, must reallocate the remaining jobs internally as well. The effect nonetheless is similar to the more restrictive provisions in France and Italy: Layoffs become more expensive, and the workers subject to the provisions begin, in the eyes of those who organize and control production, to take on some of the aura of capital as factors of production whose unemployment, if possible, ought to be avoided.

The difficulty with these efforts of organized workers to deal with their own unemployment through job security at the enterprise level is that it attacks a symptom of the problem and not the problem itself. The problem is the flux and uncertainty that inheres in economic activity. So long as the flux and uncertainty remain, the specific prohibitions create an incentive for employers to look for some way to evade the rigidity that workers' organizations introduce into their operations. The secondary sector constitutes a means of evasion: a sector of the labor market that is not subject to restrictions on layoff and discharge to which the unstable portion of demand can be transferred. The precise institutions through which that transfer occurs vary from one country to another, following the variations in the way in which restrictions on layoff and discharge are imposed. In Italy, the distinction is between small and large enterprises; in France, it depends upon subtracting and temporary help services; in the United States, all three institutions are utilized, as well as a variety of other institutions, for placing workers outside union jurisdiction. Despite the variations in the particular institutions, the institutional distinctions that permit escape from job-security arrangements closely parallel the distinctions between the jobs of migrants and the jobs of natives.

It is to be emphasized, however, that although these distinctions between secured and unsecured job opportunities create the dual-labor market in its extreme form, the tendencies they express are present even when they fail to achieve uniform expression throughout the national economy, and migrants, because of their temporary attachment to the labor market, will always be more adapted than permanently attached native workers to secondary labor-market types of employment opportunities. And indeed, as will be seen below, one can identify particular cases in which migrants were clearly recruited for these purposes in historical periods when the distinctions were nowhere near as clearly drawn as they seem to have become today.

The dual labor-market hypothesis as an explanation of the role of migrants in the labor market is not necessarily exclusive

of the preceding hypothesis. The unsecured jobs in the secondary sector generally do lie at the bottom of the job hierarchy.
The existence of these jobs may serve to motivate the work of
natives as well as to secure their employment opportunities.
Having created a set of institutional distinctions for one purpose, the economy may utilize it for other purposes as well, and
a secondary sector, whose institutional history is dominated by
the politics of employment security, may house all of the low-
status, menial jobs.

A dual labor market is not exclusive of the conventional explanation either. Indeed, one might well argue that the last jobs
created in an employment expansion, when the demand for
labor outruns supply, are likely to be the least secure jobs. If a
dual labor market exists, they will, therefore, be disproportion-
ately concentrated in the secondary, or unsecured, sector, and
in the sense that migrants are recruited for one purpose, they
will be recruited for the second purpose as well.

The particular version of the dual labor-market hypothesis
just outlined does appear, however, to provide a more comprehensive account of the characteristics of the demand for
migrant labor than does either alternative taken by itself. First,
it clearly moves the focus away from particular industries and
occupations to other characteristics of employment and, indeed, because virtually all industries and occupations share to
some extent in the variability of economic activity, suggests that
migrants may be attractive throughout the economic system.
That they are not in fact uniformly distributed, it suggests, has
less to do with the underlying structure of the problem than
with such complicating factors as the fact that not all jobs are
unskilled and, hence, readily filled by migrants. But where
skilled migrants can be found and the market can be structured
in such a way that they are confined to the variable portion of
demand, the theory suggests they will be utilized even in jobs
that otherwise would belong to the primary labor market. In
the United States, this has indeed happened with the use of
foreign doctors in the medical profession and undocumented
Canadian craftsmen in construction.[26]

Second, although the theory implies that migrants will be
fairly widespread throughout the industrial structure, it also

leads one to expect concentrations whenever especially high variability of demand coincides with relatively large numbers of unskilled jobs. The industrial concentration of migrants in France and Germany in automobiles, construction, and agriculture appears to conform to this pattern: In all these industries, the bulk of the jobs involve little or no skill, and in each demand fluctuates widely, with the season in the case of agriculture and in construction and automobiles over the business cycle as well. The difference between Europe and the United States with respect to construction and automobiles appears attributable to differences in the institutional arrangements through which these fluctuations are handled. In the automobile industry that difference embodies the distinction noted above between the European tendency to impose absolute restrictions on layoff and discharge and the American system of temporary layoff by seniority. Apparently the latter gives employers much more freedom to adjust to variations in demand, especially in the automobile industry. In Europe, the large size of automobile assembly plants and their high visibility and symbolic political significance facilitate worker resistance to layoff. The American construction industry has been much more dependent upon skilled labor than its European counterpart, and a set of institutional arrangements apparently related to that fact, which protect the labor force against variability, such as hiring-hall and job-rationing procedures, substitute for a migrant labor force. The peculiar organization of American industry is closely associated with the highly unionized character of the labor force,[27] and it is, therefore, interesting to note in Table 2-1 that in the South and Southwest, where unions are much weaker and the work structure is apparently closer to that prevailing in Europe, the penetration of migrant workers has been much higher than in the rest of the country.

Third, this view points to the connection between migrants' jobs and the characteristics of the jobs of native workers and suggests a reason why workers, as well as their employers, might have an interest in the continuation of the migration process. That interest, moreover, is not open-ended, such as their interest in the standard of living or the productive structure under the first hypothesis. It thus not only explains why the demand for migrants is as large as it is, but also provides an explanation of why it might be limited. If the cost of production in the secondary sector becomes too low relative to that in the primary sector, then the secondary sector will no longer function merely to absorb demand that cannot be sustained: It will begin to expand into the stable portion of demand, acting to undermine job-security arrangements in the primary sector rather than to sustain them. This presumably explains why workers in the primary sector might act through such measures as the minimum wage and institutional restrictions on migration to limit the market.

One final characteristic of the dual labor-market hypothesis requires comment: The hypothesis in the form we have developed here places the politics of worker organization at the very center of the way in which the society utilizes migrant workers and the way in which that utilization evolves over time. It suggests that, at root, the migrants provide a way in which workers in the native labor force are able to escape the role to which the system assigns them. To a certain extent, this is a Marxist perspective of the problem. It makes the nature of the economic system and the struggle of various different groups and classes within it the pivots around which the analysis of migration revolves. Because the analysis resembles so closely a Marxist perspective, however, it is in danger of being submerged in one or another Marxist interpretation; therefore, the various features of the theory that is being put forward must be clearly distinguished. First, the term "capitalist system" has a very specific meaning here, and it is properly used in this context instead of other terms used elsewhere in the text to refer to the recipient country, such as, for example, "industrial economy." The meaning of the term "capitalist system" is one in which, from the point of view of those who organize and control the productive process, capital is fixed and labor is the variable factor of production. To the extent that labor succeeds in imposing upon the system the obligation to treat it, in one respect or another, like a fixed factor, the system becomes less capitalistic. One might call it instead a quasi-capitalist or a quasi-socialist system. Somewhat paradoxically, in terms of the conventional Marxist wisdom, the migrants are called upon not because the system is capitalistic but because it has become quasi-capitalistic. Second, however, it is not simply the quasi-capitalistic nature of the system that is important in creating the need for migrants; another feature is also critical: the flux and uncertainty that inheres in economic activity. This feature presumably has no necessary connection to the relationship between those who control the productive process and the factors of production. It is something to which all *industrial* economies, whether capitalist or socialist, are subject; possibly it is something that affects all economies. Third, it is easy, and essentially within the spirit of the analysis, to see in the process a struggle among socioeconomic classes: a struggle first between capital (in the sense of both those who organize production and those who own capital and bear the cost of its unemployment) and labor, and then among different groups of workers, in particular natives and migrants. It is also essentially within the spirit of the analysis to describe migration as a way in which capital is able to stave off the pressures from the labor force by dividing the working class. This characterization of the process is, however, incomplete without some subsidiary points not present in most Marxian analysis. One such point is that, in the case of migration, the capitalists do not seem to create the distinctions among members of the working class. It would be more accurate to say they find and exploit distinctions that are already there. This statement of the problem fails, however, to give sufficient weight to the complicity of the native labor force in the process. Such complicity in conventional Marxist analysis is misguided: Divisions among the working class serve to postpone the revolution that would otherwise be inevitable. But nothing in the analysis here assures that the alternative would not be a return to a more purely capitalist system in which native labor bore flux and uncertainty.

Summary and general policy conclusions

What do the three approaches outlined in the preceding sections imply about the ability of public policy to control the migration process?

Of the three, the first, which views migration as the result of a tendency for demand to outrun supply, is the most optimistic. It implies that migration can be curtailed simply by slowing the pace of economic growth. This, of course, involves certain costs in terms of the proceeds of the growth process, but these presumably would be weighed against the cost of migration before a decision to curtail such population movements was made. The alternative to slower growth in this view is the development of a substitute labor supply. The theory itself says nothing about where such an alternative might be found, but because it views the characteristics of migrant jobs as reflective of the characteristics of the workers who hold them and is not basically constrained by the nature of the economic system itself, it seems to imply that virtually any alternative source of labor would be a suitable substitute and, in this sense, leaves the impression that the options are plentiful and resort to alternatives easy.

The second approach, which sees the migrants as the resolution of society's attempt to staff a set of jobs at the bottom of the job hierarchy, is the most pessimistic. Because the hierarchical structure of employment opportunities is critical to the motivation of the entire industrial work force, the jobs at the bottom cannot be eliminated without undermining the productive system. It is still presumably possible to find other workers who will substitute for migrants in the bottom-level jobs. But since the job characteristics are rooted in the nature of the system itself, not just any supply of labor will function in this way. The view as developed in this chapter moreover does not explore in any detail the motivation of the migrations: It does not explain why migrants accepts jobs that natives reject, and, hence, it does not provide guidance as to where to look for a pliant alternative work force. For these purposes, the view must be supplemented by examination of the migrants themselves, toward which we turn in the next chapter.

The third, or dual labor-market, hypothesis lies intermediate between the perspectives inherent in the growth and the hierarchical explanations. Like the latter, it roots the characteristics of migrant jobs in the structure of the economic system, and, in so doing, shifts much of the burden of analysis in the formulation of public policy to an explanation of why migrants accept these characteristics, an explanation that it does not itself provide. Unlike the hierarchical explanation, however, the dual labor-market hypothesis, in focusing upon the variability of demand as the underlying explanation of the adverse job characteristics, identifies a set of factors that may themselves be open to manipulation and control.

Two ways of accomplishing this are implicit in the foregoing discussion. In one the character of the economic system is changed to eliminate the flux and uncertainty to which dualism is responsive. The other involves changes in the institutional arrangements through which existing variability is handled. In both respects, the search for public policies points toward complex issues of economic and social theory, which are the subject of considerable controversy and debate.

Concern with flux and uncertainty among professional economists has focused upon that generated by the business cycle. For most of the post–World War II period, a consensus prevailed, grounded in the work of Keynes about the principal causes of cyclical instability and about the kinds of public policies that were required to contain it. Had that consensus survived, it would be relatively easy to summarize and endorse the traditional Keynesian policies in the present context. In the last decade, however, the postwar consensus has dissolved and the ensuing debate is too far ranging and complex to be easily summarized. Two comments would appear nonetheless to be warranted. First, a good deal of the dissatisfaction among professional economists with the conventional Keynesian formulations of macroeconomic theory derives from the assumption of Keynesian theory that certain market mechanisms upon which orthodox economic theory is predicated will fail. The consensus has dissolved because much of the profession has simply asserted that those market mechanisms are operative. This assertion is in direct conflict with the analysis of labor-market behavior in terms of which the dual labor-market hypothesis is conceived, and in particular with the notion that the labor-market operations must be understood as embedded in a larger social setting and dominated by forces introduced by that fact. In this sense the present approach is in the spirit of Keynesian analysis. It implies that economic aggregates can, and in certain contexts *need* to, be controlled by the fiscal and monetary policies of the national governments. Second, however, the characteristics of the economic system with which we are here concerned are not exactly those that were the focus of Keynesian economics. Keynes, and most postwar analysts, were concerned with the *level* of economic aggregates. The job characteristics with which we are here concerned are derivative of *variation* in those aggregages and not in their level. A series of policies that were successful in achieving the traditional postwar goals of low levels of unemployment and high rates of growth might nonetheless do so in a way that generated considerable variability, and, to this extent, that tended to favor secondary jobs and resort to workers, like migrants, who were tolerant of that kind of work. Many of the critics of active government policy have focused on precisely this kind of instability, and their concerns, if not their analytical presumptions, are thus very much to the point in the analysis of migration.

Apart from the continuing debate about cyclical variations, the literature offers few relevant insights into the causes, and possible cures, of economic variability. There is some material about particular sources of instability in specific industries. Seasonal variability in construction, for example, has been of concern to policy makers in North America for some time. The Canadian government instituted a program of subsidies for home building during the winter season and that program has apparently been relatively successful in smoothing the demand for labor.[28] Another example is provided by a Hungarian official who reported in private conversation about efforts in that country to mute seasonable variability in rural employment by locating manufacturing plants with seasonal production patterns complementary to agriculture (or with the ability to inventory output) in rural areas, although there does not seem to be a literature about this. Neither of these examples provides a handle on the overall problem. They point instead to an elaborate policy of special programs, each specifically tailored to a particular industry. The complexity and variety of such programs would undoubtedly make such a policy extremely difficult to institute and administer. For this reason, it does not appear a very promising approach to the demand for migrant workers.

The second range of policies designed to control the demand for migrants that the dual labor-market hypothesis suggests are those aimed at institutions controlling job security. The differing importance of migrants in automobiles and construction on the two sides of the Atlantic was attributed above to differences in job-security arrangements. Implicit in this attribution is the possibility that adjustments in those arrangements might change the characteristics of migrant jobs so as to attract nationals to them. The American models, in other words, presumably offer the French and the Germans one avenue of escape from dependence upon foreigners.

In the United States, the Labor Department has in fact sponsored an experiment with institutional changes that derive from an analogous line of reasoning. The experiment is designed to substitute native for foreign workers in citrus production in southwest Texas, an agricultural area that is highly dependent upon Mexican migrants. The thrust of the experiment is to change the whole structure of labor utilization at once, substituting a system that combines stable employment, higher wages, and greater mechanization for one that generated a high seasonal demand for low-wage, stoop labor. One way of understanding foreign experience is that it is a cheap way of widening the range of alternatives that such experiments serve to generate. To this view, however, there are several objections.

First, as was stressed above, differences in institutional arrangements seem to reflect the outcome of a conflict between labor and management in which the relative power of the two sides is deciding. Certainly this is true of the differences in construction in the North and the South of the United States. It is more difficult to make this kind of comparison internationally, but the greater job security provided native workers in Europe is at least arguably attributable to the electoral strength of labor parties there and the credibility of the threat of a general strike. To this extent changes in the balance of power would appear to be critical in affecting any particular institutional change. Foreign experience or experiments with alternative organizations of work might be useful indicators of the kind of organization for which workers might pressure once the balance of power was altered. But a reliance on such experiments alone to produce fundamental changes in institutional arrangements would seem to suggest that the existing arrangements are attributable to the accident of history or a lack of imagination on the part of the actors, which, in the light of existing evidence, does not seem credible.

A second and perhaps more fundamental reservation goes to the relationship between institutions governing job security and other aspects of industrial relations and of the broader socioeconomic structure in which industrial relations occur. Job-security arrangements may be embedded in these more fundamental structures in such a way that they cannot be changed without changing other facets of the system. Perhaps their dependence upon more fundamental characteristics of the system is such that the range of variation suggested by existing alternatives is simply not obtainable. To know whether this is the cause – and to identify, if it is, the precise nature of the constraints – will require research on comparative institutions. The very limited research that is available certainly points in this direction. Thus, for example, Clinton Bourdon's study of the union and nonunion sectors of the American construction industry suggests that the differences in job-security arrangements are parts of systems that also differ systematically with respect to technologies of production, skill levels, the way in which tasks are distributed among different groups of workers, and the procedures for training the labor force.[29] International comparisons suggest that the roots of the differences are even more profound. A detailed comparison of French and German plants, for example, while not focusing specifically upon job security, uncovered differences comparable to those that Bourdon identified in the sectors of the construction industry in pairs of plants in a number of different industries, each pair producing precisely the same product in the two countries.[30] These differences seem to reflect parallel differences in the industrial relations and educational systems and are possibly the product of these. Alternatively, it is hypothesized that all these structures reflect differences in the French and German attitudes toward authority and personal relations that are deeply rooted in the two cultures. A study comparing factories in Britain and Japan identifies differences of similar magnitude and arrives at similar conclusions about the locus of the explanatory factors.[31]

Finally, it should be emphasized that it is not clear how much the differences in institutional arrangements reflect actual differences in the amount of job security as opposed to differences in its distribution. Clearly, the American system of layoff by seniority, which prevails in automobiles, provides less security for the workers whom it "protects" than the European (or Japanese) system of job guarantees. The survival of the latter, however, is predicated in some measure upon the ability to transfer the insecurity generated by the system to a source of more malleable labor, like migrants, and to avoid immigration through the institution of American systems, which would impose a real cost in terms of security upon native workers. On the other hand, the different job-security arrangements in American construction may increase overall employment stability.

None of these objections, of course, forecloses the possibility of institutional change as an approach to dependence upon migration, and the final chapter of the book incorporates several suggestions for such changes in the United States. But the objections do discourage excessive reliance on such changes as instruments of policy and, in so doing, reinforce the need for an understanding of the character of the migrants themselves, to which we turn in the next chapter.

3

The migrants

The kind of migration with which this book is concerned has played a central role in American economic development, and, hence, perforce, in the evolution of American society. Many of us are the children and grandchildren of such migrants; those who are not have parents and grandparents whose lives were vitally affected and fundamentally changed by the immigrants' arrival. Most of us, therefore, have reason to think we understand something about migration. That understanding affects in a number of ways our conception of who we are as individuals and how we came to be that way. It is also central to our conception of what we in the United States are as a nation and how our nation is distinguished from the other countries of the world from which our parents came.

Our image of migration tends to be very particular. In that image the migrant at his home makes a deliberate decision to move to some other place. The move is viewed as *permanent*. The migrant may indeed go back. But in the conventional view, to *go back* is to *change one's mind*. Often, in the conventional view, those who go back are spoken of as *failures*.

This view, as an image of contemporary migrations between industrial societies and less-developed areas, is wrong. Most such migrations in the beginning are *temporary*. The typical migrant *plans* to spend only a short time in the industrial area; he then expects to return home. *Staying* represents a change of plans. In fact, to the extent that success and failure are useful terms of reference in analyzing the process, it is probably more accurate to say that it is the failures who stay on.

This cleavage between the conventional view and reality is

curious; perhaps it is a convenient reinterpretation of the family history for most of us who come from immigrant stock. In some cases, most notably that of West Germany, the temporary length of stay does seem artificial, a product of the institutional form that the migrations have taken: The Germans wanted the migrants to stay only a short period of time. They deliberately recruited people with this in mind. The migrants entered on temporary visas; they were brought as a group, often housed together in separate facilities; and returned home on specially organized government transportation. It would have been very difficult for them to stay on had they wanted to do so.[1]

However, the migration pattern seems to take a temporary form even when it is not explicitly organized for this purpose. There is an important difference here between the original intention of the migrant and his or her actual stay, which is often longer. But, studies of migrant populations who are free to move back and forth invariably show that both the actual and the intended stay is short. Thus, for example, a recent study of Mexicans apprehended in the United States as illegal aliens found that they had returned home on the average of every six months.[2] The pattern of Puerto Rican migrants to Boston is similar.[3] In France, in the late sixties, it was projected that 50 percent of the immigrant workers would return home.[4] As will be seen in Chapter 6, one-third of the immigrants to the United States in the decade prior to World War I returned, and for certain countries the numbers were much higher. Most of the returnees appear to have been temporary migrants who never intended to stay.[5] Internal migration in developing countries exhibits a similar pattern in virtually all parts of the world with the exception of Latin America, and there is some indication that there too the initial pattern was one of temporary migration.[6] A recent econometric study of internal migration in the United States found that the propensity to return *increased* with distance.[7]

When long-distance migration is not temporary, it seems to be a response to institutional restrictions that impede the migration process. Thus, undocumented aliens on the East Coast of the United States stay much longer than the Mexicans, but that seems to be the result of the fact that they are visa violators who would have a great deal of difficulty reentering the United States once they leave. In Western Europe it was also found that restrictions upon entry during the last recession had the effect of lengthening the stay of those already there.[8]

The central thesis of this chapter is that it is chiefly the temporary character of the migration stream that makes these migrations between industrial and underdeveloped areas of value to industrial society and equips the migrants for the particular roles they play in industrial society. Unfortunately, from this point of view, the migrant communities seldom remain temporary. Though nobody may intend to stay, a nucleus of more or less permanent migrants seems inevitably to grow up. Although the industrial society may find this permanent settlement undesirable, it appears unable to prevent it. As the migrant community settles down, it becomes increasingly less adapted to the role it initially played, and it is in this transition from temporary migration to permanent settlement that most of the social conflict and political problems surrounding the migration process arise.

This chapter is devoted to a discussion of the relationship between the temporary character of the migration and the motivation and attitudes of the migrants, the transition to a permanent settlement, and how that transition affects the migrants and the roles for which they were initially recruited.

The migrant as economic man

Most people work in a community setting. Each job is one of a series of interlocking social roles in terms of which the individual is defined as a person by the community in which he or she lives and which he or she in turn uses to define himself or herself. Of course, a job also yields income. This makes it doubly important. In addition to being directly part of what one is, the income that a job yields is permissive (or prohibitive) of the other roles in the family, in the neighborhood, and in church that the individual plays (or would like to play) and which completes the self.[9]

The ability of jobs to serve this second function is dependent on the income they yield. As income rises and falls, we are better or less able to meet the various different expectations of others of what we are and what we should become. Undoubtedly, this is largely responsible for the drive that most of us have toward a higher income and our resistance to income decline. Most economic theory is predicated on the notion that the production of income in this sense is the only function of work, and that people will thus move around from one job to another in response to variations in economic rewards.

But to the considerable extent that the job, and the work that it entails, serves itself to define our social and personal selves, there are decided limits upon what we feel willing and able to do simply to earn money. The very fact of having a job generates inertia: to give it up is to change who one is. For craftsmen and professionals, their occupation is like this as well: Even when they do not have a job they are reluctant to work at something else. In choosing jobs at the beginning of a career, people are less constrained, but there are certain things they would not or could not do, no matter what the price. In a great many other career comparisons there is probably some change in the income differential that would induce people to shift, but given the income differences that exist, the choice is dominated by who one is. To some extent, this is a personal matter: As each of us is a different individual, we each have different ideas about what would be appropriate, or fitting, for us to do. But to a certain extent, attitudes toward work and the acceptability of certain work roles are uniform throughout a society: There are certain jobs that everybody views as humiliating and degrading; other careers that carry a kind of prestige that dignifies anyone who follows them, in their own eyes and those of others.

The social role of the job itself limits considerably the degree to which people will respond to economic incentives. Some analysts have argued that in most of the labor market the social role is so constraining that it does not make any sense to talk about the effect of variations in wages and incomes, as economists are prone to do in commodity markets and have increasingly come to do in analyzing markets for labor. To understand labor-market behavior, in this view, one must concen-

trate instead on the process through which people develop the
self-conceptions and social orientations that determine their
job choices.

However valid this view in general – and I personally think it
has considerable merit – it does not apply to the labor market
for *temporary* migrants. The temporary character of the migration flow appears to create a sharp distinction between work,
on the one hand, and the social identity of the worker, on the
other. The individual's social identity is located in the place of
origin, the home community. The migration to the industrial
community and the work performed there is purely instrumental: a means to gather income, income that can be taken
back to his or her home community and used to fulfill or enhance his or her role within *that* social structure. From the
perspective of the migrant, the work is essentially asocial: It is
purely a means to an end. In this sense, the migrant is initially a
true economic man, probably the closest thing in real life to the
Homo economicus of economic theory.

This divorce, which the migration creates between the worker's social role and self-perception, on the one hand, and his or
her work, on the other, is something quite conscious, even deliberately created. It is illustrated by any number of anecdotes
about migrant workers and comments of the migrants themselves. As one Mexican, who worked frequently in the United
States, put it in an interview in his home in Mexico: "I work
there: Then at home, I am king."[10] Or a Puerto Rican explaining why he continued to travel to the mainland for work despite the economic development in the island and the fact that
the wage differentials, after allowing for transportation and
other expenses, were practically nil: "If I'm going to do that
sort of work, I'd rather do it over there. Then, I can come
home and be myself." The same theme is implicit in the remarks of a New England employer commenting on Latin
American workers: "They work really hard, and they'll do anything. The new ones, sometimes if you give them a broom on
the first day, they might not want to take it, but when I make
clear there is no other work, they accept it. And once they have
started sweeping, I never hear any complaints about it. In fact,
if you offer them something else to do, they don't seem to

care." And a local priest who had worked as a missionary in Latin America talking about the same group of workers: "It is a funny thing. They have a very clear conception of what is men's and what is women's work, and the first job in that factory is almost always sweeping the floor. They go right in there and do it. At home, they would never pick up a broom. I really don't understand it: In the village where I worked, it would destroy a man to do something like that. It would have been inconceivable. But here they don't seem to mind."[11] An ex-Peace Corps volunteer, who also worked in a Latin American village and is now a social worker in New York, said: "You get five or six guys living together, sometimes ten. The places are a mess – they'd never live that way at home – but they work all the time. People sleep in shifts and nobody cleans or cooks. A friend of mine went into one of those apartments and tried to get the men to set up some kind of housekeeping system, like in a frat. I thought he was crazy – I mean, you know, just to suggest that a man might cook or sweep the floor. I know the places they come from and men just *do not do those things.* But this guy didn't know anything about it and the thing was it worked. Of course, it didn't last very long – the people in those houses keep changing. You'd have to set it up every week. But it was amazing that it worked at all."[12]

Each of these comments, in one way or another, reflects the same basic point: a group of people divorced from a social setting, operating outside the constraints and inhibitions that it imposes, working totally and exclusively for money.

The underlying motivation of the immigrants and the quality of their living standards while in the developed country are also indicated by the quantity of money they succeed in sending home. Remittances of Mexican workers apprehended in the United States who send money home averaged $169 a month, compared to average weekly earnings of $106.[13] Foreign workers in Germany in the mid-sixties who were unaccompanied by their families sent one-third of their wages home.[14] It is not possible to make precise comparisons of earnings and remittances of this kind for other migrant groups, but for migration flows in their early stages, the Mexican and German cases do not appear atypical.[15]

The other side of this story is what they want the money for. I have never seen a questionnaire survey of the precise motives for migration. The comments of the migrants suggest, however, that the money is desired to maintain or advance social status in the home community. In the early states of a given migration stream, this is generally viewed in terms of retrieving some place within the economic structure of the home community or of advancing in it. Thus, rural migrants typically think of buying land or livestock, more rarely a store or truck, bus, or taxi; urban migrants talk about a business or the professional education of their children. In the latter stages of the migration, the home economy has often collapsed and the earnings are sometimes used simply to maintain consumption patterns, although most often the focus seems to be on durables, especially housing and home appliances. These patterns appear to be remarkably consistent in the comments of migrants, not only in the United States but in Western Europe and in reports from the towns and villages from which the migrants come.[16] They have important implications for the impact of the migration upon the place of origin, which are explored below.

The heavy emphasis upon the temporary character of the initial migration decision needs to be qualified in two important respects. First, there are certain groups whose immigration has been permanent who, at certain particular junctures, have been significant components of the total migration stream. In the United States, the most important groups in the late nineteenth and early twentieth centuries appear to have been the Jews and the Irish. In recent years, the numerically most significant group of permanent migrants have been the Cubans. There are also major exceptions in Western Europe: the Algerian refugees in France, for example, and the East German migration into West Germany. Typically, such permanent migrations are the result of major political and economic upheavals, which undermine or destroy the place of the migrants in their society of origin. Such migrants have a reputation for being more aggressive and more successful than temporary migrant groups. This is perfectly consistent with the nature of temporary migration as we have characterized it above: permanent migrants may be initially confined to menial secondary jobs, but because they view their stay as permanent, their ambitions clearly extend to the same economic positions occupied by natives.[17]

Second, the kinds of migrants upon which we are focusing possess, in addition to the temporary nature of their initial migration decision, a second distinguishing characteristic: They tend to come from underdeveloped rural areas. Consequently, they are frequently illiterate, naive in the ways of urban, industrial society, and quite often they do not know, and have great difficulty in learning to speak, the native language or dialect of the industrial region. It is difficult to know exactly what independent effect this constellation of factors has or to distinguish the possible effects from those of the temporary commitment, but two factors would seem to be of some importance and must be noted.

First, the fact that the region of origin is less developed than the region of destination establishes an income differential. In the conventional model, this income differential is made the pivot of the analysis of the migration process. That approach seems deficient in that it fails completely to explain what would seem to be the central mystery of the process: why two regions can coexist for years without any significant movement between them and then suddenly at some subsequent historical juncture develop significant migrant flows. It also seems to imply that the recipient country would draw upon the areas whose income is lowest relative to its own, something that does not seem to be the case. One can in fact cite some exceptions to the basic hypothesis – rural Puerto Rico appears to be one – when people preferred to work abroad even though the income was essentially equivalent, or even somewhat lower, than that available at home because they were thereby able to avoid the social stigma of menial jobs. As explained in Chapter 1, the framework developed in the present model is, in part, a response to those difficulties.

The second effect of the relative backwardness of the place of origin appears to be more important than the income differential and has to do with the status hierarchy of jobs in the two regions. In most cases, these hierarchies seem to overlap: They do so, moreover, in such a way that jobs at the bottom of the hierarchy in the recipient area lie in the middle or upper reaches of the hierarchy of the donor region. The bottom jobs in the hierarchy of underdeveloped areas are typically jobs associated with menial, heavy agricultural work as day laborers. Menial jobs in manufacturing or service jobs in urban areas or in rural resort hotels, because they are associated with modernity, generally have much higher social status. In the urban industrial areas, however, the traditional agricultural jobs no longer exist, and the menial manufacturing and service jobs lie at the very bottom of the hierarchy. The migrant moving into these low-level jobs because he sees them through the glasses, as it were, of his rural background has a sense of upward mobility that the native urban worker cannot possibly experience. To the extent that the migrants return home frequently, the perspective that they bring with them is renewed and reinforced. And this probably constitutes a distinct factor, operating independently of the short-term horizon, to render the migrant population particularly suited for jobs that native workers reject. The role of the alternative view of job status is underscored by the fact that in the underdeveloped region from which migrants come traditional agricultural jobs are often degraded by the migration process to the point where they are no longer acceptable on any terms, and one can find in these regions, despite what is often massive unemployment, the kinds of labor scarcities for low-status jobs that in the developed region serve to spark the migration process.[18] In several parts of the world, areas contributing migrants to developed countries are actually recruiting migrants from still more backward regions to fill jobs as agricultural laborers that the migrant population once filled.

The fact that the hierarchies in the developed and underdeveloped regions overlap is, of course, no accident. Population flows in one direction are generally accompanied by flows of technology, information, and apparently some jobs in the other. Exactly how the two flows are linked and, in particular, the extents to which job export and labor import occur simultaneously is an open question. But whatever the technical and economic factors linking the two processes, it does appear that the same institutional ties between regions, or countries, that facilitate population movements also facilitate the movement of capital and jobs in the other direction. This is, of course, obvious when the movements occur within national boundaries, but it is also true of international flows. The implantation of industry in the underdeveloped regions must serve to expand the horizons of the native population and is quite possibly a critical factor in the development of a conception of the world that accords a place within the recognized job hierarchy to the kinds of employments the migrants find abroad. The fact that this has not happened may account for the fact that migrants to urban, industrial areas are seldom drawn from the most backward regions in terms of income or social structures and that, instead, these areas serve to provide migrants to other agricultural regions as the tolerance of the population of these regions in traditional agricultural jobs declines.

We shall return to this range of questions again in Chapter 5 when we examine the impact of migration upon the donor region. In this context, however, it is important to underscore the difference between the idea of relative social status as the motivating factor in the migration process and the alternative, emphasized elsewhere in the text, based upon the time horizon. To the extent that the latter is the critical factor, much can probably be done to eliminate the need for migrants by restructuring the jobs to enhance the job-security and promotion opportunities they afford. But to the extent that it is social status that is critical, it may be much more difficult to reduce reliance on migrants through job changes. To even begin to evaluate this alternative one would need to develop an understanding of how the labor market comes to be conceived in hierarchical terms. But to the extent such perceptions are intrinsic to human nature or to the economic system as we know it, any attempt to eliminate the jobs currently at the bottom of the hierarchy will cause other jobs, which now carry some social status, to be perceived as menial and be rejected, for that reason, by native workers.

The settlement process

The central argument of this chapter is that the migrant's function in the developed economy is fundamentally dependent upon the temporary nature of his stay and a set of motivations that gives rise to it. This temporary commitment, however, is itself transitory. The migration streams that start out as temporary seem to develop over time into settlements of more or less permanent residents; these residents, in turn, have children who are natives – native in terms of their attitudes and motivations, and often quite literally natives as well. The social problems and tensions surrounding migration are related to this transition from the original temporary state. We shall term it the *settlement process*.

Settlement as success or failure

The settlement process may be understood in several ways. These ways are not necessarily mutually exclusive, but they do provide different perspectives upon the process. They point toward somewhat different normative conclusions or, rather, emphasize different dimensions that might enter into a normative evaluation. They also suggest different types of policy instruments that might control and direct the process.

One of the ways of understanding settlement is in terms of the *success* or *failure* of the migrants in the industrial society. This is the perspective in terms of which settlement is probably most often discussed, and the terminology is borrowed from that discussion. As we have already seen, the terminology can be misleading. But it is in trying to straighten out the terminology and in clarifying what is actually going on that the perspective upon the settlement process is most instructive.

As suggested at the beginning of the chapter, the conventional view tends to see *settlement* as success: The people who do well in the industrial society stay. Those who cannot manage to get an economic foothold go home. This view, as we have seen, derives from an erroneous conception of the initial motivation of the immigrants. But while the reasoning may be faulty, the conclusions it suggests are probably sound: People who advance within industrial society tend to develop a permanent attachment to it. This is an extremely important point because it suggests that the rate of permanent settlement is related to, and can be controlled by, developments in the industrial economy itself. In order for successful settlement to occur, however, the motivation of the migrants must change, and in order to develop the idea of *settlement as success* and relate it to policy, it is necessary to describe the process through which the change occurs. That requires a rather more complicated conception of the nature of settlement, to which we come below.

It is absolutely essential to dispel the notion that seems to emerge in naive versions of this idea of settlement as *success* that the essential aspect of *success* is *income*. As was stressed earlier, migrants tend to be target earners, and *the effect of rising incomes, all other things being equal, is to increase the rate at which they return home.*

This last effect occurs because, in terms of the original motivation of the migrants, settlement is the product of failure. People who manage to accumulate enough funds for whatever project at home that originally sparked the migration return to the home country and invest there. It is, in these terms, people who, for one reason or another, cannot accumulate those funds who end up in the industrial country, staying on and on, or who keep coming back until their attachments there are permanent.

The view of settlement as failure tends to shift the focus from events in the industrial economy where the money is earned to events in the underdeveloped economy that determine success. The ability to successfully invest in these areas depends on the ability of the underdeveloped economy to absorb the kinds of projects that the migrants wish to undertake. Since these seem to be primarily commercial and agricultural projects, it largely depends on the vitality of these sectors, although there are, as we shall see, certain important industrial exceptions.

Settlement and community development

The view of the settlement process as either success or failure is extremely superficial. It certainly overlooks a number of critical dimensions of what is going on. It probably also exaggerates the degree to which it is subject to control simply by manipulation of the economic variables at one or the other end of the migration stream. The underlying process in settlement is one in which a permanent, stable community develops among the migrants in the developed country. The danger with the success or failure terminology is that it is suggestive of an economistic way of thinking about human nature, that is, a way of thinking in which the radical individualism of economic man is seen as natural and the development of inhibitions upon that kind of behavior is something that has to be explained. The radical individualism that characterizes migrant behavior in the very early stages, which underlies the conventional economic theory of man, is essentially not a human condition. People do not live naturally so totally divorced from social ties and a structured set of community relationships and they do not live long together without the rudiments of such a structure developing.

The artificiality of the initial conditions of the Latin American migrants in New York City, mentioned earlier, with whom the ex-Peace Corps volunteer was working are obvious: twenty men leasing three rooms, eight beds, which they slept on in shifts, eating canned food uncooked out of the tins, working two jobs and occasionally three, and sending home every month two or three times what it costs them to live. People do not plan to live that way very long; probably it is easier to plan such a life than to maintain it. At any rate, people describe the development of community as a gradual encroachment, at first unconscious, or at least unwilled, upon the extreme asceticism that such an existence implies. The men, living impersonally side by side, take off a Saturday night to get drunk; the drunk extends into Sunday morning and begins to conflict with some of the extra work. Or people begin to sacrifice overtime work for the companionship of their fellow men to have time occasionally to drink in the evening, to play cards or dominoes. They are in the apartment more often; other things begin to happen around the apartment; things begin to "feel" more crowded. It is harder to sleep there on the second and third shifts, and the number of people that can be accommodated declines. What does all this mean? The migrants work less so they earn less money; they spend more for consumption; on both counts, they have less money to send home, so they have to stay longer to meet their initial target, and as their stay continues, the need for community grows.

But it also implies that community has developed. The men, who begin simply by sharing their sleeping quarters and spending most of their time working, end by creating a space in their lives for leisure activities in which they engage together. In so doing, they start to rely upon each other in other ways as well: for help perhaps as medical or personal crises occur, for moral support, for advice, for financial assistance. They begin to see each other as differentiated in terms of the ability to provide these things: as more or less friendly, more or less knowledgeable, generous, or financially secure. And these perceptions give a structure of prestige, status, and respect to the community that is developing. That structure may build upon – if not, certainly it grows up with – other structures of status and prowess that are connected to drinking, to women, and to games.

Something similar begins to happen not just in relationships among men (or among women) but also between men and women. Most people who migrate, it seems, have some kind of attachment at home: at least a girlfriend (boyfriend) or fiancée, very often a spouse and children. The idea of coming is very often conceived in terms of these attachments: to accumulate the funds to marry or to support and advance the family that already exists. But it is not easy to live long without the companionship of the opposite sex. Prostitution helps but it is not enough. So people begin to form liaisons, most often thought at first to be temporary but which develop a kind of permanence. Some of these liaisons then become a second family or a substitute for the family the migrants had planned to form at home. Quite frequently, in some migrant cultures very frequently, there are children born as well. Here too the story is the same: less work, and hence a lower income, higher levels of consumption, and overall, less money sent home, a longer stay and a more intensified need for community but also the rudiments of community development.[19]

As migration proceeds, structural elements from the home community are also introduced into the incipient community at the industrial end. People begin to anticipate their inability to maintain the ascetic existence they had originally planned, and they begin to bring their wives, and occasionally their children, from home. Very often, younger brothers and sisters follow.

All of this adds to the sense of community in the industrial country and begins to add to the viability of life there as a continuing, more or less permanent existence.

Because many of these changes are unintended, unplanned, and even undesired, it is properly seen as a kind of wildcat development: something that just happens. But to say this – and to say as well that it is a complete distortion of what is going on, to describe it as the rational, calculated decision implicit in the view of settlement as success or failure – is not necessarily to argue that the process is uncontrolled by economic variables; certainly, there is no intention here to argue that it is uninfluenced by these variables. But the influence is not always in the direction usually supposed. Thus, as we shall argue in the next chapter, high levels of unemployment will under some circumstances hasten settlement, but under others discourage it. Similarly, to the extent that high wages make it possible to achieve any given target rapidly, they will discourage settlement, but to the extent that they occur late in the migration process and encourage people to bring their families, they will tend to promote settlement.

The settlement process we are discussing appears almost invariably to include a shift in job aspirations. As people develop a more permanent attachment, their time horizon expands: Instability of employment is no longer a matter of indifference. They see themselves as staying "after the season" or "beyond the boom." Once the family has joined the original migrant (or family attachments have been formed in the industrial region) it is not so easy – indeed it may become impossible – to go home if unemployed. And obviously all of these things create an interest in job security, and sometimes career advancement, that was not there before. The income of the job and the characteristics of the income stream are moreover not the only job characteristics that appear to interest settled migrants. People in migrant communities are intensely conscious of the social status of the jobs as well: Temporary migrants are, as we have seen, able to divorce themselves from the status of the job because it is so far removed from the physical and social space of the world in which they understand and conceive themselves. Obviously, as they become more permanently attached to the place where the work is performed, and more and more of a social structure grows up around them there, this kind of detachment becomes more difficult, and in this sense a "status consciousness" develops along with an interest in the long-run earnings prospects. Since social status, job security, and career opportunities are generally the characteristics of work that attract natives, the shift in attitudes toward work that accompanies settlement brings the migrants into competition and conflict with the native population. This is the basic dilemma of migration as a social process and the heart of the problem that it poses for social policy.

The shift in attitudes toward the job market is seldom complete for the first-generation migrants. However settled they actually become, they continue to see themselves in a certain sense as belonging to some other place and retain an idea, albeit increasingly vague and undefined, of returning "home." If the parental generation maintains a residual distance between themselves and their work, however, and the possibility of return in a true economic catastrophe remains a realistic if increasingly complicated alternative, none of this is true for their children. The second generation reared in the industrial region knows no other life. For all practical purposes they are native and retain a native outlook on the labor market.

If this is the basic model, it needs, however, to be modified in several important respects. First, the generational distinction needs to be extended. Second, it is important to explore alternative models of the settlement process.

The first and second generations: some qualifications and complications

Generically, the terms "first" and "second" generation refer to the place of birth: The first generation is born "abroad"; the second generation is born in the industrial society. This however is a much too literal interpretation of the terms. To capture the essence of the transition that occurs in the settlement process, the terms must be extended in at least two respects.

First, in relation to individual attitudes and behavior, the critical distinction appears not to be the place of birth but the place where one grows up and, in particular, spends his or her

adolescence. The importance of adolescence as the dividing
line in terms of cultural affinity emerges repeatedly in contact
with migrants and migrant communities. People who come to
the industrial region in their late teens and early twenties seem
to retain an affinity with their place of origin: If they learn to
speak the language of the destination at all, they speak it with
an accent; they also retain the mannerisms and attitudes of
their home and a nostalgia to return. Children who migrate
before adolescence, on the other hand, seem to adopt the culture of the destination. In the migrant community, they are
viewed, and view themselves, as "streetwise." When they do return home they have trouble reintegrating themselves into
their native environment and are seen as a disruptive element
there. Adolescence is the true divider between these two pos-
tures vis-à-vis the industrial culture. Something, although it is
not quite clear what, happens during this period of personal
development. The orientation and attitude of children who
migrate during adolescence itself, in early or mid teens, is un-
predictable. This emerges clearly in conversation with migrants: From the migrant's perspective, the effect of migration
on the adolescent is critical because the adaptation of industrial
values creates a painful cleavage within the family. They worry
a lot about it, because they see the difference as the product of
a largely random play of people and events beyond their control – a friend at school, an adolescent love affair, the
neighborhood. As one Latin American in New York City put it:
"You can't tell." When she left home her two children were
fourteen and fifteen. Three years later, the elder boy was an
American who spoke only English, even to his parents, and
seemed (to his mother at least) to live on the street on the
fringes of the drug culture. But the younger child remained a
"Latino," so much so that they were thinking of sending him
home to live with his grandparents.

A second modification of the distinction between the first
and second generation is that, for many purposes, the proper
referent is not the individual at all: It is, rather, the *community*.
The attitudes and behavior associated with generations, in
other words, may depend less upon where the individual
grew up than upon where most of the members of the

neighborhood or community into which he or she moves as a migrant were born and reared. At the very least, one must recognize the existence of second-generation communities that have developed a permanent settlement and a social structure comparable to that in the area from which the original migrants first came. Very often, these second-generation communities are in terms of mores and kinship patterns viewed by those within them as extensions of the place of origin abroad. People who migrate into this kind of community setting from those home communities will have an attitude toward the labor market much more like those already there than like that of the original pioneers. That this is so is implicit in the notion that what distinguishes the original migrant is the asocial, purely instrumental character of life and work abroad. For a migrant moving into a settled community, this obviously cannot be true. And the migration decisions of latecomers thus, perforce, must more closely resemble the permanent migration of the popular imagination. Typically, this is not simply true "by construction" as it were. The decision of latecomers is often anchored quite concretely in a set of community roles as well. Sometimes new migrants are recruited as marital partners of older settlers. Or they come because a death at home leaves their closest relatives abroad. At the very least, they move into a household whose head is closely related and is expected to serve in locus parentis.

Migrants to settled communities often have not only a predetermined family role there, but often an assignment in the labor market as well. Sometimes this assignment is in the secondary labor market of the ethnic community where the newcomer is expected to serve an apprenticeship before moving into the preferred positions in the family business or opening his own shop. But very often it is within an ethnic enclave of the primary labor market. Thus, in Boston it is alleged that jobs on the street crews of the gas company are allocated to new migrants from Ireland *county by county*. But even when a labor-market role is not preassigned, the range of work that will be acceptable is limited by the fact that the migrant enters a settled community and the job that he or she takes will reflect upon his or her social status and those who sponsored his or her migration. And the effects may in fact set in relatively early in the settlement process. It was clear, for example, in the interviews with Puerto Rican migrants to Boston in the early 1970s that an important reason for selecting Boston over New York was that the limited character of the Boston settlement left people freer to, as one man put it, "just make money." In New York, with a much older, more settled Puerto Rican community, people felt constrained to avoid the most menial jobs. And in New York itself, marginal manufacturing concerns, which in Boston would employ Puerto Rican labor, hired aliens. One manufacturer, on the edge of a large public housing project inhabited by Puerto Ricans and American blacks, makes quite clear that this was not by choice.

A variety of other social processes complicate the hard distinction we have attempted to draw between first- and second-generation communities. Some of these relate to the political organization of migrant communities and are discussed in the next chapter. The other processes emerge most clearly through a comparison of the view of settlement developed here with alternative understandings of community development.

Alternative patterns of community development

The preceding model of community development is a composite derived largely from interviews with members of migrant communities at various stages of settlement. As such, it must be viewed as something of a hypothesis. To substantiate that hypothesis, one would need a series of detailed case studies of the settlement process, that is, longitudinal studies of the evolution of migrant communities over time. Although studies of precisely this kind are not available, there are, in fact, a number of sociological and anthropological studies of "ethnic" or poor communities.[20] These studies were not designed to study migration as such, but the communities upon which they focus are composed of migrants, or derivative of the migration process, and can be used to throw the view that we have just developed in relief. The studies suggest two alternatives to the model of the inevitability of a permanent settlement with a value structure that brings the migrant community into competition with natives for jobs.[21] These alternatives are the culture of poverty and unassimilated settlements. Each requires some consideration here.

The culture of poverty

Any number of authors can be said to develop the perspective associated with the "culture of poverty," but the two most prominent are Oscar Lewis, particularly in *La Vida*,[22] in which he explicitly presents the idea of a *culture of poverty*, and Eliot Liebow, in *Tally's Corner*,[23] who develops the different components of that life-style and, of special interest in the present context, the relation of the life-style to patterns of work. The central notion in this literature is that there is a whole cultural pattern that is typified by unstable and volatile social arrangements. That pattern is reflected in labor-market behavior by continual job turnover, a weak and mercurial attachment to the labor market, and a highly personalized relationship between supervisor and subordinate on the job. It is also reflected in personal relationships, which often result in unstable unions between men and women in which the women are frequently left with children, producing female-headed and, in many interpretations, as a consequence, matriarchal families. The same pattern is reproduced in relationships among people of the same sex: extremely intense friendships that are very short-lived.

Such a cultural pattern would seem uniquely compatible with the characteristics of jobs in the secondary labor market. Indeed,it has been argued that the culture is in fact reflective of, and a response to, the kinds of employment opportunities provided by that market. To the extent that industrial societies can find or create a cultural pattern of this kind, and that pattern is "stable" in the sense that it will reproduce itself from one generation to the next, they do not need continuing waves of the kinds of migration upon which we have been focusing (although, it should be added, such migration might well be a preferred alternative).

If such cultural patterns can become a substitute for continued migration, however, they are certainly not *independent* of the migration process. Virtually all the case studies upon which the notion of a culture of poverty is based are migrant societies in the sense both that the settlements are relatively recent and that there continues to be considerable movement in and out. The literature on the early community life of ethnic groups that now constitute stable communities is replete with incidents and anecdotes that could be drawn from *La Vida* or *Tally's Corner*. They even creep into the oral narratives of aged immigrants, where one expects that the social disapproval of the life-style and morality have led them to be greatly suppressed. Contemporary black novels about ghetto life reproduce the theme, sometimes the very episodes, of early twentieth-century Jewish immigrant literature: Adjusting for style and shifting the perspective of the Jews who tend to write as adult immigrants to that of the blacks who tend to write as the children of migrants, they *could* be the same.

All of this suggests that the patterns identified with the culture of poverty may be interpreted as one stage in the process of transition to a stable, permanent settlement. Because of the prominence of the culture of poverty in the literature, it is worthwhile to identify how this interpretation would proceed. First, a part of what the investigators in these communities took to be basic cultural traits was probably just a manifestation of the temporary character of migration. Thus, for example, people had short-term, ephemeral sexual liaisons *because* they had a union that they regarded as permanent and which they wanted, and expected, to return to at home. Their job attachments were also short term and erratic because they planned to return home or because problems at home forced them to return prematurely.

Second, the very fact of living in a community with a large, transient population is likely to produce the kinds of behavioral patterns associated with the culture of poverty, even for people who are themselves permanent residents. The probability of finding sexual partners who are themselves looking for a temporary attachment is, for example, extremely high even if you want a permanent relationship. In a job market attuned to a high turnover labor force, it is hard to find out about stable jobs; as a member of a group identified by employers as unreliable, it is not easy to gain access to a stable job even if they are known to exist. In a community where a very large portion of the population is living outside the normal social restraints and inhibitions, the opportunities for crime and promiscuity are greatly enhanced.

Third, and perhaps most fundamentally, the transience and turnover associated with migrant communities in the early stages of settlement may be disruptive to what sociological studies take to be the "normal" maturation process. The disruptive effects of migration are best appreciated in terms of a rather unconventional view of what is involved in the culture of poverty. The conventional view has tended to characterize the *culture of poverty* by the time horizon and the capacity for delayed gratification of its members. The central idea is that people who share that culture are unable to contemplate and plan for the future in the way that the rest of us do.[24] In the labor market, this implies that they do not think in career terms and, hence, fail to make the educational and earlier job commitments that are necessary to gain access to and develop the skills required for the higher level positions. This characterization seems implicitly to incorporate an economistic view of life history as planned out in a series of conscious, deliberate decisions taken to achieve clearly defined goals.

An alternative way of looking at the evolution of life-style and career is that these consist of a series of roles played out in particular, often interlocking, social settings, and that the individual is propelled through those roles as he or she matures by the social pressures that surround them, by the expectations of others, and by his or her own expectations. One tends in this view in fact to define culture in terms of the constellation of social settings, the roles that the individual is expected to play within them, and the way in which those social settings and their expectations interrelate.

If this is indeed the process that is being played out in career decisions and in family formation and development, the migration process that we have described becomes disruptive in a most fundamental way. It is a process in which the individual is placed outside a structured social context. He or she is physically distanced from the family network, which at once serves to display the roles one is expected to play and to generate the pressures to play those roles and to move from one to another over the life cycle. To a certain extent, the migrant is divorced from those roles as well. This may or may not be disruptive of the migrant's own development. That depends upon how closely he or she remains tied to the original community in which the roles are anchored; how often he or she returns to that community; how closely his or her activities in the industrial society are linked as instruments to roles he or she means to be playing out at home; how much he or she has internalized community expectations. But for children growing up in the migrant community, who are not anchored like their parents in the community of origin, the migration process is likely to be completely destructive of maturation. The migration community in the early stages is a community in name only: It lacks the full range of social and familial roles. And, hence, the child grows up both without the models of "normal" maturation and removed from the social processes that compel him or her to adapt these models in turn. In this interpretation, the hallmark of the culture of poverty becomes the *absence* of culture and community. To the extent, however, that the transient phase of the migrant community is unstable, and a more permanent settlement and structured community starts to appear almost immediately and gradually comes to dominate the social setting, the so-called culture of poverty is also a passing phenomenon.

This interpretation of maturation and career development in terms of movement through a set of social roles tells a different story from an interpretation as deliberate, conscious decision making, but from a certain perspective they are not so very different. For the decision-making model to work, one must ascribe to the individual some conception of how the world operates and of the various attributes of the alternatives he or she is choosing among. In the case of career decisions, for example, the model assumes that people somehow know what the alternative careers are, that they know the economic advantages and disadvantages of those different careers, and that they know how the careers are pursued. The most likely sources of this kind of information are the career models of those surrounding them in the various social settings in which their lives are played out. The community setting can thus be said to provide the *information* upon which the decisions in the decision-making model depend. The difficulty with this interpretation of community structure is that it somehow leaves the impression that its absence can be overcome by handing the individual a pamphlet or putting him or her through a class. The record of a whole variety of manpower projects tried in the United States over the last ten years attests to the fact that this is not the case. If, however, one does not take a too literal and simplistic view of what information is, contrast between the two interpretations becomes largely semantic.

An example: the American working class. It will be useful to develop these ideas more concretely. It is not possible, however, to present a *typical* example. The work, career positions, and family roles through which individuals typically move over a lifetime, and the precise sequence in which these roles and positions are usually held, presumably vary from one society to another and, within any given society, among social classes. Generally it is different for men and women. For the kind of migration with which we are concerned, the example of men in the American working-class culture may be taken as strategic because it is generally into that class that upwardly mobile migrants in the United States most often move. It has been argued, moreover, that the culture is an outgrowth of precisely the settlement process we have attempted to describe.[25]

The culture of the American working class appears to be played out in two parallel social entities: the peer group and the family. The peer group is composed of friends of roughly the same age who grow up together in the neighborhood, entering school and subsequently starting work at about the same time, often forming a cohesive group within the classroom or the shop, and sharing their leisure time together as playmates in childhood, in street-corner gangs during adolescence, and in bars as adults. Within the group, each member assumes a distinct role, defined in relationship to leadership, entertainment, physical and sexual prowess, skill in one or another game, and so on. The roles within the group tend to be invariant with age. At the same time, however, there are other roles, within the family, that the individual moves through with age: childhood, adolescence, husband, father, grandfather, and patriarch. The movement through these life-cycle roles within the family involves distinct shifts in the locus of activity and the relative importance between the peer group and the family. In childhood and adolescence the peer group is the central focus of activity and family roles are secondary. Maturation involves a shift in priority with family roles and family responsibility achieving precedence and peer-group activity becoming secondary and, essentially, diversionary. This shift is signaled by marriage and the birth of children. It tends to be accompanied by certain changes in attitudes toward work and in labor-market behavior. Adolescence is a period of casual labor-market attachment: Jobs serve primarily to support peer-group activity. That activity is, in turn, adventurous and episodic; it frequently conflicts with work commitments, and since these are seen as instrumental in peer-group activity, the latter is given priority. With marriage and family formation, work becomes essential to family support: The work itself thus becomes much more important. Job stability and security become valuable job attributes and the behavior in the labor market steadier.

In terms of labor-market behavior, the critical juncture in the working-class life cycle is the shift from adolescence to adulthood. This involves a movement from unstable, short-term job attachment to a permanent labor-market commitment and an awakening of career interests. The cultural changes involved in that shift appear to be, first, a shift in family roles occasioned by marriage and, second, a shift in the priorities accorded social roles. The roles within the peer group that held priority during adolescence are downgraded and the roles in the family assume dominance. The pressures for this transition probably come from within the family. People are expected at a certain age to settle down, to move out of their parents' house, and to form their own family unit. But the pressures are successful in part because the peer group as a competitor for the allegiance of its members disappears; to the extent that most of its members are under similar pressures to marry and form families at about the same time, the whole nature of the peer group and the activities that it engages in is forced to change. It no longer really exists as an alternative to the family in the way it did during adolescence. It becomes, in other words, complementary to family activity. And this, in turn, puts its own pressure on the remaining single members because the kind of companionship that the peer group once offered is no longer available; indeed, the substance of activity and conversation begins to presuppose a family.

It is easy to see how all of this might break down in a transient, migrant setting. The family pressures are no longer present. The aunts and uncles, brothers and sisters, parents and grandparents, all with the same expectations for the individual, giving mutually reinforcing signs of encouragement or disapproval, which one finds in stable working-class neighborhoods and, generally, in the rural, peasant cultures from which the migrants come, are absent. At best there are pieces of the family, whose own lives belie any single model of family formation and provide instead a confusion of alternatives. Indeed, there may never have been a stable household from which the individual was forced to move to form his own. Absent also is the stable group of peers in relationship to which one molds one's own activities. The typical experience of growing up in the slums appears to be one of constantly moving in and out of different peer groups, of forming and reforming attachments.[26] The disappearance of one's friends into marriage thus is as likely to be the occasion for the development of new friends as it is to be the occasion to enter into marriage itself. Indeed, the essential characteristic of the culture of poverty as it is generally described seems to be a continuation in adulthood of patterns of behavior, in the labor market and in other activities as well, that are typical, and generally unremarkable, in adolescence. In American society, in fact, the patterns of labor-market behavior are typical not only of working-class adolescence but of middle-class adolescence while in high school and college as well. This is a point of interest beyond the immediate issue at hand because it implies that the labor-market role of youth is similar to that of migrants, and we return to it for that reason below.

The basic thrust of this excursion into the culture of poverty is to reinforce the view that migration and settlement must be understood as processes relating to communities rather than to individuals. It suggests that even migrants who are born and reared in industrial societies, and who in these terms clearly constitute the second generation, are likely to resemble in their behavior, if not also their motivation, the temporary migrants of the first generation if they grow up in communities dominated by the latter. From the point of view of labor-market attitudes, it implies that perhaps settlement and community ought to be viewed as a three-stage process. In the first stage, the community will consist almost exclusively of temporary migrants. In the second stage, it will develop a more permanently settled component, but the continued transience of many community members and the fact that the "second generation" among the permanent settlers grew up in a transient community and were affected in the ways just described may generate what has been identified as a culture of poverty. Such a culture, while different from the culture of the migrants themselves, may lead to a comparable perspective on work and indistinguishable labor-market behavior. As settlement continues, one might expect the culture of poverty to give way to a third stage in which the permanent community with a stable labor-market attachment and a demand for permanent jobs emerges.

The discussion does not establish that the culture of poverty is *only* a manifestation of the general climate that large-scale, circular migration imparts to a community. The possibility remains that these patterns could develop into a permanent response of a stable community. That, in other words, what we have just identified as the third stage might never emerge. In this sense, the culture of poverty might also be taken as an alternative to the model of settlement presented in the earlier part of the chapter and as a substitute, albeit an extremely unappealing one, for further migration.

A second alternative model, which might also serve as a substitute for further migration, is settlement without assimilation.

Settlement versus assimilation

In the United States, the conventional view of the immigrant experience has revolved around the notion of American society as a "melting pot." There are certain parallels between this view and the idea of settlement in that both make central to the interpretation of immigrant experience a critical transition in the values of the community, which occurs in its early history. It is important, therefore, to emphasize the difference between the two interpretations. The transition envisaged by the melting pot is a process of *assimilation* in which the migrant, *through contact with the industrial culture,* absorbs its attitudes and values. The transition involved in settlement is an autonomous process that occurs within the immigrant community independently of whatever contacts that community has with the larger cultural environment in which it is situated. To the extent that settlement results in a set of values coincident with those of the native population, it is because in the settlement process the subjective relationship of migrant worker to his economic environment comes to resemble that of the native population, not because the former has *borrowed* the values of the latter.

In the present context, the distinction between settlement and assimilation is important in two respects. First, it creates the possibility of a stable community with a value structure independent of, and therefore potentially complementary to, the value structure of the native population. Second, it renders problematic the capacity of the immigrant communities to meet the aspirations that develop as the initially transient community disappears. In terms of social stability, these two implications work against each other.

All of this is perhaps most graphically illustrated by *The Urban Villagers,* Herbert Gans's famous study of Italians in Boston's West End.[27] The West End *is* a "settled" community with an independent value structure. The dichotomy just described between peer group and the family is central to the culture of that community, and the basic values that adult members seek to implement through work are associated with family roles. The status hierarchies of work and family however are such that it is really only possible to integrate work roles with family roles in a small family business. Such a business, therefore, constitutes the *ideal* for virtually all West Enders and is the ambition of many. But it is an ideal that very few are able to realize. For those who do not, work is essentially instrumental, and, as Gans described it at least, people seem able to disassociate themselves from their work roles by viewing the latter simply as a means to an end in much the same way that temporary migrants view work as instrumental. To this extent, the settled migrants seem willing to accept jobs that the larger community views as demeaning and degrading and, hence, though "settled," might continue to complement native work roles.

On the other hand, the family roles that do motivate the West Enders, which constitute the ends for which the work is the means, impose certain requirements upon the work that the ends of the temporary migrants do not. The chief requirement is precisely that which was earlier associated with settlement: namely, a steady, stable, and preferably rising source of income. Without income, it is difficult for men to maintain and support a family. The settled West Enders are no longer plastic factors of production in the sense that their transitory forebears were.

The potential significance of this, of course, depends upon the particular theory of the jobs that migrants hold to which one subscribes. If one believes that the salient characteristic of such jobs is the inferior social status that they carry in the eyes of the native population, then the possibility of settlement without assimilation will seem very attractive. If, however, one subscribes to the dual-labor market hypothesis, the independent value structure of the migrant community will be of marginal interest. The hypothesis admits the possibility that the social status of work may play some role in the rejection by natives of "secondary jobs," but it also considers that the salient characteristics of such work, the insecurity of employment and income and the attitude of the community toward these characteristics, are bound to change with settlement whatever happens to the evaluation of social status. In the conventional view, which sees in migration a way of overcoming a tendency for demand to outrun supply and attributes job characteristics to the attributes of the migrants, settlement without assimilation is of essentially no interest at all.

It should also be noted that Gans's understanding of settlement without assimilation is only one of several possible interpretations of how such a process might operate, and in terms of the advantages it offers in the labor market is in many ways the most optimistic. What happens in the West End is that the clash in values between the ethnic enclave and the larger society leads the citizens of the former to "suspend" judgment about the work experiences that occur in the latter. As an alternative, the ethnic workers might continue to make such judgments but simply apply a different set of criteria in doing so. Under these circumstances, it would simply be a matter of luck whether or not the ethnic and native value structures coincided. Settled immigrant communities *might* then offer the industrial economy an escape from the dilemmas that migrants were recruited to solve, but there would be no *necessary* reason why they should be expected to do so. The Jewish settlers who appear in *The Urban Villagers* on the periphery of the Italian life that was the book's central focus have a value structure that nearly coincides with that of the native population, and while Jews are, as a result, much more "successful" in American society than Italians, they constitute for that very reason a much greater threat to the native population. From the point of view of the forces generating the migrant streams out of which the two communities grow, the one value structure is as likely as the other.

Finally, there is still another facet of the value structure of unassimilated ethnic communities that may be of considerable importance in judging its suitability for the roles that its migrant forebears were originally recruited to perform. Judging from interviews with members of those communities about jobs that the most recent wave of Latin American migrants is being recruited to perform, the historical experience of the community becomes an independent factor in generating values that are antagonistic to certain jobs, quite independently of any tendency to assimilate the values of natives. Thus, in the Boston area, undocumented Latin American workers are moving into the jobs once held by Italians, French Canadians, and other older immigrant groups in shoes, textiles, leather tanning, and the like. Employers are quite explicit about the fact that the new migration is necessitated by a labor shortage and attribute the labor shortage to the refusal of the children of older migrant groups to move into their parents' jobs. But it is clear from the comments, not only of employers but also of the workers themselves, that it is not simply, and possibly not primarily, the attitudes of the younger workers that are at issue. Apparently the parental generation looks back upon its own employment experience as humiliating and degrading: They see it justified only by the social advancement of their families; for their children to move into the very jobs that they saw as an instrument of escape would belie the meaning of the parents' work life, and there is thus tremendous parental pressure upon children to refuse the work. The way in which the social status of the job comes to be rooted in this way in the community makes it very doubtful moreover that anything one could do to the work in terms of changing relative wages or even improving working conditions would greatly affect supply, since the governing attitudes are not those of the people who would reap the higher wages or experience the improved conditions. As one young worker explained: "That job would kill my grandmother. Even if I wanted to take it, I would never be able to explain it to her. When I came home, she would smell [the chemical dye], and it wouldn't matter how much they paid *me* to do it."

Whatever they may be, moreover, the advantages that accrue from settlement without assimilation must be weighed against the threat that such a process poses to the capacity of immigrant communities to meet the aspirations that develop in settlement. Again, Gans's study is to the point: In the West End, the very distance from middle-class American society that leads the West Enders to see work roles differently also leads them to distance themselves from other social institutions. And that distance makes it difficult to acquire the skills and other attributes requisite for admission to stable, steady employment. Gans's own focal point here is education and the school system. The Italian immigrants initially did not appreciate the value of education at all. But in the West End community, the settled second- and third-generation migrants do see education as important and pressure their children to remain in and do well at school. They view education, however, like they view work, as essentially instrumental. The substantive content of what is taught in school and the values upon which that teaching is predicated, and upon which the school as a social system operates, are alien. The result is a clash of values. Faced with this conflict, the children have a great deal of difficulty remaining in the school and tend either to drop out entirely or to do poorly in acquiring exactly the instruments that they need to fulfill their ambitions in the labor market. The parents are thus unable to operationalize their interest in education for their children: Because they cannot bridge the gap between their values and those of the school, they can neither motivate the children nor force the school to accommodate to the community.

In Gans's study, the failure of the West Enders in their dealings with the educational system is symptomatic of a general failing to deal with the larger society. In the specific case that he studies, it ultimately leads to the destruction of the community itself through an urban renewal process that the community cannot stop because it cannot comprehend. In this sense, the basic message of the study is that settled communities with unassimilated values, however viable sociologically and in the short run, are not viable politically over the long haul. The problems posed by such communities as a substitute for new migration stand, however, even without this last point.

Some general implications for public policy

The central argument of this chapter is that migrants are recruited for industrial society because they are essentially transient. They view themselves as strangers and their work as instrumental. They are willing to accept a series of jobs that, because of the low social status, the insecure income, and the lack of opportunities for advancement, native workers reject. The difficulty with temporary migration as a solution to the problem of manning these jobs is that migrants do not typically remain transient: Transitory migration movements seem inevitably to generate permanent migrant communities. The members of those communities, the original settlers and their children, have a very different attitude toward the labor market from the people caught up in the transient migration flows out of which the communities grow, and these attitudes bring them into competition for jobs with the native population.

This implies that one set of parameters of the process, which is of critical policy interest, is that which determines the rate of settlement. The settlement process appears to have several other dimensions, which should be separately distinguished. In principle, it is possible to distinguish between settlement in the narrow sense and the process through which members of the settled community *assimilate* the values and attributes of the larger society in which the settlement occurs. It would appear useful, in addition, to distinguish between the assimilation of the *values* of that society and the assimilation of *traits* important in advancement within the labor market.

Settlement alone, that is, the development of a permanent commitment to the industrial society, will create an interest in employment security and career advancement that, in turn, will make aspirations more nearly coincident with those of the native population. It will, moreover, create incentives to political organization, education, and other activities important in realizing those aspirations. But it is consistent with the maintenance of a separate value structure in which employment opportunities devalued by the native population retain a certain prestige (or at least lack negative connotations) in the immigrant community. This will obviously reduce the competition between the immigrant and the native population in the second generation. On the other hand, the possibility that the immigrant community may settle without assimilating the value structure of the larger society also implies that it may fail to assimilate the cultural traits required to advance into the secure jobs that its residents seek.

All of this suggests that from the point of view of the industrial society, it is desirable to delay settlement as long as possible. It might also be desirable to delay assimilation. That will depend upon whether the immigrant community does indeed have a distinctive value structure, whether the assimilation of values is really a process distinct from the assimilation of productive traits and other characteristics important in mobility, and, if so, whether the former process can be retarded without retarding the latter.

The current state of knowledge does not permit definitive answers to these questions. The case-study literature on communities that are the product of the migration processes with which we are concerned does not speak directly to these issues. It seems to imply that the distinctions we are making are real. But the material is fragmentary. In particular, it provides no real help on how one might, in practice, work to foster the assimilation of productive traits without changing the value structure of the immigrant community. Indeed, if anything, it suggests that the dominant cultural values with respect to job opportunities are much more readily assimilated than the traits required to obtain them. And that, in any case, immigrant communities with distinctive cultural values that are complementary to those of the native industrial population are accidents of history and in no sense inherent in the processes that call these communities into being. Available evidence would thus seem to argue for a policy that fosters the assimilation of settled communities as rapidly as possible.

Contemporary experience also suggests, however, that there is a certain amount of conflict between the goals of delaying settlement in the first place and fostering the assimilation process once settlement has occurred. This is clearest in respect to the access of the migrant population to education and training institutions. Such access is critical for upward social mobility, but it obviously tends to encourage settlement as well. The same conflict is present, albeit in a less acute way, in the case of health, public welfare, and, indeed, in the provision of any social service that enhances the contact between the migrant and the larger society in which he is moving.

Contemporary experience does, however, suggest a variety of ways of organizing the migration process so that settlement will be delayed. The model structure designed to do this was that instituted by West Germany in the sixties. A similar model, which operated to much the same effect, is provided by the Puerto Rican agricultural workers in the United States. The Puerto Rican government contracts with individual farmers who hire for a fixed term. The contracting farmer meets the workers at the airport and transports them directly to the farm, where the workers live, isolated from all but the farm family and permanent help. The basic characteristics of these systems, single-sex recruitment, fixed short-term contracts, isolated

housing, and (in the German case) no reentry, are incorporated piecemeal in a number of other countries.

Neither the Puerto Rican nor the German system, it is to be
noted, has been successful in preventing settlement. They undoubtedly have delayed the settlement process, but to what extent it would be difficult to say, because many of the features
imposed institutionally arise naturally when migration is uncontrolled. However, immigration policy in Germany today is
dominated by precisely the settlement problems that the institutional arrangements were designed to prevent. And, after
thirty years of Puerto Rican agricultural migration, every New
England village has a small Spanish-speaking community composed of permanent settlers who dropped out of the agricultural stream.

One reason why the institutional barriers are unsuccessful in
preventing permanent settlement is the inherent tendency of
men to form permanent, structured communities, which we
emphasized in the body of the chapter. But a second, and
probably more important, factor is the character of the demand for migrants emphasized in the preceding chapter. The
agricultural demand in the United States is unstable, but its
variation is predictable; the employer is thus able to meet that
demand through fixed-duration contracts, which carry substantial fixed costs for transportation and housing. The labor
demand of the industries that made initial use of migrant labor
in Germany and for whom the system was originally designed
had similar characteristics; they were large oligopolistic industries like automobiles, where demand fluctuations were either
seasonal or in the short run foreseeable. Many of the industries
that utilize migrant labor are not of this character; their demand is not only variable, but the pattern of variation is also
uncertain: They want the migrant to bear not only the variability but the uncertainty as well. And because of the uncertainty
they are not prepared to finance either transportation or housing. Indeed, it is desirable from the point of view of these industries that migrants move around freely and easily in the
economy following the flux of productive activity, and any ar-
rangement that isolates migrants will interfere with these
needs. The settlement processes in both Germany and New

England have been the result of these industries seeking out migrants who were originally recruited by others. So long as these industries exist and find it advantageous to use migrant labor, it is questionable whether it is possible to maintain the institutional barriers that will forestall settlement for any length of time.

4

Particular characteristics of
the migrant labor market

The characteristics of migrant workers outlined in the previous
chapter give a particular cast to their behavior in the labor
market. This, in turn, affects the structure and operation of the
market and its evolution over time. At certain junctures it can
produce results that are in conflict with conventional notions
about how labor markets operate and about what parameters
are important in evaluating the impact of migrant flows and
attempting to control such flows for policy purposes. This
chapter discusses such effects in four specific areas: the competition between migrants and other labor-force groups, wage
determination, unemployment, and worker organization.

Migrants and other labor-force groups

At the heart of most discussions of migration policy lies the
question of competition between migrants and native workers.
On the one hand, it is argued that migrants take jobs from
natives: The extreme version of this argument, not uncommon
in the current policy debates in the United States and Western
Europe, is that, were the migrants to leave, they would free
enough jobs to absorb domestic unemployment.[1] On the other
hand is the argument that migrants are largely complementary
to native workers and the migration process thus works to preserve native jobs and sustain native consumption patterns. At
the heart of this position is the contention that migrants take
jobs that native workers will not accept, and that by so doing
they preserve industries and technologies that would otherwise
move abroad or drop out of our consumption patterns as im-

portant sources of employment for native workers as well.

The thrust of the two preceding chapters is to suggest that migrants are not in competition with the primary native labor force. This, however, is true in only a limited sense. One important qualification involves the inevitable settlement of the migrant community and the emergence of a second generation whose members are essentially native and in competition with other native workers for stable, respectable jobs.

A second important qualification is that migrant workers of the kind upon which we are focusing are but one part of a broader class of industrial labor. All the members of that class share with the migrants the general characteristic that their commitment to industrial work is marginal. Particularly, they view their attachment to the job, and often to the labor market, as temporary and define themselves in terms of some other activity from which they derive their personal and social identity. The other major groups of workers, in addition to migrants, that compose this class of labor are youth (and in earlier periods, children), housewives, and peasant workers. The members of these other groups are natives.

It is impossible to do justice to the distinctive characteristics of these other groups here. To begin to do so, in fact, would require separate books for each. They do, however, constitute the principal substitutes for migrants as a source of labor. Moreover, to the extent that migrants are in competition with native workers and serve, as has been alleged, to undermine the economic welfare of natives, it is, at least in an immediate sense, principally these groups that are concerned. Their character thus becomes of some importance in discussions of migration policy, and certain comments, however abbreviated, are in order.

Those workers closest in social origin to that of migrants are peasant workers: people who live on the land, which they often own themselves, and define themselves as agricultural workers and proprietors. They work in industry to supplement their agricultural income. The rationale for doing so is various: The landholdings may be insufficient to maintain a family and industrial work may be necessary to sustain consumption. But industrial work may also be seen, as it is seen often by the migrants, as a way of accumulating funds to expand existing land-holdings or to buy agricultural equipment, livestock, and the like. In the latter case, industrial work is likely to be something that people do in the off-season, in winter, for example, or in their "spare time." Peasant workers are like migrants in two critical respects. They see their industrial work as temporary: *Eventually* they will be able to devote full time to farming. In the meantime, the farm provides a cushion against economic adversity and unemployment in the industrial sector. And they are able to distance themselves from the job: They *are* farmers, not workers.[2]

The peasant-worker is a prominent character in accounts of the early history of modern industrial societies and in under-developed countries.[3] But, he is still quite common, if possibly less visible and certainly less prominent, in the collective consciousness of industrial economics. In modern Italy, for example, the peasant-worker has been a critical component of the dual labor-market structure of the postwar economy: Peasant men have been a source of industrial labor for small enterprises attempting to evade union restrictions and to take advantage of exemptions from legal requirements imposed upon large productive units; rural women have been an essential element in the revival of the putting-out system.[4] In the United States, the terminology is different but the phenomenon is basically the same; at the current stage of economic development, in fact, farmer-workers are a large component of the labor force in virtually all rural areas. Their role is attested by the popularity in such areas of manpower programs that train people in welding, machine repair, and other skills useful on the farm, despite the general paucity of industrial jobs employing such skills. This phenomenon is reflected statistically in the size of the rural-nonfarm population.[5]

Housewife-workers are like peasant-workers. Their major social and economic activity is as a wife and a mother, and they define themselves in these terms. The job is a source of income to *supplement* other family earnings. Sometimes it becomes a permanent part of the family budget. But often housewives work for specific consumer items: a sewing machine, a washer, or a new car. In these cases their motivation approximates that of the farmer accumulating to buy more land or a piece of agricultural machinery. Like the migrant or the peasant-worker, the housewife-worker can separate herself from the job and view it as purely instrumental. Like these other workers, too, she has a commitment that limits her interest in job security or career opportunity, and she has a source of other income, in the form of her husband's earnings, which serves as a cushion in times of economic adversity.[6]

The third category of workers in this class of marginally committed labor are youth. Youth in modern society appear to pass through a series of stages in terms of their commitment to economic activity. Paul Osterman has labeled the transitional stage the "period of moratorium."[7] During this period – in American society generally late adolescence and the early twenties – the primary commitment of a large portion of the young labor force out of school is to leisure-time activities. Income is a means of earning money to finance these activities. Actual income needs are limited because the youth remain unmarried and often live at home, and their parents' household provides the kind of cushion that the husband's income provides for the housewife and the farm for the peasant. In-school youths constitute a very similar type of work force: Their pursuits outside the labor market are arguably more serious, but their economic characteristics are the same. They define themselves socially in terms of their studies; work is instrumental, a way to finance school. They remain economically linked to their families, which serve as cushions against economic adversity. Sometimes the school as an institution or the legal status of a student provides a cushion against adversity as well.

While these appear to be the principal components of the marginal labor force, there are undoubtedly other groups that have a similar relationship to the labor market. It has been argued in the United States that a principal function of the public-assistance system, particularly Aid to Families With Dependent Children (AFDC), is to operate in this way, creating a stable base of income for the clients, who are then able and willing to take low-status, insecure, dead-end jobs, which they hold either illegally while also drawing public assistance or intermittently, alternating between work and welfare.[8] Low-income employers with whom I have talked do indeed express a great tolerance for the public-assistance system – a tolerance that contrasts markedly with the views of management in industrial enterprises paying higher wages and would thus seem to confirm this view. But the precise impact of welfare upon the organization of low-income markets remains to be documented. One effect of the AFDC system has clearly been to enable mothers of illegitimate children to move out of their parents' households where they once lived in shame and humiliation. In the process, some of these women must have escaped the role of secondary family earners and assumed an identity in the eyes of themselves and of the community as full-time parents. They tend either to demand stable, full-time jobs, which will enable them to support their families, or to withdraw from the labor force completely and maintain themselves through public assistance. On the other hand, it is clear from contacts with welfare households and low-paying establishments that the welfare system constitutes a cushion for a variety of people (older children, men, even distant relatives) who are attached, often surreptitiously, to welfare households and share the same types of employment as migrants.

How do these other groups compare to migrants as a source of labor for secondary jobs? They can be compared along three principal dimensions: (1) the plasticity of the work force, (2) their durability, and (3) their susceptibility to manipulation and control.

The basic difference between migrants and other groups with a marginal commitment to industrial work is that migrants appear by far to be the most plastic, the most readily adaptable to the requirements of the labor market. For each of the other groups, the social roles and community settings to which they owe primary allegiance significantly constrain their adaptability to job needs. The most general of the constraints is upon geographic mobility. In virtually every case except the migrants, the geographic location is determined by factors external to the labor market and cannot be changed without destroying the very marginality of the workers' commitment, which renders them an attractive source of labor in the first place. Thus, the location of youth and women is determined by the household of the primary earner to whom they are attached. This location generally restricts movement, not only to a particular city but often to jobs that are quite close to the place of residence within that city. Youth, and to a much lesser extent women, can be attracted to jobs beyond the limits the immediate residence imposes, but only by inducing them to leave home and set up a separate household, a move that generally implies a much more fundamental labor-market commitment and leads, sooner or later, to demands for stable, higher-paying jobs. The geographic mobility of peasant workers is, of course, constrained by the locations of their landholdings. In addition to these geographic restrictions, the labor-market activities of each group are also subject to a variety of specific constraints imposed by their primary social roles: Peasants will not work during the harvest and in other peak agricultural seasons; students cannot work during school hours; housewives sometimes can work only when their children are at school and not too generally at night. Perhaps the most outstanding example of the substitution of migrant workers for women occurred in French textiles in the late 1960s when the industry began to work night shifts.[9] Other constraints derive from the limited physical strength of women and youth.

In most industrial countries, these constraints have been embodied in law, so that, in fact, women and youth are not *allowed* to work nights or in jobs involving heavy lifting. It is difficult to know to what extent such laws impose artificial employment barriers. Recent experience in the United States, when such laws have been successfully challenged by advocates of equal employment opportunity, suggests that the laws do in fact restrain women from performing work that they can and want to do.[10] This point is, of course, an important one in consideration of public policy. But from the larger historical perspective, the legal restrictions may also be viewed as a reflection of a social structure that, by defining a series of sex- and age-related roles, creates the marginal labor force.

It would appear that the tighter constraint upon the labor-market activities of these other groups is balanced by the fact that, relative to migrants, they constitute a more durable source of labor. There is no obvious pattern whereby participation in the labor market acts to change work attitudes and commitments in the way that the shift from the first to the second generation does in migrant communities. Youths, it is true, mature into adult workers, but they are generally replaced by succeeding generations. However, the durability of the labor-market roles of the other marginal groups, particularly women and peasant-workers, may be illusory. Some case studies, as well as the broader social movement involving women's rights, suggest that marginal labor-market participation works over time to undermine the original social structure, and in the emergent structure, the level and stability of income and the social status of the work itself become more important. The dynamic suggested here for women is one in which they begin working in order to finance specific consumer durables that enhance and reinforce their self-conception as housewife and mother: But they discover, through work, that they enjoy the freedom it provides from household routine and from financial dependence upon their husbands. And this, in turn, leads them to a changed image of themselves, one in which work becomes more central to their lives, and they, in turn, begin to impose increasing demands in terms of the psychological and financial rewards of the job. The inevitability of this process, however, remains an open question.[11] That labor-market participation acts to change preexistent social roles seems indisputable, but it is less clear that the changes apparent in recent years are inherent in the process itself as opposed to the particular historical moment in which they have occurred.

Finally, it appears that the deployment of these other marginal workers has been less open to control and manipulation by the dominant classes than is the case with migrants. But, here too, while the basic point may be valid, especially at the present time when most migrants are foreigners, the difference may be a matter of degree. It is difficult to argue that employers, acting either individually or collectively, have *created* youth or women or peasant-workers. But the social roles of each of these groups and the way in which they participate in the labor market have been importantly influenced by the institutional framework. Some of these institutions can, in fact, produce very rapid changes in worker attitudes toward labor-market roles. The system of conscription and military service, for example, has dramatic effects upon a youth's decision to marry and settle in a permanent employment commitment. A second example is provided by patterns of education. These have a decisive effect upon both youth and women. Imagine what the impact upon participation rates of both groups would have been if the resources devoted over the last thirty years to the expansion of higher education had been devoted instead to preschooling. Clearly, this would have strengthened the commitment of both women and young workers to the labor market and, in so doing, enlarged the primary labor force.

Wage determination

We argued in the initial chapter that most migrants work at the bottom of the job hierarchy in low-wage, menial employment. In virtually all modern industrial societies the wages on those jobs are governed by statute. Either they are directly fixed by law or they are part of a wage hierarchy that rests upon a statutory minimum and in which the various wage components move up (and presumably down as well) with changes in the base. The economics of wages for migrant workers is, therefore, by and large the economics of the minimum wage.

One can distinguish two basic analytical perspectives upon the minimum wage. These perspectives more or less correspond to the distinction we have attempted to draw throughout between an economistic view of the labor market and a social view. The economistic view attempts to treat labor, at least for analytical purposes. like any other commodity. The wage, in this view, is then simply the price paid for labor. In the absence of outside interference, it will be set by the forces of supply and demand. Except under conditions that in a commodity market would be deemed extremely unusual, it should vary so as to ensure that supply and demand are brought into balance. If there is excess demand, the wage will rise and more people will be brought into the market. The process should continue until the demand is satisfied, and at that point the wage rate will stabilize. Conversely, if there is excess supply, the wage will fall and demand will expand until the excess is absorbed.[12]

A statutory minimum in this view serves at most to generate unemployment: It will definitely generate unemployment if it is set at a level above the competitive wage, for at such a level labor will be in excess supply. (If it were set below the competitive wage, of course, it would have no effect.) To a certain extent, the unemployment might be compensated by the higher earnings of the employed. Obviously, however, one's views upon that matter will depend upon how the employment (and unemployment) is distributed. And obviously as well, whatever the distribution, there will be some level beyond which the employment loss cannot be balanced by the wage gains. Overall, this view tends to see the minimum wage as an outside force introduced artificially into the labor market; at best, it is an instrument of policy, the use of which requires a careful weighing of costs and benefits. But because it is believed that the policy tends to see the benefits and lose sight of the costs, it is viewed with great suspicion.

In the social view of the labor market, the minimum wage is perceived as a good deal more natural. It tends, at the very least, to be accepted with a certain amount of fatalism and is generally viewed with considerably less suspicion. This position is not very well articulated in the literature, especially with respect to the statutory minimum, but the essence of this perspective is more or less as follows: Labor is performed, and wages are paid, in a community setting. In that setting, the wage is seldom perceived as a price whose function is to allocate labor as if it were a commodity. Rather, the wage tends to be perceived as defining the social relationships among people in the productive process, conferring prestige and establishing patterns of authority and subordination. Generally, these perceptions lead people to operate in various ways to establish a wage structure and freeze wage differentials. One way in which they operate is through trade unions and professional associations. In the absence of such formal organizations, the wage structure is critically affected by the actions of informal social groups in the workplace. The political process through which the minimum wage is set is simply another expression of the same set of social forces. No doubt, the fact that the wage is fixed by statute has *some* effect upon its level and its flexibility. But it would be a mistake to conclude from this that in the absence of a statute, the wage would be set through a market process as if labor were a commodity, and, in fact, very often there is a "social minimum" that actually exceeds the statute.[13]

The view of the migration process developed in the preceding chapters is one in which any *single* migrant group begins with people whose labor-market orientation is essentially economic, in precisely the sense in which that term is used in conventional theory, but then changes over time as a community develops, and their orientation toward the labor market at the destination in the developed country includes more and more of the social elements emphasized in the second view. To this extent, we would expect that the relevant model of wage determination shifts over time as well; that the first model captures the wage-setting process, and the effect of legislative regulation, at the beginning of the process; the second model captures the end point; and to understand the interim one must develop some hybrid of the two. It is probably true that the character of the wage-determination process, as well as other aspects of the labor market for migrants, does shift over time, but it is *not* true that the two alternative models can capture that shift, at least as these models are generally conceived. The central relationships of the competitive model are distorted, and its results are fundamentally changed, by the nature of labor as a commodity when it belongs to, and is being sold to, the kinds of migrants we are describing. The problem is twofold. First, the migrants are target earners. Second, it is not clear what the *supply* of migrants actually is.

Target earning

The fact that the migrants are target earners means that the supply curve of any individual migrant worker is backward bending, that is, increases in the hourly wage *reduce* the number of hours the individual worker is willing to supply. This, moreover, is a characteristic not simply of migrants but also of several other types of workers who share low-income jobs (women, for example, working to provide a specific commodity or income supplement to the family earnings, and youth, living at home and working for pin money to finance leisure-time activities). This fact, we argued above, is probably not coincidental but, rather, is intimately related to the kinds of jobs that are at stake.

While it is clear that the conventional model does not capture the behavior of markets composed of large numbers of target earners, it is not easy to know what model would fit such a market. The fact that the supply curve for individual workers and for the market as a whole is backward bending does not necessarily imply that this is true of the supply curve for individual firms. When the firm is small relative to the market as a whole, it can expand its own labor supply by drawing labor from other firms. Thus, it is conceivable that in such a market any wage equilibrium is very unstable. Each individual firm experiencing a labor shortage will raise its wage in an attempt to attract labor from other firms: The result will be a higher market wage. At that wage people will want to work less, and firms will be driven to drive the wage still higher. Conversely, any labor surplus would set off a downward wage spiral: Employers, noticing the existence of unemployment, reduce wages; workers respond by staying in the market longer, thus increasing the pool of available labor and providing an incentive to lower wages still further.

These, however, are really only theoretical possibilities. An understanding of how such low-income labor markets actually operate would require empirical studies of a kind that, to my knowledge, have never been made. My own conversations with employers in these markets in the United States are, in the light of the foregoing theoretical considerations, very difficult to interpret: The employers themselves – even quite small employers – place tremendous emphasis upon the backward-bending supply curve. Indeed, it is through conversations with them that I was led to recognize this aspect of the migrant labor supply and to search for its origins in the nature of the migration process. The preoccupation of employers is such as to suggest that they may actually believe, and behave, as if their *own* supply curve were backward bending. How is one to interpret such a finding in the light of theoretical considerations? It seems to me three interpretations are possible, all of which however lead to rather similar conclusions with respect to the minimum wage.

First, employers may *actually* be very confused about what the supply curve is. Economic theory assumes that the supply curve to the firm is a known relationship or at least one that can be quickly discovered by experimentation. However, in fact, experimentation is viewed as costly by the firm and it tries in other ways to infer the nature of the labor supply. It knows that a wage increase will serve to reduce the supply of labor offered by its existing employees. It also sees applications of new employees as a kind of random process generated by a floating population that comes from afar and does not have enough information about the labor market to know where any particular firm stands in the local wage structure. Fears of a labor shortage, and possibly the effects upon it of costs and competitive position in the product market, forestall experimentation with higher wages. The statutory minimum forestalls lower wages. In short, the firm may not actually believe that its supply curve is backward bending, but it is unsure, and the effect of the uncertainty is a considerable inertia in its own behavior and a tendency to welcome the statutory minimum as a way of resolving its problems.

A second interpretation of the way employers talk about their labor supply is that, despite the quite unskilled character of most of the work in this labor market and the consequent ability to tolerate what seem to·be incredibly high turnover rates, there is in fact an independent concern about turnover. The jobs, one can argue, are quite simple but involve enough skill so that new workers must be shown how to perform them and spend time, albeit a *short* time, perfecting what they have learned. In this atmosphere, there is a premium placed upon labor-force continuity: The older workers show the newer ones how to perform the job and maintain a base level of output while novices are being absorbed. Employers may know, therefore, that higher wages will attract more new workers and still fear sufficiently the effects of these wages upon existing employees to deter any effort to meet labor shortages through wage increases. It is obviously impossible to resolve this problem by paying higher wages to only new workers, as the problem arises because the old workers are more productive and such a pay scheme would, therefore, violate the most elementary standards of equity.

The third interpretation is that employers almost never behave with respect to the labor market as isolated competitors: They virtually always have a sense of community and operate in collusion with each other, conscious of the effects that their actions will have on the market as a whole. Local labor-market studies seem to suggest that this is the case.[14] And it is conceivable that employers, in their comments about the backward-bending supply curve, are actually expressing a concern about the market as a whole, which they have developed through conversations with each other or, more likely, mixing that concern and confusing it in their own minds with a more parochial concern about the behavior of their existing employees.

Ambiguities about the supply of labor

All of this must be read, however, against a backdrop that recognizes the second peculiar feature of the labor market for migrants: the ambiguous nature of the migrant labor supply. That supply is extremely elastic. For practical purposes, it should perhaps be viewed as infinitely so. Employers are generally in a position to stimulate an increased supply of workers through existing channels simply by spreading the word among their own employees that they are recruiting. Given the wide disparities in income between developed and undeveloped areas and the size of the underdeveloped world, there are an infinite number of new sources of labor to draw upon as existing channels dry up. Thus, employers are under the impression at any time that a labor shortage can be met through other means besides increasing the wage rate, and, in particular, by stimulating further migration. This is an atmosphere, then, that is quite conducive to acquiescing to social pressure exerted by their peers and colleagues against actions that tend to "ruin the market" and to resolving confusion about the actual nature of the supply curve in favor of wage inertia.

Taken together, then, these features of the labor market for migrants lead to a rather different view of wage determination and the role of the statutory minimum from that arrived at when one thinks of the labor market as simply a market for another commodity. If it is reasonable to think of the supply of labor as being restricted at all, the market in the absence of government regulation has a strong tendency to be unstable and behave perversely. Employers are uncertain and confused and to a great extent welcome statutory regulation as a means of resolving that uncertainty. To a large extent, however, it is not reasonable to think in terms of a limited labor supply: The supply of migrant labor is, in the long run, virtually unlimited at any conceivable wage. Without some regulation, the wage therefore is likely to fall eventually to a level at which it threatens the employment of native workers and offends their sense of equity, and it is simply not reasonable to expect that the society will let this occur.

Finally, from a public policy point of view, it is important to underscore one particular aspect of the market's perversity: Because migrants are target earners, the labor supply increases as the wage falls because each worker stays longer. The length of stay of the migrant, however, is a critical policy variable, probably much more critical than any other variable in the process. It is critical because the length of stay determines the speed with which the migration shifts from a flow of temporary workers toward a permanent, established community, and hence, from a process complementary to native labor to one competitive with it. To the extent that one can control the wage rate, one would probably want to do so in the light of this effect, and a relatively high minimum would then be preferable to a low one.

Minimum wage determination in permanent communities

The other element in analyzing the wage-determination process in migrant labor markets concerns the effect of stable communities upon wages of low-paying jobs. Stable communities affect these jobs in two ways. First, some of these jobs may be held by members of such communities, and when this is the case, the wages paid for these jobs can come to be governed by the community's mores even though all the workers employed there are not community members. Second, the wages of menial employment are sometimes a part of a larger wage structure whose movements are governed by the stable native workers and their organizations. In such cases, the workers who hold higher-level jobs normally expect a customary wage differential to be maintained between their work and that of those below them, and their organizations operate to do so.

To understand both effects would require the kinds of extensive study of wage determination at the bottom of the labor market that, as we noted, have not been undertaken. Examples of the second kind are fairly common in the United States. Typical is a New England shoe plant that employs new migrants only in the warehouse; all of the workers are organized by the union and the whole wage structure is established by collective bargaining. Normally, a fixed differential is maintained between jobs in the plant and jobs in the warehouse; some plant jobs and warehouse jobs, in fact, share the same job category. But the union does not provide effective representation to warehouse workers on a day-to-day basis and warehouse workers do not transfer to plant jobs. Other examples can be cited in the textile and garment industries. It can be argued that the association between migrant and native workers in this way is largely a historical accident: a decision of a governmental body (like the National Labor Relations Board) that failed to recognize in defining the unions' jurisdiction existing ethnic distinctions or the vestiges of a past in which the workers who dominate the organization once held the migrant jobs, perhaps because they were then migrants themselves. But the very turnover of the migrants provides certain incentives to include them within the organization; because the migrants have such a high rate of turnover, they contribute to union finances, most notably to pension and welfare funds but also to union dues, without staying around long enough to become eligible for assistance or to demand union services. To this extent, they are a financial windfall to the unions and, it is sometimes alleged, certain unions have deliberately sought out migrants for this reason. Migrant workers, it may be noted, have a very similar effect upon the financing of national social security and medical care systems.

The first effect may be even more important, but our knowledge about it is even more limited. Here the problem is not only a lack of study but the extremely sketchy nature of most notions about the social minimum wage. Essentially, the argument is that in a market completely dominated by migrants with a temporary attachment to industry and a high turnover, there would be no social minimum. And if all worked well, and migrants (or their children) who developed permanent attachment moved up the job hierarchy, a social minimum would not develop. In fact, however, the jobs are not held exclusively by migrants: They are shared with women and youth who, while similar in a number of respects, do belong to a resident community that is capable of incorporating the wage rate within its own mores. All settled migrants do not, moreover, move up; and thus new, temporary migrants often share the work with preceding generations who belong to settled communities. In the United States, where blacks have been denied upward mobility, this phenomenon is particularly apparent. For whatever reason, employers in the northern United States seem to feel that there exists a social minimum that is above the statute and below which they cannot attract and hold labor. And it is apparent from contracts with the migrants themselves that their fellow workers have succeeded in instilling these standards, even among relatively recent arrivals, so that newcomers who land the few jobs that pay below the social minimum are pressured and driven out of them, even though they might otherwise be contented to stay. This is perhaps too sketchy a view of the process to see clearly its operational relevance, but it does at the very least suggest that the behavior of wages in migrant labor markets is .critically influenced by the relative isolation of the migrants from other workers, especially with respect to the wage floor. To the extent that the floor is an important variable in limiting the extent of the migrant labor market and in enhancing the turnover within the migrant community, this is important to bear in mind.

Unemployment

It is generally believed that unemployment in low-income neighborhoods is extremely high, and insofar as these neighborhoods are composed of migrants, it is inferred that their unemployment rate is relatively high as well. To a large extent, this belief is based upon rather impressionistic evidence, and in underdeveloped countries—possibly in developed countries as well—such impressions have probably been distorted by the failure to recognize the existence of what has come to be termed the "informal" sector and, hence, by a tendency to see employment as limited to the kinds of activities that we have been accustomed to associate with modern, industrial activity. Nonetheless, in industrial countries like the United States, where unemployment is systematically defined and scientifically measured in ways that one would not expect to be seriously biased in this regard, the unemployment rates of low-income communities *are* extremely high. Generally double, and sometimes three or four times the national average, these high unemployment rates have often been made the focus of economic and social policy.

Unemployment in low-income labor markets, however, must be interpreted in the light of the character of the migrant labor force and the shift in that character that occurs over time. Again, a sharp distinction can be drawn, on the one hand, between the early stages of the migration process for any given migrant group, when the basic commitment of the migrants is to their place of origin and there is a high turnover among the population at the destination, and, on the other, the late stages of the process, when settlement has occurred and the population is dominated by the perspective of the second generation, with a permanent commitment to the destination and a native's perspective on the labor market.

The high turnover in the early stages of the migration process can be expected by itself to generate a certain amount of unemployment both at the origin and the destination. At the destination, newcomers may spend time looking for jobs after they arrive. People who have left their jobs but not yet returned home may also be accounted as unemployed, especially if their departure is precipitated by the loss of work rather than a voluntary resignation. Similarly, at the place of origin, migrants may quit work some time before they actually leave and spend time after they get back "readjusting" before they manage to reinsert themselves into the local economy (or, as very often happens, decide to return whence they came). The very fact of being tied to one place while working in another undoubtedly acts to raise this kind of "frictional" unemployment. People can be drawn home suddenly for all sorts of personal reasons: a major event, an important holiday at home not recognized abroad, illness in the family, emotional problems, which lead one to seek the comfort of home, or just loneliness. Employers of migrants are full of stories about workers who leave suddenly for these kinds of reasons, sometimes without notice, sometimes sending a friend to take their place, and then return weeks later to claim a job that is no longer open.

One must be very circumspect, however, in attributing the bulk of unemployment among migrants to "frictions" of this kind. Roughly speaking, migrants in the early stages of the migration process appear to fall into two groups. First are what might be called "free-floaters" – workers who move toward the industrial area with no particular job in mind, often apparently with no specific destination. A large portion of pre–World War I migrants to the United States were of this type. They were met at the ports by agents for canals and railroads or – less often – by recruiters for manufacturers in inland cities, hired, and dispatched to the job. In periods of slack employment, such workers presumably waited around the ports until such contracts materialized or moved inland on their own.[15] Juan Diez-Canedo argues that a substantial amount of contemporary Mexican migration to the United States is of this kind as well:[16] The migrants make their way north from the border by foot or by bus with no specific destination in mind. When they run out of funds, they stop to take a job. Most towns seem to have a particular block where there is a shape-up for odd jobs early in the morning. The transient migrants apparently find its location through the grapevine and hang around until they are picked up. When they have replenished their funds, or if they cannot find work, they move on to the next town, until, eventually, they arrive at a manufacturing center that offers relatively steady work. The second group of migrant workers has a much more specific destination in mind: They are planning to join relatives and friends who have pioneered a migration route, perhaps as migrants of the first kind; very often, these relatives and friends have a specific job opening for which they have actually recruited the migrant. But even when they do not, they generally know the labor market to which the migrant is coming, keep him abreast of the general availability of job opportunities before he leaves home, and help him find a job once he arrives.[17]

Both of these two groups of workers tend to be under-counted in the unemployment statistics. Indeed, there is some question whether the first group is even captured at all, for they seem, when unemployed, to have no residence and even when employed to operate in a kind of quasi-legal, under-ground labor market. The second group of migrants is also unlikely to be counted as unemployed. Since the underlying motivation of the migrant is to accumulate a fund of resources that can be invested at home, expenditures at the destination are viewed as an unavoidable cost of accumulation. If they are not working and cannot quickly find a job, they figure they are better off at home.[18] The financial requirements are minimized because housing tends to be free and meals are shared with the family. In the case of international migration, moreover, the value of currency earned abroad is greater if spent in the country of origin. For all of these reasons, there is a tendency to wait out periods of economic difficulty at home and to migrate only when, on the basis of information supplied by people already there, they can be relatively sure of finding a job in a minimal amount of time. While at home, on the other hand, they are likely to resume traditional roles in the local economy.

Although we cannot argue that the frictions involved in the movement of migrants back and forth, from origin to destination to origin, are not responsible for any of their unemployment, the foregoing does suggest that it is unlikely to be the major cause. Their unemployment appears rather to be caused by the nature of these employment opportunities themselves.

The fact that the jobs are often relatively unstable, offering little job security and subject to cyclical and seasonal fluctuations in demand, leads to periodic displacement of workers; in addition, the nature of the social relationships in the workplace, which are such that even on stable jobs workers are frequently fired or quit over personal differences with each other or with their supervisors, also contributes to the instability. Such a casual attitude toward employment relationships on the part of the employee is encouraged by the lack of job security and opportunities for advancement: When such jobs are relatively easy to come by, as in a tight labor market, there is no particular reason to remain in a job one does not like. The fact that the jobs are basically unskilled encourages a similar attitude on the part of the employer. As we have noted, these features of the jobs that migrants hold are not incidental but rather integral to the process: The features that generate the unemployment – the instability, casual social relationships, unskilled work, and so on – are precisely those features that render the jobs unattractive to native workers. And it is the attachment to a foreign home from which employee-initiated turnover derives that makes the migrants a willing source of labor. Thus, the argument is not that the unemployment is unconnected to the migration process, but that the connections are indirect.

All of this, however, is characteristic only in the early stages of a given migration stream. In the later stages, the explanation for the relatively high levels of unemployment in migrant communities is different. If the migration process worked smoothly, the attachment of the migrants and their children to the receiving country would become permanent, and they would be able to move upward into higher-level employment opportunities. Such opportunities tend to be associated with less unemployment than those at the bottom of the labor market. They are insulated from fluctuations in the demand for labor; they offer chances for internal advancement and other special benefits that discourage employee turnover; they tend to involve a certain amount of employer investment in hiring and training, which acts to discourage layoff and discharge; and they are surrounded by a set of social relationships that act in a more fundamental way to discourage job separation. To the extent that advancement occurs as the migrant community ages, therefore, its unemployment rate should decline.

The settlement process – as we have noted repeatedly in this text – seldom works this smoothly. The black migration in the United States is probably the most outstanding case to the contrary, but in practically all migrations where the newcomers are distinguishable from the natives, barriers impede advancement. Again, this is not accidental; the security offered by high-paying jobs is, as was argued previously, very artificial, dependent upon an institutional structure that limits entry to secure jobs and maintains other positions that can bear the variability and uncertainty against which the secure jobs are insulated. Ethnic and racial traits provide a convenient criteria for limiting entry and justifying the distinctions among the work force that such limitations maintain. The retarded organization of migrant communities acts, as will be seen shortly, to delay efforts to overcome such barriers until it is too late for the second generation. The result, in most cases, is a second-generation migrant community permanently located in the destination but trapped in the parents' jobs.

Unemployment in settled communities with a labor force entrapped in this way tends to be higher than among communities of recent arrivals. It is higher for essentially two reasons. First, although temporary migrants tend to return home when they cannot find work, permanent settlers clearly remain. In part, this is an accounting problem: The temporary migrant, when he is unemployed, tends to be accounted in the unemployment of his home community, whereas the permanent resident is accounted in the unemployment rate of the destination. There may also be certain real effects. In the early stages of migration, temporary migrants often have a place within the traditional economic activity of their homes, and when unemployed in foreign industry, they simply resume that place. In a sense, therefore, they are never unemployed. As will be discussed shortly, however, migration works over time to destroy traditional economics, and temporary migrants at late stages in the process, though they may return home when they lose their job, remain unemployed. Thus, in the late stages of migration, the difference between permanent and temporary migration unemployment in this regard is indeed largely due to accounting.[19]

There is a second reason for high unemployment in the late stages of migration. The permanent residents despise the work. They may work because they need the money, but they resent the job, often quit, and pose numerous discipline problems for employers, which are likely to lead to their being fired. Employers are very quick to contrast the job attitudes of natives and migrants in this regard: The contrast sharpens the picture of the migrant as an extremely hard-driving, dedicated worker. This approach to work does not apparently prevent migrants from becoming involved in personal disputes on the job, which will cause them to leave (or be fired), or, as noted earlier, from leaving suddenly and without notice to return home. But employers distinguish all this from the attitude of natives in the same position, which tends to create similar problems of turnover, absenteeism, and insubordination but which is accompanied by a sullen hostility on the job, a slow pace of work, and a sloppy attitude toward the work itself and toward the workplace.

The employers' comments imply then that the children of migrants have a turnover in their parents' jobs that is comparable to that of the first generation, albeit for very different reasons. Unlike their parents, moreover, the motivation of the children is such that they are likely to be reluctant to take a new job when they leave their old one. The high turnover, thus, would seem likely to be accompanied by a longer duration of unemployment as well.[20]

In sum, then, one must distinguish two distinct causes of the unemployment among migrants: One of these is the transient character of the migrant population and is associated with migrant streams in the early stages before substantial settlement has occurred. The second is a distaste for the available work and is associated with settled communities where there is a sizable second generation whose upward mobility is, for one reason or another, blocked. It is unclear, however, whether unemployment in the early stages of migration is accurately reflected in statistical measures, because the very transience of the population, which generates the unemployment, implies that the unemployed are likely to escape official notice.[21]

Finally, it is perhaps worth emphasizing here the contrast between this interpretation of unemployment and the interpretation most prominent in contemporary economic models of the process. The contemporary models are largely built upon the pioneering work of Harris and Todero, who focused on high and institutionally rigid wages of industrialized areas.[22] Given these high wages, they argued, people would be attracted from low-income underdeveloped regions in numbers much larger than the available employment opportunities, on the chance that they would luck into a job. It would pay the rational economic man, in other words, to migrate even if employment was not assured, and "equilibrium" in the market would be associated with a relatively high level of unemployment, which equated the "expected" income, that is, the high wages of the job discounted by the probability of getting it (which was equal to one minus the unemployment rate), with the low wage levels prevailing in the place of origin. Later refinements of the Harris-Todero model recognize that the migrants are not actually unemployed but work instead in an informal sector, whose wages are flexible and, therefore, low, but continue to see the migration flow as governed by the high and rigid wages of "modern" industry and the probability of lucking into an industrial job. There is thus a complete contrast with the transient migration process we have been analyzing in which migrants in the early stages do not plan to remain long enough to advance to the higher-wage jobs and in which their children, who aspire to such jobs, are no longer migrants.

The organization of migrants

Finally, in discussing the peculiarities of the migrant labor market, some comments about the political organization of migrant communities in general and the organization of migrant *workers* in particular would seem to be important. Just how important depends to some extent upon the particular labor-market theory to which one subscribes. Even the most conventional human-capital theory, however, suggests that such organizations play some role. In that theory, education and training are critical to economic advancement; the school system, which provides these, is a public institution; and the degree to which that institution is open and responsive to the needs of migrant children will depend upon the political pressure that the migrants can exert on their behalf. Even in the United States, where the issue of open access to education was supposedly resolved in the nineteenth century, it has been a central issue for the offspring of black migrants to northern cities and is still a factor with respect to the most recent immigrants as the ambiguous legal position of undocumented workers and their children provides local communities with a new way of restricting access to public schools. Access, of course, is only part of the issue: There is the further question of how well the schools meet the special needs of immigrant populations, particularly when there are cultural and linguistic barriers to instruction. In addition to the educational system, conventional theory has also recognized the possibility that economic mobility might be affected by artificial entry restrictions, imposed either by trade-union organizations at the workplace or through the political process in the form of licensing requirements, civil-service regulations, culturally biased tests, and the like. In the version of the dual labor-market hypothesis developed in Chapter 2, organization becomes even more important: The very structure of the demand for migrants in the first place results from the organization of certain groups of workers to secure their employment opportunities and the attempt of employers to escape the rigidities that these groups impose.

The development of political consciousness and organizational structure in migrant communities has become a separate area of study.[23] We cannot do justice to the complexity of the phenomenon and the issues that it raises here. Our comments must be confined to those aspects of the process that seem most critical in shaping the labor market in which migrants operate and the way in which they respond to it. From this perspective, the following observations seem important.

First, the shift from temporary migration to permanent settlement implies a fundamental change in perspective, which has repercussions in political and other forms of organizations. Temporary migrants do not have a long-term interest in the community, and this is bound to affect their interest in political participation. As a general rule, they simple do not see themselves as being around long enough to make most issues of community development and structure relevant. This no doubt goes a long way to explain the poor political participation of many ethnic communities, like, for example, that of the Puerto Ricans in the continental United States, which, in the face of the intense interest and high levels of voter participation that politics generates on the island itself, would otherwise be something of a mystery. It is also undoubtedly a factor in the slow political organization of black communities, although in that case the long history of repression-of community organization in the South must also have been an important retarding factor.

Second, the temporary character of the migration generates a leadership problem, which is quite distinct from the problem of arousing interest in the migrant population and which retards effective political action even on issues in which the community is, or might be, concerned. A part of that leadership problem is the fact that potential leaders, like other members of the community, are temporary migrants and turn over rapidly. The more serious problem, however, appears to derive from the high turnover among the potential constituency. As a result, even a permanent resident leader must be continually rebuilding his base of support. This fact removes all the advantages of incumbency. It leaves every leader open to perpetual challenge and results in considerable instability among community leaders, on the one hand, and, on the other, to a preoccupation with activities in the community designed to retain power, which precludes activity outside the community on its behalf. All of this has been especially apparent in the late 1960s and early 1970s in the United States when various political and programmatic positions have been reserved for representatives of the newer ethnic groups. The effect of these reserved positions, which confer a certain amount of income and prestige, is to attract more challengers to existing leadership, further aggravating the problem of instability.

All of this, of course, changes as the community stabilizes.

Residents then do have a genuine interest in the community development, and the problem of organization becomes one of convincing them that the interest can be effectuated in a particular way. By the same token, the stabilization of the community resolves the basic leadership problem. From the point of view of the labor-market problems generated by the migration process, however, this change in political consciousness and organization appears to come too late.

The central labor-market problem in the process as we have characterized it is that of assuring channels of upward mobility for the second generation. To meet the aspirations of these workers it is necessary that a variety of institutions be opened to this population and made responsive to it. The most important of these institutions are probably the educational system and union and other craft and professional associations, although one might want to include here in addition institutions granting credit, commercial licenses, health and safety inspection, and the like. The opening of these institutions to the second generation, it should be noted, is important whether the institutions play the functional role in preparing people for jobs attributed to them in conventional theory or, as is sometimes argued, serve simply to limit access and provide economic shelter for favored social groups. The paradox is that the political power to open these institutions is only available after the second generation has emerged, whereas access to these institutions is required in order to meet the aspirations in the first place. By the time, for example, that the community can organize to force the school system to cater to the needs of its children, a whole generation of children will have emerged from the schools uneducated. To the considerable extent that the political organization is required to gain access to channels of upward social mobility, the nature of the process seems to imply that the aspirations of the second generation are bound to be frustrated.

These observations, which apply to organizations in general, also seem to apply to trade-union organization. Unions might be expected to be a somewhat unique case to the extent that they are not necessarily limited to the migrant community and can, therefore, draw upon more stable groups for the bulk of their constituency and leadership. In principle, the migrants could simply be drawn into a much larger organizational entity. There are, of course, examples where this is the case. But for the process to work effectively to overcome the problem created by the differential emergence of the aspirations and the political capacity to gain control over the means of achieving them, there would have to be more of a community of interest between migrants and nonmigrants than appears in fact to exist. Indeed, if, as we have tended to argue, migrant labor is complementary to primary native labor, and many migrant jobs are created in an attempt to restore to the economic system some of the flexibility that the native union organization works to remove, the incorporation of migrants as equal partners with natives in their organization is basically antagonistic to the interests of the natives. Where migrants are incorporated, they seem, therefore, to have a secondary status within the union, which they must subsequently organize to overcome. The nature of the problem is exemplified by the garment unions, which, it is reported, have had considerable trouble adjusting to federal laws requiring the vesting of pensions because the financial structure of their pension programs was heavily dependent upon high-turnover migrant groups who contributed to the funds without remaining in the industry long enough to draw upon them. This case is of special interest because it seems doubtful that the system was deliberately designed in this way, but it did nonetheless produce a system in which the newer black and Hispanic migrants were effectively subsidizing the retirement of the older, more stable Jewish and Italian communities. In any case, it would appear that union organization in both the United States and Western Europe has largely emerged out of the migrant community in the process of stabilization. Thus, as we shall argue in a later chapter, the waves of organization in the United States in the late 1930s can be understood as the outgrowth of the stabilization of the "new immigrant" communities, following the cutoff of foreign immigration in 1923. In Western Europe, the organization of migrant groups into unions occurred in a series of spontaneous strikes in the late 1960s, which also seems to reflect the stabilization of the migrant communities and the emergence of a second generation.[24]

It appears at first glance as if the peculiarities of migrant communities and the attitudes toward work might explain the distinctive characteristics of the labor movement in the United States, which has drawn so heavily in its development upon foreign workers. Attempts to develop explanations along these lines, however, have not proved very convincing.[25] First of all, as we have argued, most industrial societies rely quite heavily upon migrants in their development, and while the heavy reliance upon foreign migrants especially early in the development process may distinguish the United States, the characteristics of migrant communities upon which we are focusing here does not. Secondly, it is not clear which way the characteristics of the migrants and their particular attitudes toward the labor market cut. It might, for example, be argued that their overriding interest in income and their short time horizon render them less susceptible to union organization than natives because they see no purposes in "investing" in a strike. On the other hand, they also have a great deal less to lose than native workers and can much more easily move elsewhere if they lose the strike. Although it is true that migrants were often used as strikebreakers in the United States, it also seems that they played this role largely out of ignorance, for when efforts were made to inform them of what was at stake, they often joined the strikes.[26] If it is possible, therefore, to develop a theory of the American labor movement that hinges upon migration, the pivot would have to be the attitude of natives and not that of the migrants themselves.

The nature of migrant attitudes might also explain the role of business unionism in the United States with its concentration upon short-term economic gain to the exclusion of long-term and allegedly more ideological issues. Again, however, such explanations seem to be undercut by the fact that, on the one hand, the bulk of union organization among migrants appears to occur in the second generation, when the time horizons are no longer foreshortened, and, on the other, the migrants in the first generation have such *extremely* short time horizons that they could not possibly expect to gain from union organization, particularly the kind of protracted battles that such organization has required in the United States, and, hence, the only possibly successful appeal to them is in terms of a broader ideology of worker solidarity.

5

The impact of migration on the place of origin

The migration process discussed in the preceding chapters is anchored in the place of origin, generally an underdeveloped country or a backward region of an industrial economy. The changes in the place of origin produced by the migration constitute the "other" half of the process. They are not the immediate focus of this volume, but it is obviously impossible to discuss the process in the receiving area without some reference to them. This chapter is directed toward that end.

In public-policy analysis, and in most scholarly publications as well, migration from backward to developed areas has been thought to affect the place of origin in two critical ways. First, migration is supposed to contribute to economic development. Second, it is often argued that the out-migration serves as a "safety valve," relieving both the physical pressure of growing populations and the political and social pressures generated by the aspirations for higher income, which the developing country cannot, or at least cannot yet, meet. Both of these factors are discussed in this chapter, along with the relationship between external and internal migration patterns in developing countries.

Migration and economic development

The most prominent views of the relation between international migration and economic development have been articulated in the context of the postwar population movements in Western Europe between the industrialized North and the less-developed countries on the southern and eastern fringes

of the continent, and in Africa and the Middle East. These envisage two principal contributions to the development process.
First, the migrant remittances have been thought to provide
critically needed foreign exchange. Second, the migrants
themselves are supposed to develop industrial skills that they
then return to apply, overcoming in this way barriers to development generated by the shortage of skilled manpower.[1]

As noted in the introductory chapters, these contributions
have proved in actuality to be rather elusive. The migrants and
their families have not been eager to spend their foreign earnings on locally produced goods and services in a way that would
enable the government, or the private capital market, to siphon
off the foreign exchange and allocate it to development projects. The earnings are often used instead to finance imports,
and attempts of the government to forestall such spending are
frustrated, either by bringing in the earnings in cash or, worse
still, holding them abroad. The migrants themselves have not
been a significant source of industrial skills. The most skilled of
the migrant workers are reluctant to return home. Those who
do return often turn out to have acquired little in the way of
useful industrial skills and are, in any case, loath to enter in
their home country the kinds of industries and occupations
in which they worked abroad.

In light of the functions that the migration serves abroad, the
failure of return migrants to provide critical industrial skills is
not surprising. The migrants are not recruited for jobs in
which they could acquire skills. Given that their acceptance of
the jobs for which they are recruited results in no small measure from their status as temporary migrants, working outside
the social structure in terms of which they define themselves
and from which they obtain status and identity, they obviously
view the same work very differently in their native environment, where they are not migrants but permanent residents.
Because many jobs for which they are recruited, moreover, involve work that prevailing values abroad discourage, any cultural assimilation and social integration that does occur in the
industrial society will only increase the migrant's reluctance to
perform the work when he or she returns home. At the same
time, assimilation of industrial values also leads to the very kind

of consumption patterns that foster expenditures on foreign imports and lead to pressure for the social overhead expenditures on such things as roads and rural electrification that will support them.

The migrants themselves, in fact, envisage a role for themselves at home very different from that foreseen in the rhetoric of public-policy pronouncements on migration and development. Typically, they plan to utilize funds acquired abroad to establish themselves in an activity that will give them independent, entrepreneurial status.[2] Treating all such migrations as of a piece, the most common migrant fantasies probably include agricultural investment, the expansion of family landholding, and investment in farm machinery, buildings, and livestock. But a wide variety of other ambitions also turns up in interviews with contemporary migrants: farm-equipment rentals; interurban taxi and bus services; various commercial ventures and repair services; and investment in machinery for small-scale manufacturing, most often, but not exclusively, sewing machines. The resistance to dependent status is so strong that it seems to explain why many migrants prefer not to spend time at home in productive activity and instead use their foreign savings to create a consumer environment and provide a fund capable of supporting their retirement.

It is perhaps possible to understand this in terms of the peasant tradition: The pattern here appears at least to involve the projection into a commercial or industrial setting of the attitudes normally ascribed to peasant proprietors. A second explanation is that of Gans, discussed in Chapter 3, who ascribes it to the *working-class* subculture.[3] A third alternative, of course, is that the ambition for independence, which a small business seems to confer, is somehow basic to human nature. The ambition is so pervasive among migrants that there is a sense in which it might as well be so. The single important exception of which I am aware is the migration of blacks in the United States from the rural South. The paucity of entrepreneurial activity among this group might be attributable to the fact that relatively few blacks were, or ever had the opportunity to operate as, independent peasant proprietors, an explanation that links this ambition to agricultural landholding patterns. But an equally plausible alternative is the long, systematic repression of independent black economic activity in the southern United States, a repression that left the professions, particularly education and religion, as the only avenue for social mobility. This latter view is more compatible with a view that independent entrepreneurial status fulfills a basic human desire.

The failure of return migrants to assume the anticipated role at home is not simply a result of their initial ambitions. It is also a product of the processes through which the skills that have been thought to be critical to development in the place of origin are acquired in industrial society. Those processes require a degree of cultural assimilation and social integration that seems, perforce, to weaken the ties that bind the migrants to their homes and to motivate the high rate of return among the unskilled and untrained. This is most apparent in the case of middle-class professional and managerial workers who attain their skills and status through prolonged formal classroom education. Obviously, these people must become proficient in the language of the industrial area and through time and exposure, if not through absolute necessity, are likely to acquire the kinds of social skills and a circle of friends that anchor them "abroad." Indeed, the length of the educational process and the degree of social integration required are such that people who begin migrating as adults are foreclosed from utilizing this route to advancement, at least in large numbers; for practical purposes, it is open only to the "second generation," that is, those who move with their parents as children or early adolescents and the children of migrants born abroad. A significant population of this kind only begins to emerge at a relatively late state in the migration process, by which time a stable community has often emerged at the destination and the "natural propensity" to return, even among first-generation migrants, is declining. The second generation, moreover, has only the weakest ties to the place of origin. Their memories of "home" are vague, more often the product of their parents' reminiscences than their own experience; very often, they cannot really speak the home language.

It is not that such professionally trained people never return home. They do. But the process of return is very different from that of first-generation migrants and is not really organic to the migration process itself. The returnees are tied to their home area by nostalgia rather than by realistic experience. They often have problems of cultural assimilation, which are as extreme as those of other foreigners, and, indeed, in terms of minimizing these problems and the frictions that they generate in the workplace and in the society at large, it is not clear that return migrants are a better source of labor than workers trained abroad with no historic ties.

The other major source of industrial skill is informal on-the-job training. It is more open to first-generation migrants than formal education and is thus apparently more promising, but, in fact, it also is a process that acts to reduce the probability of return. It does this because, for any but the most trivial skills, on-the-job training occurs in a social setting and depends heavily upon the social integration of the trainee. The critical components of knowledge are transferred directly from the experienced workman to the novice, through conversation and demonstration in spare moments in the production process. The workmen must like and accept the trainee or they will not cooperate in the training process. The social and ethnic distance between migrants and natives is very often sufficient to foreclose the training process, and when it does so, that in turn acts to heighten the migrant's sense of frustration and loneliness, frequently hastening his return home. But the other side of the role of social acceptability is that when learning does occur it involves overcoming the social distance in a way that makes the migrant feel more at home abroad and substantially reduces his desire to leave.[4]

The development process

It would be a mistake, however, to place too much emphasis upon the character of the migrants in assessing the failure of the migration to make the anticipated contribution to development. It would be a mistake in part because that motivation is organic to the migration process. It is not that people with a particular motivation happen to migrate, but rather that people with that motivation are useful and attractive to the industrial society that is offering the jobs. People more inclined to return home with skills, even if they could be found, would not be wanted abroad. A second, more important reason not to overemphasize the characteristics of the migrants is that the migration process itself calls into question the model of the development process from which the original anticipation about the role of return migrants derives.

The impact of international migration has been generally analyzed in terms of a model in which development in general and industrialization in particular are viewed as a more or less continuous evolution from a primitive subsistence economy toward an increasingly complex, sophisticated productive structure. The technical requirements of the job structure are thought, in this model, to follow the technical evolution of the economy itself so that steadily increasing levels of education and training are required of the labor force as development proceeds.[5] For early developers, this model implies that the qualifications of the work force might evolve pari passu with the requirements of the productive structure. But for late developers, and perforce for underdeveloped nations now attempting to industrialize today, the model implies a tremendous gap between the skills of the labor force and the requirements of the technology they are seeking to introduce. It is this gap that the migrants, through their sojourn in the developed country, were supposed to overcome.

The migration, however, belies these propositions. The migrants are being recruited to fill a set of jobs that do not require sophisticated education and training. The migrants originate, in fact, in agricultural areas accustomed only to quite primitive agricultural techniques, are unable to speak the language of the country to which they are moving, and are often illiterate even in their own tongue. And, moreover, not only do industrial countries seem to generate, and generate quite regularly, jobs into which such unskilled recruits readily fit, but it is in such jobs that acute labor shortages seem to occur. The native labor force, which has the sophisticated education and training that one would have thought a modern economy required, does not want the unskilled jobs, and if there is indeed a problem of structural imbalances in the labor market, it is one of overabundance of highly skilled manpower and not vice versa. Conventional ideas about the nature of industrial society and the industrialization process are also belied by another characteristic of the migration process: The conventional view is that technological development involves a progression toward larger productive units and larger conglomerations of capital and labor. It is this idea that makes the aspirations of the migrants for self-employment, and their rejection of industrial job opportunities at home in favor of activities in which these ambitions can be realized, apparently so detrimental to the constructive contribution that had been expected of them. But, in fact, the job opportunities to which they are attracted abroad are quite frequently found in relatively small enterprises managed directly by the proprietor. In Europe, for example, the largest single employer of migrants is construction, an industry dominated by small-scale enterprises. And migrants have been important in service establishments, which are also small scale, and in the lower range of establishment sizes of most major industries. Migrants, to be sure, have also been employed in industries characterized by much larger productive units, such as automobiles. But this does not detract from the basic point: In order to account for the migration phenomenon and its role in the productive structure of industrialized nations, analysts have been forced to recognize and accord a greater importance to smaller production units than the conventional development model allows.

All of this suggests that perhaps there is an alternate way of understanding the development process, one that accords more closely with the realities of the migrants' role in industrialized countries and also suggests a role in the underdeveloped countries that is both more constructive and more in accord with the returning migrants' desires and expectations than the role that migrants have been accustomed to playing, at least as that role is conventionally interpreted.

A full-fledged alternative understanding of this kind has not yet been developed. But it is emergent in a growing literature focusing upon "dualism" and a set of related phenomena that have been discussed somewhat misleadingly under that heading. Some of the findings of this literature were incorporated into the discussions of the demand for migrants in developed economies in Chapter 2. The study of the phenomena in less-developed areas has been given particular momentum in the last several years by the International Labor Organization's interest in the so-called informal sector of the urban economies in its less-developed member nations.[6]

What the literature highlights is the continuing presence and dynamic character of small-scale enterprises and the importance of many of these small enterprises to the large establishments conventionally associated with development and modernity. Analysts appear undecided as to whether the small enterprises should be treated as integral to industrialization, conceived either as a process or a state, or as the product of "lags" and distortions, manifestations of the preindustrial society into which the process of development is injected. But it is apparent that the smaller enterprises are a sufficiently pervasive and durable feature of the industrial sector so that, however interpreted, they cannot be readily eliminated nor the effects completely ignored, and that, however important the past in explaining their continuation, they serve many functions that are preeminently modern and industrial.[7]

The chief functions that the small-scale enterprises seem to serve are fourfold. First, they provide a source of flexibility when large enterprises are prevented by legal restrictions and union rules from responding quickly to variations in the level and composition of demand. Large enterprises either refuse customer demands that cannot be profitably met given existing restriction, thereby forcing people to contract directly with smaller firms, or they accept such customers themselves and then subcontract the production involved to smaller satellites.[8] We emphasized this phenomenon in the examination of duality in the structure of developed economies in Chapter 2. The phenomenon is equally pronounced in a number of underdeveloped countries where the size, the backward nature of most of the economic structure, and very frequently foreign ownership and/or management make certain modern enterprises extremely vulnerable to regulation and control. Second, small enterprises are apparently more efficient than large ones in catering to small, specialized markets. Such markets will not sustain the elaborate division of labor or the highly specific capital equipment that generate the economies of large enterprises. Small enterprises use more versatile tools, and workers are thus able to shift back and forth from one kind of output to another, piecing together a living out of an extremely heterogenous demand. In many cases, this enables small enterprises to fill in the interstices of the economys, exercising a considerable leverage on the development process. Thus, for example, a major obstacle to expanded markets in underdeveloped countries is restricted transportation, communication, and storage facilities. Interurban buses and taxis, which are a prime "target" for the earnings of many migrant workers in the United States, help to overcome these obstacles and pave the way for large enterprises to reap economies of scale in production and marketing. Similarly, automobile repair and body shops, a typical outlet for immigrant remittances in the Caribbean, serve to prolong the life of productive equipment and consumer durables.[9] (Among their other contributions, in fact, is the lower cost of interurban transportation projects.) Not all of the advantages of small business, however, derive from the state of underdevelopment. Thus, small firms seem particularly efficient in catering to the specialty tastes and services in which the income of highly developed countries enables the population to indulge on a large scale. They are also more efficient than large organizations in the repair and maintenance of the expensive, specialized equipment utilized in large-scale mass production in the so-called modern sector and of the automobiles and other consumer durable goods that absorb an increasing fraction of income as development proceeds. They seem generally to dominate in the provision of professional services, such as law and medicine, and are apparently capable of competing quite effectively with large-scale organizations in agriculture. Finally, small-scale enterprises often seem most effective in the development and initial introduction of new products that have not yet developed a mass market.

The outstanding example of the contribution of migration to industrial development is a study by Juan Diez-Canedo[10] of a town in Jalisco, Mexico, where an extensive textile industry has grown up from nothing, financed by immigrant remittances.

The industry began when one returning migrant invested his savings in a single piece of machinery, which he operated in his home. Since that time, the original entrepreneur has expanded substantially. He has also been imitated by most of his neighbors, starting first with proceedes from work in the States and subsequently expanding by investing the earnings generated by the business itself. The town, which in 1968 had no industrial activity and was an "exporter" of labor, is now experiencing a substantial labor shortage of its own and is recruiting migrants from the surrounding countryside. The industry that has grown up there competes successfully on the national market with large-scale mechanized factories in Mexico City and Monterey and is recognized as an important factor in the business decisions of the socially established elites who manage those "modern" enterprises.

Diez-Canedo sees the major function of migration in the development of Jalisco as that of providing scarce capital. Private capital funds in the rural villages of Mexico are largely in the hands of local moneylenders, who charge exorbitant rates of interest and lend only to customers with a sizable collateral, which peasants often lack. Government programs obstensibly designed to overcome the obstacle to rural development inherent in this kind of private capital market are politicized and bureaucratized. The funds allocated to these programs are virtually all diverted to the support of the *ejidos,* a form of collective agriculture originating in the Mexican Revolution in which the peasant-proprietor has an inherited right to certain landholdings but cannot sell or expand them. The *ejidotarios* form the backbone of the regime in rural areas, and the "loans," which pass through rural credit institutions, have become a form of subsidy provided in return for their political support. Given the nature of the land-tenure system under which they operate, the *ejidotarios* are not in a position to expand their agricultural activity through land purchase or improvement, and their offspring, when they migrate, move permanently to Mexico City. They do not go to the States. The migrants to the States come almost exclusively from among the non-*ejido* peasantry, which does not have access to the official rural credit institutions but which is free to purchase additional land when they have the resources to do so. Their primary motive for migration, at least initially, is to accumulate these resources.

The acquisition of skills in the narrow sense of the term was not apparently important in Jalisco. The migrants while in the States worked in heavy industry, in service, or in agriculture but not in textiles or in garments. Diez-Canedo does argue, however, that the broad exposure to industrial processes and organization has been a factor in the success of industrial development. The new entrepreneurs, his interviews suggest, have a sophisticated view of production layout, methods of wage payment and of worker motivation and control, which can be traced to their personal experiences as industrial workers in the States.

Jalisco may be extremely unusual. Clearly, it is impossible to generalize on the basis of a single case either about the frequency of such a development pattern or about the peculiarities of the environment that might have produced that pattern in Jalisco or might be fashioned in an attempt to reproduce the same pattern elsewhere. Nonetheless, several features of this particular study are noteworthy. First, the phenomenon was not uncovered in a search for the impact of return migration on development but was discovered, quite by accident, in a study conducted by Wayne Cornelius and directed at a quite different phenomenon, that is, the political impact of out-migration.[11] Second, the textile development was only the most dramatic example of the investment of immigrant resources and a good deal of its drama derived from the sheer size of the industry in the area, its novelty, and the close relationship between that industry and what we normally think of as industrialization. And one might even argue, given the competition it offered to large-scale factories in Mexico City, that it is not such a net contributor to social welfare. Diez-Canedo found a number of other examples of the investment of remittances in small-scale enterprises in agriculture, in commerce, and in services of one kind or another. The agricultural investments are less remarkable because they represented an expansion of traditional activities. But they may quantitatively have been more important. And as a subject of further study, the pattern of development may prove more promising because there is considerable variation across the territory. Diez-Canedo's preliminary hypothesis, that much of this variation can be explained by land-tenure systems and the interplay between those systems and the nexus of public and private credit institutions, seems to dovetail with literature on the pattern of return migration in contemporary underdeveloped areas.[12] Recent studies of early twentieth-century migration to the United States also suggest that the migrants came not from the poorest regions but from those where the system of land tenure provided the opportunity to invest remittances.[13] Third, as suggested above, the investment in commercial activity and services may be a good deal more productive than is generally recognized. Such investments, however, are too scattered in terms of the normal units of observation, so similar in character to what was there before, and so far from what we normally think of as modern and industrial that they are likely to go unnoticed relative to such industries as textiles and agriculture. The significance of such development is magnified by the fact that both case studies and anecdotal evidence suggest that, that kind of development accompanies virtually all migration, with the possible exception of blacks in the American South for whom, as noted earlier, the display of resources, which it might have entailed, carried prohibitive risks of confiscation and physical retaliation.

Would it be possible to take advantage of this type of development to design development policies in ways that capitalize upon the migrants' desires to open small businesses? To evaluate this possibility would require a more complete general understanding of the role of small enterprise as well as a more detailed list of the activities in which small business plays an important, strategic role. But it must also be recognized that it is not clear that the role of small business can or should be *planned*. The several functions ascribed to such institutions above all derive from the underlying ability to deal with those aspects of the economy that cannot be readily planned, because they are too uncertain, too various, too minute to be meaningfully described by the categories in terms of which planners conduct their analyses, or involve innovation that cannot by definition be foreseen. In the case of Jalisco, in fact, it can be said that the migration and the income it generated were a means of escaping or circumventing the institutions that had been planned. To this extent, perhaps, the lesson for public policy makers is indeed a negative one: that the greatest contribution of migration may be obtained by an official restraint, by an effort to minimize the control to which the process of return migration and the remittances of migrant income are subject.

The same point may be made by focusing on the role of those large enterprises whose jobs the migrants are rejecting and whose activities appear to be supplemented by the small businesses that the migrants enter instead. The success of these large-scale enterprises is critically dependent upon deliberate organization and planning. They utilize specialized labor and capital equipment, which can be kept fully employed only if the market is structured so as to maintain a steady demand for a standardized product.[14] This seems to imply that such enterprises do not and cannot function in the kind of uncontrolled, competitive market upon which conventional theory has focused in its positive, "scientific" analyses and which it has advocated as a normative policy prescription. It requires instead the kind of directive planning by government or by dominant corporate entities toward which conventional economic theory has been hostile but which provides the perspective in terms of which migration and development policies in underdeveloped countries are usually formulated. The argument about small business made above amounts to the proposition, however, that while conventional theory is wrong and the planning perspective right about large enterprises, and perhaps even about the basic thrust of the development process, the conventional model does correctly describe the role of small business in that its function is best left unplanned, to be coordinated and controlled by the market.

Migration as a "safety valve"

The second advantage of external migration frequently claimed for developing countries is that of a "safety valve," an outlet for a surplus population whose aspirations and expectations cannot be met at home.[15] From an analytical point of view, the difficulty with this claim is that it is not rooted in any understanding of the process through which aspirations and expectations are generated. It has generally been advanced at times when the migration process was already in full swing, and both the aspirations and the population movement seemed to be rising together. It could be that the migration is indeed acting as a safety valve to meet aspirations that would otherwise be pressed more vigorously through the political process at home. But it is also possible that the migration, by exposing the population to foreign standards of living and patterns of work, is actually generating the aspirations that public policy makers feel pressed to meet.

In attempting to unravel these possibilities, it is important to recognize a point developed in the next section of the chapter: The character of the external migration stream is not stable. Rather, it appears to shift systematically over time as the migration process ages and the economy at the place of origin develops. In the preceding discussions, we have focused upon peasant migrants from rural agricultural areas. The preponderance of migrants from underdeveloped to industrial societies are of this type and they are the sources of the characteristic social and political problems to which the migration process gives rise in the developed area. Migrants of this type, however, are not *pioneers,* or not at least in the case of international migration. In the *initial* stages, such migrations are composed of an aspiring middle class seeking to circumvent barriers to upward mobility in large urban areas. These people have already been exposed to the consumption patterns they are likely to encounter abroad: In fact, it can be argued that their whole migration is motivated by the patterns of living associated with urban industrial society (although such a view probably underestimates the role of social status as an independent motivator). The role of migration as a means of meeting aspirations thus probably outweighs any effect it has in generating or enhancing them, and in this sense, the process may indeed relieve social pressure that the society would otherwise be forced to accommodate in other, possibly politically explosive, ways. Since these people are also socially and physically more prominent in the eyes of the ruling elites than the peasants who follow them, one may well argue that they loom larger in policy decisions of underdeveloped areas than their relative number or visibility in the industrial country would seem to warrant.

By the time external migration has become the focus of public attention and deliberate policy abroad, however, the composition of the migration chain has generally shifted from one dominated by the aspiring urban middle class to one dominated by agricultural workers and peasants from the relatively backward regions of the country. The initial motivation for migration of these people is rooted in a desire to attain advancement within the social structure of the rural setting from which they come. The migrants have relatively little previous exposure to the urban industrial patterns of living they encounter abroad; the migration must thus work fundamental changes in their conception of what is possible in terms of patterns of consumption, routines of work, and, in the broadest sense, styles of life. It does not take much of a theory about how aspirations and expectations evolve to believe that this exposure works to change conceptions about what is *desirable* as well. The migrants bring these changed conceptions back to the countryside when they return, and at this stage it is not at all clear that the process operates, on balance, as a safety valve and not the reverse.

Finally, in assessing the effects of external migration processes upon the aspirations of the population and the way in which these are expressed at home, one must also include the impact felt in the very late stages of the process, possibly after net out-migration has actually already ceased, of the second-generation migrants reared abroad. In the case of migration to the United States at least, the second generation has a tendency to become involved in the politics of the countries from which their parents came in ways that have often been disruptive. These efforts seem to be related to the problems of the second generation abroad: frustrations in their attempts to achieve assimilation and upward mobility and a consequent desire both to establish a positive individual identity and cohesive political groupings in which the home country and its image become critical points of reference. These tendencies are manifest most recently in the role of northern blacks in the southern civil-rights movement[16] and in the relationship between the Young Lords, a New York youth organization, and the Puerto Rican Independentista movement.[17] Historical manifestations include the role of Irish-Americans in the Irish Republican movement, of American Jews in the Zionist movement and more recently in the support of the Israeli state, of Greek-Americans in the Greek Independence movement, and so on.[18]

Of these various ways in which migration is related to aspirations and expectations, the effect on rural agricultural communities appears to be the most important because it seems, in many respects, most integral to the migration process itself and potentially most detrimental to economic development. That it is not, of course, a purely negative factor is suggested by Diez-Canedo's argument that the kind of development that occurred in Jalisco was critically dependent upon exposure through migration to the managerial and organizational patterns of an industrial society. Other effects, although possibly not conducive to development (and one might argue, therefore, of little general value to the country or region as a whole), are nonetheless balanced quite nicely by the resources generated by the migration process itself. The consumption patterns supported in rural Yugoslavia and southern Italy by migrant remittances, for example, will offend the esthetics of the tourists who traditionally sought in these places relief from the visual monotony generated around them at home by the industrial society. It would undoubtedly never have occurred to the people there to want such things, let alone to buy them, without exposure to industrial society through migration, but the consumption patterns and the satisfaction with which they are displayed testify to the ability of the migration process to generate resources commensurate with the desires to which it seems to give rise.

It is also true, however, that external migration has a tendency to degrade and devalue the occupational structure of the economies in which it occurs, especially in those occupations involving traditional patterns of subordination and authority.

The process through which this occurs appears to be essentially the same one through which second-generation migrants in the destination come to devalue and disparage and finally reject the occupations that their parents' generation performed. Like the latter process, it can work to create labor shortages in affected occupations, despite a dearth of alternative employment, and in this way may work to undermine traditional economic activities. The effect is not serious if, as occurred in Jalisco, the migration also generates new activities to replace the traditional economic structure. Indeed, where new developments are occurring, the decline of traditional activities may actually be a facilitating factor, releasing resources critical to the emergent industries. But migration appears to adversely affect the attractiveness of traditional activities whether or not it generates replacement for them.

Rural Puerto Rico provides the most dramatic illustration of this process.[19] There the traditional activities are sugarcane and coffee. Those activities had, in fact, constituted such a large proportion of total employment in the generally labor-surplus rural economy that public policy was directed at the preservation of these employment opportunities and, for this reason, acted to retard mechanization and other productivity improvements. The result of prolonged migration to the continental United States and the generation of new employment opportunities through development at home was to devalue the traditional occupations in the countryside. The devaluation was very much a generational phenomenon. The older generation continued to find the traditional work acceptable, but the younger generation did not. As the older generation began to age and die in the middle 1960s, the Puerto Ricans suddenly found themselves with a rural labor shortage. The shortage grew despite very high levels of unemployment – in some regions exceeding 50 percent – and continued despite the introduction of a government wage subsidy, which rose to cover half the wage and, adjusted for other costs, created a rough parity with earnings through migration to the mainland. It is now clear that even at relatively high earnings, the younger generation finds traditional agricultural work to be humiliating and degrading and prefers to remain unemployed. The consequent labor shortage has become so severe that employers have been pressuring for the import of labor from Colombia. In the absence of labor migration, the industries appear to be declining. Conventional economic theory, in analyzing a labor shortage of this kind, is prone to concentrate upon relative wages and to argue that the shortage could be overcome by the introduction of higher wages or the elimination of alternative income sources available either through migration or such income maintenance programs as unemployment insurance, welfare, and food stamps. To a certain extent, this is true. Or at least it is true that in rural Puerto Rico high unemployment does not imply starvation or anything close to it. Because people do migrate, it is not even a permanent condition. But it is *not* true that the low wages are the cause of the labor shortage. It is clear that the labor shortage is the result of the changing value structure produced by the migration process. Migration to the mainland has expanded employment and income opportunities for both the younger and older generation and both take advantage of these. But the older generation is also willing to work in the traditional jobs: The younger generation is not. It is unclear, moreover, what amount of income would attract the younger generation into their parents' occupation. It is conceivable that no viable wage would compensate for what they view as the humiliation of traditional jobs, and it is certainly apparent that the wages that would begin to attract an adequate native labor force would destroy the industry.

The Puerto Rican case is not unusual. Indeed, allowing for institutional variation, it is fairly typical of sugarcane cutting in the Caribbean. In the French Antilles, whose relationship to metropolitan France is similar to that of Puerto Rico to the continental United States, a parallel labor shortage developed; there, it was, in fact, overcome through the importation of labor, in that case, from French Guiana on the South American coast. In Santo Domingo, and also in Cuba, at least before the revolution, the process of out-migration generated a vacuum in the market for cane cutters that was filled by migrant workers from Haiti. In the Dominican Republic, which borders Haiti, this migration in turn posed a threat to territorial claims on the border region.[20]

The pattern also appears to be prevalent on the European continent. North African workers are reportedly being recruited to do agricultural work in labor-surplus regions of southern Italy, Sardinia, and Sicily; Portuguese workers are being recruited for regions of heavy out-migration in Spain.[21] The contemporary border problems in the Dominican Republic and Haiti find parallels today in Venezuela and Colombia and historically in East Prussia and Poland, where the Poles were recruited in large numbers to take places vacated by migrating Germans.[22]

External and internal migration

Finally, in examining the role of migration in developing countries, we must consider the relationship between external migration and internal migration. Although this chapter as a whole focuses on the donor country, we shall examine this question from the perspective of the recipient nation's development pattern as well as that of the donor. To the very considerable extent that the current recipients were once themselves underdeveloped, an examination of their experience may be of some relevance to contemporary donors as well.

In recipient countries, external migration appears to be a substitute for internal population movements. We have argued that industrialized nations need a steady supply of new labor from relatively underdeveloped regions, but they can get that supply either from within their own borders or from abroad. Thus, we noted that U.S. development drew initially upon migrants from abroad and, in this way, avoided reliance on domestic labor reserves in the rural South. This pattern presents at least an apparent contrast with the European experience where heavier reliance was placed initially on internal migration and extensive reliance on immigrants is a phenomenon of the later stages of development.[23]

It can be argued that reliance on foreign immigration has certain characteristic advantages for a developing nation. In the case of the United States, for example, the long-run impact of internal migration, when it finally did occur, appears to have been the destruction of the traditional southern rural

economy. The immediate causes of the economy's demise were
the civil-rights movement and changes in agricultural technology, which produced mechanization.[24] But as the preceding
sections of this chapter suggest, the civil-rights movement can
be seen as an outgrowth of the migration process itself. The
two factors that produced it were organizers who grew up in
industrialized regions and became interested in the fate of
their relatives who remained behind and a receptivity among
the resident population produced by a growing dissatisfaction
with patterns of subordination and authority associated with
traditional occupations. Both of these are, as the preceding section suggests, quite typical of migration processes. The revolution in agricultural technique may be viewed in this light as
endogenous, a response to the "shortage" of pliable labor that
the civil-rights movement produced (or if you prefer, revealed). And one is led to wonder what would have happened
to southern agriculture if the out-migration had occurred immediately after the Civil War. The country might then have
paid for an expansion of the industrial North with a corresponding decline in the agricultural South. Or, alternatively, the
composition of southern agricultural output might have
shifted to less labor-intensive crops. Or the South rather than
the North might have drawn upon foreign immigrants in the
same way that the French Antilles have drawn upon a foreign
labor source to harvest cane.[25] Quite possibly, the southern
immigration pattern would have depended more heavily upon
the Caribbean basin and less heavily upon Europe. It is possible
that the costs of these alternatives, however vaguely perceived
and indirectly felt in the political process, were responsible for
the particular historical pattern of U.S. development.

The U.S. case may be unusual, but it is not unique. The
European country with the heaviest reliance upon foreign
workers in the postwar period is Switzerland: Immigrants
there have come to constitute 25 percent of the labor force.
And, in that case, it seems apparent that a highly mobile and
fluid foreign population is a substitute for the internal mobility
of the Swiss themselves, who are subdivided into several distinct linguistic and ethnic groups, each tied to certain geographic territories where they have gradually relinquished tradi-

tional economic pursuits.[26] As with the case of the American South, one can speculate about what would have happened without external migration. Perhaps the linguist groups would have maintained their geographic inertia. They would, however, clearly have sacrificed for this the tremendous economic prosperity with which Switzerland and the Swiss pattern of existence have come to be associated. Alternatively, internal migration might have substituted for the foreign immigrants, resulting however in direct face-to-face encounters between the different groups that claim Swiss citizenship, possibly creating the very kinds of linguistic and ethnic confrontations that have plagued other European countries in the 1960s.

Indeed, one must wonder whether the apparent reliance upon internal labor reserves in the early development of the rest of Europe is not, to some extent, a product of reading the past in terms of modern categories of thought that are the outgrowth of those very historical processes. The nation-states that now compose Western Europe are the product of relatively recent historical developments. Now that clear national boundaries have emerged, it is obvious that movement within them is easier than movement across them (although the U.S. and Swiss cases make clear that even that notion is somewhat deceptive). But the political processes through which those national boundaries have come to be drawn have themselves been influenced by migration movements between territories that originally conceived of themselves as distinct but came through migration to think of themselves first as economically and eventually as culturally associated. In the preceding pages, we cited several examples in which the migration process and the politics of frontier territories had become intertwined: the German-Polish border, Venezuela and Colombia, Haiti and Santo Domingo, and in a certain sense, even Mexico and the United States.

The donor country

In the case of modern long-distance migrations between developed and underdeveloped nations, the nation-states involved are clearly defined entities. From the vantage point of the underdeveloped region, internal and external migrations are not so clearly alternative, substitute patterns but from many points of view can be considered complementary. They occur simultaneously and are complexly interrelated. The interrelationships are so complex that it is not easy at this stage of research to generalize, but several general points do seem to emerge from the U.S. and European experience, and several more, albeit more speculative, points can be made.

First, external migration is clearly a phenomenon of the early stages of economic development. In the later stages, once the donor countries' own urban areas are experiencing rapid growth, they are able to absorb their own rural populations directly, and when this occurs, it seems to cut off external migration. This suggests, and much anecdotal evidence seems to confirm, that people really do prefer to migrate within their own linguistic and ethnic territory provided economic opportunities are comparable.[27] The clearest examples of countries in which internal developments seem to absorb the potential migrant populations, acting eventually to cut off external flows, are Italy and Spain.

Second, the external migration, once it is in full swing, appears to involve a direct migration from the countryside in the country of origin to the city of the destination. Thus, two-stage migration, which is often discussed in the literature, appears to be neither necessary for migration nor typical of it. And the result in the underdeveloped country is that at certain stages in the evolution of migration patterns there are both internal and external movements occurring simultaneously. Apparently the two movements are distinct. In some cases, the distinction is geographic. Thus, for example, northern Italian development depended for some time upon a labor force recruited from adjacent rural regions, whereas the southern Italians sought work abroad. As suggested above, Diez-Canedo argues that in Mexico the two movements depend upon land-tenure arrangements and the possibility of reinvesting earnings. Private proprietors, who are in a position to improve or expand land-holdings, migrate to the United States. The offspring of *ejidotarios*, who have no opportunity to invest earnings and for whom there is really no place in the rural economy, move to

Mexico City, where they feel more at home than in the States and can establish a permanent residence. The anecdotal evidence in Puerto Rico is that the distinction between internal and external migrants is cultural. It is claimed, somewhat paradoxically, that to make it economically in San Juan requires much greater sophistication and savoir faire than the typical rural peasant possesses and that he is better off, and less open to exploitation, on the continent. The comments of Puerto Ricans in Boston seem to bear this out: The major reason for choosing Boston over either San Juan or New York is a fear of "drugs," which seems to symbolize all the threats and temptations of competitive urban life and which people see as especially strong in areas where the Spanish-speaking community is of long standing.

Third, in the case of Latin American and Caribbean migration to the United States at least, a two-stage migration pattern appears to characterize the early stages of the migration. Thus, most of the newest wave of illegal migrants from Latin America and the Caribbean seem to be aspiring members of the middle class coming from the major urban areas. They are often the offspring of a previous generation who moved from the country to the city. This pattern was also typical of the Puerto Rican migration to the United States in its earliest phases, although, as has been noted, that pattern is now basically a single-stage migration from rural areas. The Haitian and the Santo Domingan migrations at the moment seem to be shift cases: Originally composed of the middle class, or aspiring middle class from urban areas, it is now increasingly rural and lower class in background.

How might one explain these patterns? In part, the transition from the urban middle class to the rural lower class can be understood in terms of the physical and institutional structure of the migration process itself. International migration requires both transportation and documentation. People have to know where to go to obtain passports and visas; they must be able to get there; they need to know how to fill out the forms that are required; in some cases, they have to pay to obtain the necessary document, and, in any case, they must be able to purchase transportation. Initially, these are only available in major urban

areas. Foreign countries do not maintain embassies and consu-
lates in agricultural communities, and transportation companies
do not normally have agents there. Even in cities where such
offices are maintained they are only accessible to people who are
relatively sophisticated in the ways of industrial society and
have a modicum of financial resources, and this perforce is the
urban middle class.

To tap the rural population, a much more extensive institutional structure is required, a structure that consists of intermediaries that can help the potential migrant obtain the necessary documents, advance the requisite funds, and arrange
transportation. Before this institutional structure is established,
somebody must have acquired a sufficient understanding of
the labor market in the industrialized country to make the institutional structure economically viable. And it appears that it
is the initial middle-class migrants who perform this function.
Their "middle-class" background provides them with the
perspective upon society and the knowledge of its operation
required to put together the necessary institutions that will
bridge the difference between the countryside in an underdeveloped area and the immigration procedures of a developed
industrial nation: Their own experience as migrants yields the
knowledge of the industrial labor market, and their parental
ties in the countryside yield the knowledge of the peasant
population required to recruit labor and secure the financial
resources advanced for documentation, transportation, and initial living expenses.[28]

This effect is basically compositional; a middle-class migration is required to pave the way for penetration into the rural
interior. But it is possible that the initial migration of the urban
middle class is also related in an organic way to the development process itself. The comments of the current middle-class
migrants from Latin America make clear that what is involved
in their migration to the United States are obstacles to upward
mobility at home. In contrast to rural migrants, whose chief
ambition seems to be self-employment, the ambition of the
middle-class migrant is the upward social mobility of his family.
He may express an intention to invest his savings in an enterprise at home, but this is generally only a means to the end of

investment in education for his children, which will enable them to enter the professional middle class. Some of the migrants are themselves these children, who have obtained the requisite education but seem unable to find a place comparable to their educational achievement among the occupational positions open to them.

What these comments suggest is that the urban occupational structure of these developing countries is unequal to the size of the aspiring middle class or, judging from the qualification and even the performance of the migrants, of even that group that has not only the aspirations but is also educated for and equipped to assume professional and managerial roles in the economy. It is possible, however, that this is a temporary bottleneck; as development proceeds, the middle of the occupational structure eventually does begin to expand more rapidly, opening up positions for the aspiring middle class at home and simultaneously cutting off the migration of these people abroad.

On the other hand, once the rural migration begins, it is possible that its effect is simply to swamp the middle-class migration rather than to substitute for it. The total migration becomes much larger, and the middle-class migrants may remain, possibly sharing the labor market with the lower class, which is now so large a proportion of the total that the middle class goes unnoticed; but more likely, the middle-class workers find positions in the immigrant community as professionals, politicians, storekeepers, and organizers of the migration process itself, which correspond to their social status and aspirations at home.

Piecing together these various observations, the following composite picture of migration patterns in underdeveloped countries emerges: The earliest migration pattern in underdeveloped countries is one of migration to major urban areas from adjacent rural regions. This initial migration appears to generate a second stage in which the offspring of the original migrants, aspiring to middle-class status but blocked from upward mobility by the paucity of opportunities at home, move to industrial areas abroad. The middle-class migration leads to a third stage of direct rural migration from the underdeveloped country to industrialized areas abroad. The second stage, middle-class migration, appears to be a necessary link in the emergence of the third stage: The middle-class migrants create the institutional structure required to link the countryside of their own country with the industrialized nation abroad. At the same time, the earlier middle-class migrants achieve upward mobility in the infrastructure required to support the massive migration of unskilled labor at home and abroad. The third stage of the migration process may also be one in which the professional and managerial positions in the home country expand, and the barriers to upward mobility that promoted the original migration abroad recede. To this extent, economic development at home would act along with economic development abroad to shift the class composition of the migration stream. Economic development of urban areas in the donor country also seems to encourage internal migration so that not infrequently rural migration abroad is accompanied by internal rural-urban migration as well. The two streams do not typically coincide: They tend to be differentiated geographically and socially. In the final stages of the development process – typified at the current time by Spain and Italy in Europe – internal development is capable of absorbing completely the migration flows from rural areas, and net external migration comes to a halt. There may, in fact, be a certain reverse flow of second-generation migrants returning to assume middle-class positions in urban areas at home. New Yorkers returning to Puerto Rico and blacks moving from the North to the urban South suggest this pattern. But at the same time, the momentum of past migration also produces a residual flow of people leaving their native country to join family abroad. At this point, the donor country has, in effect, joined the ranks of the developed nations; in the next stage, when it has exhausted its own labor reserves, it begins itself to draw upon foreign labor.

6

The historical evolution of long-distance migration in the United States

This and the subsequent chapter review the migration experience of the United States in terms of the analytical perspective developed in the foregoing pages. The present chapter focuses on the historical evolution of long-distance migration flows. The next chapter is directed at the contemporary policy problems posed by undocumented alien workers. The chapters are designed to illustrate, through the examination of the American case, the type of interpretation that the analytical perspective implies. But they also represent an attempt to demonstrate the usefulness of the approach as a means of understanding and coming to terms with the specific problems that such migration poses for public policy.

The history of migration flows in the United States may be analyzed in terms of two distinct developments, the evolution of the job structure, or the *demand* for long-distance migrants as workers, on the one hand, and the evolution of the migration streams, or the supply of migrants, on the other. This chapter is divided accordingly.

The demand for labor: the structure of the labor market

A careful study of the historical development of labor-market structures remains to be undertaken; in the absence of such a study, our understanding of the development must remain incomplete and fragmentary. Nonetheless, available material suggests that in the United States five periods were of critical importance, particularly in the formation of the low-wage, or secondary, sector into which unskilled immigrants have flowed: (1) a preindustrial or craft stage; (2) a stage of incipient industrialization, in which industrial and agricultural activities were combined within the same productive units; (3) the development of factory production, (4) the formation of large manufacturing trusts in the late nineteenth and early twentieth centuries; and (5) the introduction of social-welfare reforms and the formation of industrial unions in the 1930s and 1940s.

Preindustrial work organization: craft production

Prior to the development of large-scale manufacturing, manufacturing work was conducted within a household unit that was largely self-contained and by modern standards relatively self-sufficient. The core production was handled by a skilled craftsman. His work was supplemented by less-skilled journeymen and apprentices, who lived as part of the household unit, and by the remaining family members who acted as helpers, providing supplementary labor when not performing other household tasks.[1] These craft production units also engaged in minor agricultural activities, producing a good deal for home consumption, and performed the larger part of home construction and maintenance. Fluctuations in demand for output were absorbed by these units in a continual reallocation of labor back and forth from manufacturing production to subsidiary home consumption and vice versa.[2] The subsidiary activities tended in any case to minimize dependence upon the market.

Incipient industrialization: the putting-out system

As the economy expanded, there was increasing specialization of labor and these self-contained units began to break down. The emergent production structure involved more specialized but less-skilled labor, employed in proportions that could no longer be contained within a household unit supplemented by a limited number of outside apprentices. The initial expansion, however, was apparently able to draw upon the large number of independent agricultural producers in the surrounding rural areas. For these people, manufacturing production constituted a supplement to agricultural income and activities

more or less as agricultural activity was, for the craft household, a supplement to industrial earnings. The now more
specialized craft units at the core of productive activity were
able to use the agricultural sector to absorb fluctuations in demand, contracting out peak loads to the countryside and curtailing this outside activity when demand declined. The agricultural sector was in turn able to support this variation by
readjusting work schedules toward more or less intensive work
on the farm. The nature of the relationship between manufacturing and other activities was clearly different here than it was
in the period of household craft production, but the labor-
market structure continued to rest heavily on the intermeshing
of different kinds of activities in polyvariant productive units.[3]
The nature of the intermesh was such that industrial unemployment as we know it today was largely unknown in the
first half of the nineteenth century, despite wide fluctuations in
the degree of economic prosperity and the level of productive
activity.[4]

In this type of production activity, built around household
units, there was no place for the unskilled, temporary immigrant, and it should not be surprising therefore that immigration was of a more or less permanent kind, formed either of
whole households or of individuals with a long-term outlook
and commitment, which enabled them to form, or integrate
into, the kinds of community structure in terms of which production was conducted.

Industrial expansion: the factory system

A third stage in the expansion of activity appears to have been
reached when fluctuations in production could no longer be
handled through a symbiotic agricultural sector. At this point it
apparently become necessary to draw into continuous manufacturing activity a labor force that could not be sustained in
slack periods. The expansion of production that necessitated
this adjustment seems also to have led to further divisions of
labor, more or less in the manner of Adam Smith's pin factory,
which reduced the skill requirements of this large labor force,
and it is at this point, which was first reached in the shoe and

textile industries just prior to the Civil War, that there begins to
be a place for a work force of unskilled and more or less transient immigrants.[5]

Industrial consolidation: the trusts movement

It is at this point in the evolution of most manufacturing industries also that the movement toward consolidation and
monopoly appears to intervene, an intervention that leads to a
further transformation of the market structure. A major study
of this movement in late nineteenth- and early twentieth-
century America has just been completed by Alfred Chandler
of the Harvard Business School;[6] that and some recent developments in economic thinking about this problem[7] suggest
that the emphasis upon monopolization in most writing on this
subject is somewhat misplaced. The impetus behind the industrial consolidation movement appears to be a series of
economies associated with control over the stable segment of
market demand. These economies seem to have derived from
large-scale production of a standard product. This is typified
by the strategy of Arthur Moxhamn of Du Pont who rejected
the notion of complete market control in favor of "60 percent
full and steady."[8] The economies are apparently connected to
major technological innovations that can be introduced into the
production process. To the extent that the innovations are capital intensive, their capital intensity provides an impetus for the
stabilization of output in order to ensure high levels of utilization. Chandler suggests that these innovations were induced by
the expansion of the market occasioned by the railroads and
the telegraph. They can thus be seen as part of the process
envisaged by Adam Smith: an outgrowth of the division of
labor and the specialization of labor that seems to accompany
the growth of manufacturing activity. At any rate, it is clear
from Chandler's study that the nineteenth and early twentieth
centuries saw the same transformation occur in a variety of industries until, by the end of the period, it was pervasive
throughout the national economy.

The consolidation movement in American industry laid the
groundwork for a dual economic structure. It divided demand

in most major industries into two components: a stable component, Du Pont's 60 percent, which the newly formed trusts attempted to reserve for themselves, and which was met through modern, capital-intensive production technologies in relatively large-scale productive units, and a fluctuating component, handled by much smaller enterprises, probably in smaller productive units and using more labor-intensive techniques.

Our knowledge about the job structure in these sectors is very sketchy, and we know a good deal less about the small-scale sector than about large-scale production. It appears, however, that some of the production jobs in the smaller enterprises must have been, relative to those in the so-called monopoly firms, much more highly skilled. The products were less standard and the workmen had to be able to accommodate a good deal of variations, perhaps to design portions of the product or of the productive processes themselves. But other jobs were probably in some sense less skilled: elementary tasks separated out from the work of the highly skilled craftsman to save his time; simple, unskilled routine work that in larger factories was performed by machines and created a demand in those factories for skilled machine repairmen and other workman, no more skilled but certainly more dependable and responsible than the usual unskilled operative, to tend the expensive equipment. To the extent that the jobs in the small-scale sector were less demanding in terms of skill and/or reliability but were at the same time more variable, the small-scale sector created a demand for labor in terms of which the transient immigrants were especially attractive.

The distinction between the employment activities in the two types of manufacturing activities in the early period should not be exaggerated. The large-scale enterprises had a number of jobs that were essentially unskilled; these jobs were readily available to immigrants and a number of immigrants were employed in them. The stability of employment, which the large enterprises were able to offer, was often relative rather than absolute, and, in fact, when workers were unskilled and easily replaced, the nature of supervision and the way in which jobs were filled after a layoff often did little to translate the theoretical possibility of employment stability into real job security. All this meant that the employment structure, even in large enterprises, created a real place for the transient labor force that was able to accommodate economic fluctuations, which the immigrants provided.

Worker consolidations: industrial unionism

The significance of these structural developments in the organization of industry was greatly changed, however, by the advent of union organization in the 1930s and 1940s. This period witnessed the growth for the first time of stable industrial unions. Membership in unions rose from 6.3 percent of the labor force in 1930 to 12.7 percent in 1940, 22.3 percent in 1950, and 25.2 percent in 1956.[9] In most of heavy manufacturing, the growth was equally dramatic. Job security was a major goal of these new union organizations; job-security provisions were among the first demands of the newly formed organizations and attempts to expand those provisions have progressed throughout the postwar period.

The effect of American trade unions on job security has been twofold. First, they have introduced a series of provisions governing the allocation of existing jobs, which act to translate security already inherent in the demand of labor into effective employment security for the work force. They do this by barring arbitrary discharge and by introducing strict procedures governing the layoff of workers and creating a right of recall for laid-off employees to return to work when employment expands. To the considerable extent that the demand for labor in general had already been stabilized by the consolidation movement a half century earlier, these trade-union measures had an important impact upon the stability of employment opportunities. In addition, unions have tried to extend job security by restricting the right of employers to discharge workers and by arrangements that divide existing employment opportunities into secure and insecure jobs. They have undoubtedly been less successful in this regard than some European labor movements, which have managed to erect legal barriers to layoff for economic reasons.[10] But every provision that increases the cost of layoffs enhances the incentives for stability, and most trade-union rules governing layoff have this effect.

In addition, unions have imposed supplementary unemployment arrangements in some industries that deliberately have this effect. Other arrangements affecting the structure of employment opportunities are membership classifications, such as those in longshoring, which make certain groups of union members eligible for permanent jobs. Similar distinctions are made in construction, not only among different categories of the membership but, more commonly, between union and nonunion workers. In most manufacturing concerns, union protection is only extended to workers after a probationary period ranging from several weeks to a couple of months, and in some firms this also is used to create a series of temporary employments staffed by workers who are always discharged before their probation comes to an end. Thus, in terms of labor-market structure, the advent of trade unions appears both to have sharpened existing distinctions between secure and insecure employment opportunities and to have acted, albeit probably secondarily, to introduce new distinctions that had not previously existed. The role of successive waves of migration and the fate of their offspring in the second generation must be understood in the context of this evolving labor-market structure.

The supply of migrant labor

The United States is a country of immigrants and, in a certain sense, immigration must be seen as a continuing feature of national development. Nonetheless, migration, particularly migration streams feeding into the bottom of the labor market, appears to fall into a series of distinct patterns. It is useful to recognize four of these: (1) the "old" immigration from Northwestern Europe, which dominated early economic development; (2) the "new" immigration from Southern and Eastern Europe, which predominated in the late nineteenth and early twentieth centuries and was brought to a halt by World War I and the legislation closing the border in 1923; (3) the internal migration of blacks, Spanish-speaking Americans, and rural whites, who moved from the agricultural South and Southwest, Puerto Rico, and, secondarily, out of Mexico itself

to the urban, industrial North. This migration stream began as
the "new" immigration from Europe was closed off in World
War I and in the 1920s but was concentrated in World War II
and the postwar period extending into the early 1960s; (4) the
"new" new immigration of the late 1960s and 1970s, which is
dominated by people from Mexico and the Caribbean basin.
Much of this migration is undocumented and extralegal.

The "old" immigration

What has come to be known as the "old" immigration was composed of people from Northern Europe, Britain, Sweden,
Germany, and Ireland. These countries dominated the immigration flows prior to the Civil War.

The movement in that period appears to conform to the now
prevalent popular image of American immigration in general
as a form of permanent settlement. It remains remotely possible that, even for these times, the popular view is in error but
the error at least is shared by virtually all historians and commentators. The Immigration Commission, writing in 1911,
states flatly that "The Old Immigration movement was essentially one of permanent settlers."[11] Kuznets and Rubin, on the
basis of an examination of available data, concur.[12] Charlotte
Erickson, working from letters of British immigrants earlier in
the century, comes to similar conclusions:

> British immigrants who went into agriculture in
> America did not emigrate in order to try to save or contrib-
> ute to the improvement of a family farm in Britain. Only
> one of them mentioned the possibility of helping to pay
> the rent on an English farm. Taking a farm in the United
> States was not a means of being able to send cash back
> across the Atlantic. Undertaking no responsibility for fam-
> ily or enterprises left behind, the emigrants to American
> agriculture made a clear break. One of their strongest as-
> sets was the fact that most of them had decided to remain
> in the United States permanently before they emigrated.
> Though they hoped to visit England, even this intention
> was frustrated as the cares and expenses of farming piled
> up.[13]

This characterization fits closely with the economic structure of the period as we outlined it in the previous section. Manufacturing and agricultural activities operated to complement each other within a single household and among households in the larger community, and their complementarity played the role that temporary migrants came to play in later periods. Since production, moreover, tended to take place within a household unit, there was little room for the kind of unattached individuals that temporary migrant labor became. It makes sense, therefore, that the migrants should have come as a household unit or with the intention of eventually forming such a unit, attaching themselves in the meantime to a settled household.[14]

The other factor that would seem to have encouraged permanent migration was the nature of the voyage. As late as 1856, more than 95 percent of transatlantic migration appears to have been by sail.[15] The cost and time must have acted to discourage temporary movement.

The "new" immigration

The composition of immigration shifted dramatically after the Civil War and the flow was increasingly dominated by new groups, not represented in the earlier period, from Southern and Eastern Europe: Italians, Jews, Russians, Slovaks, Poles, Croatians, Romanians, and Greeks. In the Civil War decade, the percentage of immigration from Northern and Western Europe was 89 percent; by the decade 1901–10, it had fallen to 22 percent.[16]

The new immigrants were not permanent settlers. The Immigration Commission, summarizing the results of a forty-two-volume study published in 1911, contrasted the new to the old immigration as follows:

> The New Immigration is very largely one of individuals, a considerable portion of whom apparently have no intention of permanently changing their residence, their only purpose in coming to America being to temporarily take advantage of the greater wages paid for industrial labor in this country. This, of course, is not true of all the new

immigrants, but the practice is sufficiently common to
warrant referring to it as characteristic of them as a class.
From all data that are available, it appears that nearly 40
per cent of the new immigration movement returns to
Europe and that about two-thirds of those who go remain
there ... As a class, the new immigrants are largely unskilled laborers ... Nearly 75 per cent of them are males.
About 83 per cent are between the ages of 14 and 45 years
and consequently are producers rather than dependents.
They bring little money into the country and send or take
a considerable part of their earnings out. More than 35
per cent are illiterate, as compared with less than 3 per
cent of the old immigrant class.[17]

Data on return migration is fragmentary, but the fragments do seem to form the picture that the text of the report
attempted to paint. Thus, the Immigration Commission reports that for fiscal 1908–10, European alien emigrants were
equal to 32 percent of European alien immigrants: The figure
for new immigrants was 38 percent; for older immigrants only
16 percent.[18] There seems to be little doubt that the bulk of the
returnees were short-term migrants: More than 80 percent had
been in the United States less than five years.[19] Table 6-1 shows
rates of return by country of origin. As can be seen, these rates
for certain particular groups are exceedingly high: 57 percent
for Croatians and Slovenians; 63 percent for northern Italians;
56 percent for southern Italians; 65 percent for Magyars; 31
percent for Poles; 41 percent for Russians; 59 percent for
Slovaks; 51 percent for Spaniards.

One might suppose that the difference between the old and
new immigrants noted by the Immigration Commission was essentially the age of the migration stream, that is, the older immigration, if examined at a comparable stage in the process,
would also have appeared transitory. but this does not in fact
seem to have been the case. Several factors point in the other
direction. One of these is a study by Simon Kuznets and Ernest
Rubin of immigration patterns in the nineteenth and twentieth
centuries, which identifies a clear shift over the period toward
an increasing transient component.[20] The rising transience is
suggested both by the size of the return flows relative to inflows

Table 6-1. *Migrants admitted to and departing from United States fiscal years 1908–10 by ethnic group*

Ethnic group	Immigrants admitted	Emigrant aliens departing	Number departing for every 100 admitted
Armenian	11,440	1,294	11
Bohemian and Moravian	25,188	2,710	11
Bulgarian, Servian, and Montenegrin	37,286	10,927	29
Croatian and Slovenian	78,658	44,442	57
Dalmatian, Bosnian, and Herzegovinian	10,331	1,991	19
Dutch and Flemish	29,004	3,085	11
English	101,611	14,481	14
Finnish	32,752	5,608	17
French	21,298	9,622	45
German	192,644	39,749	21
Greek	86,257	21,615	25
Hebrew	236,100	18,949	8
Irish	93,090	6,409	7
Italian, North	77,661	48,649	63
Italian, South	457,414	257,902	56
Lithuanian	51,129	7,189	14
Magyar	78,901	51,014	65
Polish	269,646	82,507	31
Portuguese	18,426	2,550	14
Roumanian	30,949	8,396	27
Russian	41,578	17,076	41
Ruthenian	55,106	6,697	12
Scandinavian	113,786	15,602	14
Scotch	42,737	4,345	10
Slovak	70,717	41,438	59
Spanish	10,299	5,297	51
Syrian	13,507	3,810	28
Turkish	4,261	3,010	71
Welsh	5,562	417	8
Total	2,297,338	736,835	32

Source: "European Immigrants (including Syrian) Admitted to the United States, and European Emigrant Aliens (including Syrian) Departing from the United States, Fiscal Years 1908–1910, Inclusive, by Race of People," Immigration Commission (The Dillingham Commission), *Abstract of Reports of the Immigration Commission,* U.S. Senate, 61st Congress, 3rd Session, Document No. 747 (Washington, D.C.: U.S. Government Printing Office, 1911), Vol. I, p. 182, Table 16.

and by the pattern of correlation of arrivals and departures. The two flows are positively correlated and the strength of that correlation increases over the period. This is a pattern in which the number of people leaving increases in good times and decreases in bad. It does so apparently because the number of people coming also varies in this way and this suggests that people leave not because they have trouble finding work but because they did not intend to stay very long in the first place.

Letters also suggest a difference in the motivation of the two migration streams. Thus Brody, summarizing the motivation of immigrant steelworkers as revealed in their letters, writes:

> From the peasant viewpoint the longer move to America differed from seasonal migration only in degree. Men went to Germany to add to a slender livelihood. In America they would save enough to pay off the mortgage or to buy land that would restore their social position. A Polish immigrant expected to "remain for some years and return with something to our country so that later we might not be obliged to earn [as hired laborers]." The Atlantic crossing meant a heavy investment, a long absence, unaccustomed work in mill or mine: but the essential purpose did not differ from seasonal migration. The immigrant hoped to earn a stake and return to his village. With this end, Slovaks, Poles, Croats, Serbs, Magyars, and Italians made the passage to America.[21]

What was responsible for this shift in the character of migration in the nineteenth century? Commentators at the time tended to attribute the shift to the nature of the new migrants. This theme is especially strong in the report of the Immigration Commission, which has a heavy racist flavor.[22] Even if one could trace the pattern of circular migration to the motivation of the migrants, however, it would not constitute a satisfactory explanation for the shift in the character of migration because, as noted in Chapter 2, the migrations were not spontaneous. Throughout the period, there was an active recruitment system: In Europe, that system was controlled by the steamship companies and, possibly, the railroads. But, they were, in turn, responsive to the demands of labor agents, who met arriving immigrants at the port city or at major railroad centers in the interior. The labor agents catered in their turn to employers and were responsive to their demands. Employers also recruited directly through their existing employees.[23] Had the economic system wanted to recruit permanent settlers, it seems likely that this network would have directed its efforts in other directions. Hence, it seems more plausible to attribute the shift in the character of the migration to the changing character of labor demand noted in the preceding section. This had two important components. One was the change in industrial demand connected with the expansion of industry: the progressive disintegration of the symbiotic relationship between industry and agriculture; technological shifts leading to the deskilling of many jobs; and changes in industrial organization isolating the unstable portions of demand. The second component was the demand for a mobile, unskilled construction labor force to build the railroads and canals. The second component seems to have preceded the first and declined with the completion of the national railway network toward the end of the century.[24]

The notion that the basic causes of the shifting character of migration are to be found in demand rather than in supply gains some support from another factor: There is some question as to whether the shift in the character of the migration can actually be traced to the new immigrants. The character of the old immigration appears also to have shifted in this period. Thus, steamship records in the early twentieth century show a rate of return for third-class passengers (which presumably excludes tourists) of 39 percent for British ports, a very high rate for groups with a long, continuous history of migration that would seem to imply that a large proportion of the immigrants must have been joining established family units.[25] Literary evidence also suggests a shift in the character of British migration. Thus, Erickson, again summarizing a review of letters written by immigrants, concludes:

> The industrial workers of the early period, whose emigration had social and political overtones, expressed a determination to remain in the United States . . . The new,

more economically oriented immigrants did not go to the
United States with the fixed intention of staying there.
Even among those who did remain, the possibility of returning to Britain constituted an active alternative choice
for a long time.[26]

There is one possible alternative to supply-side changes as an
explanation of this shift: the decline in the costs and time for
transatlantic crossings. This change appears, however, to pre-
date the shift in the character of immigration. By 1873, sailing
vessels accounted for only 3.2 percent of transatlantic migration in the port of New York.[27] The cost of steerage passage
between Naples and New York in 1880 was $15.[28] This com-
pares to the average daily earnings for common laborers of
$1.23.[29] Thus, it is clear that the impact of steam transport was
already felt in the first decade after the war. The Kuznets and
Rubin study makes clear, however, that the shift in character of
migration developed only gradually in the course of the late
nineteenth and early twentieth centuries.[30]

Settlement and upward mobility. The critical event in the evolution
of the ethnic communities that grew out of the new wave was
World War I. The war closed off new immigration; at the same
time, it halted the return of many immigrants in the United
States who had planned to leave. In this way it acted to hasten
the settlement process in these communities. Settlement would
no doubt have taken place in any case but probably at a much
slower pace. Immigration revived in the period immediately
after the war, but the revival was short-lived, for free foreign
immigration was foreclosed by legislation in 1923. The legislation limited entry under a strict quota system, giving priority to
relatives of earlier migrants. In this way the legislation, like the
war, acted not only to slow down the rate of inflow greatly, but
also to encourage the shift from a temporary pattern motivated
by desires to further family fortunes at home to the permanent
immigration of people seeking to form or join a family abroad.
    The effect of the shift upon the composition of immigrant
communities is suggested by Tables 6-2 and 6-3. These tables
show the relationship between the number of foreign-born and
the number of native-born of foreign stock for two ethnic

Table 6-2. *Population of Italian origin living in U.S.*

	Born in Italy (in thousands)	Born in U.S. of Italian or mixed parentage (in thousands)	Proportion born abroad	Proportion born in U.S. of Italian or mixed parentage and 10 years old or more
1900	484	255	65.4	—
1910	1,343	772	63.5	12.0
1920	1,610	1,751	47.9	23.0
1930	1,790	2,756	39.4	38.5
1940	1,624	2,971	35.3	60.0
1950	1,427	3,143	31.2	68.8

Source: Computed from data in U.S. Department of Commerce, Bureau of Census, *Historical Statistics of the United States, Colonial Times to 1957* (Washington, D.C.: U.S. Government Printing Office, 1960), pp. 65–66.

Table 6-3. *Population of Polish origin living in U.S.*

	Born in Poland (in thousands)	Born in U.S. of Polish or mixed parentage (in thousands)	Proportion born abroad	Proportion born in U.S. of Polish or mixed parentage and 10 years old or more
1900	383	327	53.9	—
1910	938	726	56.4	19.7
1920	1,140	1,303	46.7	29.7
1930	1,269	2,074	38.0	39.0
1940	993	1,912	34.2	71.2
1950	861	1,925	30.9	68.9

Source: Ibid.

groups: the Poles and the Italians. The proportion of both groups born in the United States and ten years old or older is also shown. These figures suggest that the second generation comes to predominate in the population at large in 1910–20; in this period, however, it is composed overwhelmingly of children. Those children only begin to play an active role in the community and in the labor force in the second half of the following decade, and their dominance in community life is a phenomenon of the decade that follows, that is, the 1930s. A similar shift occurred in the character of the foreign-born population itself. The nature of that shift is suggested by Table 6-4, showing the percentage of all foreign-born in the country ten years or less. The dramatic difference between the figure in 1940 and all previous decades is especially noteworthy.

This change in the composition of the immigrant communities coincided with the political events of the 1930s and with the advent of union organization. It seems likely that the two events are not independent and that the organization of labor both in the shop and at the polls can be understood in large measure as a part of the process through which ethnic communities coalesced and the second-generation communities expressed their resentment against the job characteristics that the parental communities, with a different motiva-

Table 6-4. *Proportion of foreign-born in United States 10 years or less*

1870–1880	32.3
1880–1890	44.9
1890–1900	25.0
1900–1910	36.9
1910–1920	16.2
1920–1930	19.2
1930–1940	0.9

Source: Simon Kuznets and Ernest Rubin, *Immigration and the Foreign Born* (New York: National Bureau of Economic Research, 1954), Occasional Paper No. 46, p. 42.

tion and a different attitude toward the labor market, had come to accept. Again, the evidence in support of this interpretation is fragmentary. Studies of voting behavior, however, do suggest the critical role of the ethnic vote, organized and enfranchized for the first time, in the emergence of the New Deal.[31] And, at least two case studies of union organization in the late 1930s suggest that second-generation ethnic workers were the critical factor in the climate that led to union organization and in the success of the organizational drive.[32]

The ethnic communities also experienced considerable economic mobility in the World Wars and in the periods that followed. In most major industries, the positions they initially occupied came, during the war and postwar period, to be held by blacks and Mexican workers, and they themselves moved into higher ranks.[33] But it should be noted that overall, the economic advancement of European immigrants was not simply a matter of upward mobility within a given occupational hierarchy. It also involved a substantial restructuring of economic opportunities through plant-level union organization in the 1930s.[34] This restructuring, as was noted above, eliminated many of the characteristics of existing jobs that would have been expected to bother a native labor force much more than a migrant one. The change is probably in no small measure responsible for the fact that native workers in the United States now find these jobs attractive, whereas they are generally rejected by nationals in Europe. The unionization of these jobs is generally seen as an exogenous event, attributable to the political climate of the times and the atmosphere engendered by the Great Depression. But, as we have just seen, it can itself be looked at as endogenous to the immigration process, a product of the stabilization of the immigrant communities and the shift in attitudes toward the labor market concomitant with the emergence of a second-generation labor force.

Internal migration

If the first effects of World War I and the restrictive legislation that followed was the stabilization of the new ethnic communities, the second effect was to create a vacuum in the bottom of the labor market. This vacuum was filled by a massive internal migration, of which the chief component consisted of black workers moving from the rural South to the urban industrial North. That migration began on a large scale with the war in 1915; continued in the 1920s; abated somewhat in the 1930s; was revived by the World War II boom, and continued at very high levels throughout the late 1940s and the 1950s.

The data on black population movements are virtually all net migration figures. Gross flows of blacks out of the South have not, to my knowledge, been studied. It is thus impossible to draw a precise comparison between the character of black migration and the immigration that preceded it. The dominant view appears to see the process as a one-way, permanent migration. This view seems most consistent with our notions of blacks in the South as an economically and politically suppressed population. Such a view, however, leaves a number of critical characteristics of the southern exodus unexplained. As Gunnar Myrdal, whose own analysis is grounded in this conventional view of the problem, points out, it is difficult to understand why the exodus was delayed until 1915; why, once it began, many more blacks did not migrate; why the population flowed to large urban centers in the North and Midwest and not to smaller towns where patterns of life were more in keeping with the rural backgrounds of the migrants, or southern cities where the culture was presumably more congenial, or the Far West, which was by far the most tolerant region with respect to race (or, at least, to the black race).[35]

These factors, which the conventional view of the process cannot encompass, suggest the alternative interpretation that the black migration was not fundamentally different from the migration patterns of the ethnic groups that preceded it. The black population, like these other groups, was fundamentally tied to the rural, agricultural South. However oppressive the cultural patterns of the communities in which they lived, they were comfortable and familiar, especially in comparison to the conditions of northern urban life. People were prepared to take advantage of economic opportunities, when these were offered; they may have seen these opportunities as a way of changing their life-styles; but the changes were initially conceived in terms of the southern rural communities from which they came. The new economic opportunities in the North were not seen as part of the distinct independent life-style that they later became. The blacks did not, in other words, leave to escape the South. They responded to recruitment patterns of northern industry. They sought temporary economic advantages and they expected to return. They left the South when they did and moved where they did in response to the timing and geographic recruitment patterns of industry.

There is certainly enough evidence of northern industrial recruitment patterns to make this a plausible story.[36] There is also some direct evidence of ties of the kind this interpretation would imply. Thus, one study describing the market in the 1920s reports: "Many employers declare that the industrial labor market is constantly affected by a temporary shift of Negroes from both agriculture and personal services to industry. The shifting in the case of agriculture is of a seasonal character. Colored workers go into the Northern factories in the spring and go back home in the fall."[37] Just how much of the process it captures, however, must await further study. My sense that it is essentially valid is based upon my own experience working in rural Mississippi in the middle 1960s. At that time, when statistical analysis still focused on net flows, it was clear in the communities from which the migrates were coming that the gross flows were much more important not only numerically but also socially and culturally. Academic discussion focused attention upon who left and who stayed. But it was clear in the community that virtually everybody at one point or another had left; the pertinent questions were rather who had come back and why. But even this somewhat missed the point: People were forever coming and going. They would work in the North for a while, come back to visit, to take care of a sick relative, attend a funeral, or dispose of a piece of property. Once home, they often stayed on, particularly if they could get a job or if it was summer and there was plenty of food on the farm. Often parents would bring their kids home to live with the grandparents in the South, and then return north themselves to work. By the same token, people would go north planning only to visit, but then stay because they had found a boyfriend or a job. I was in Mississippi as part of the civil-rights movement. There was continual talk of repression; it was generally acknowledged that economic and social conditions, always bad, had grown much worse in the 1960s and were likely to deteriorate further. (People turned out to be wrong on this last point.) But the South was always compared favorably with the North by both those who had come back and those who were about to leave. The "destination" was looked upon as a cold and alien land; a place one went to earn a living perhaps but not to live.

The pattern of black settlement in the aggregate can be inferred from the statistics presented in Table 6-5. This table compares the size of the migrant and the native population in the northeastern and midwestern and western states. It is comparable to the earlier tables for the Poles and Italians. It suggests that blacks born in the North began to dominate the northern black labor force only in the 1960s: The domination was perhaps less complete than at a comparable stage in the development of ethnic communities because the new black migrants were never cut off from home in the way that foreign migration was by war and legislative restrictions. Nonetheless,

Table 6-5. *Proportion of nonwhite population living in North*

Year	Born in South	Born in North and under 10 years old	Born in North and under 20 years old	Born in North and 10 years old or more
1910	39.4	8.1	—	55.5
1920	49.8	5.7	11.6	44.5
1930	57.0	12.9	16.3	30.1
1940	52.0	11.1	22.3	36.9
1950	53.0	15.0	22.3	32.0
1960	44.1	23.4	33.7	32.5
1970	31.2	29.7	46.1	39.0

Source: Historical Statistics, op. cit., pp. 41–4; *U.S. Census of Population 1960,* Vol. PC(2)-2A, Table 5, p. 3, and *U.S. Census of Population 1976,* Vol. PC(2)-2A, Table 3, p. 3.

in terms of the relative magnitude of the second-generation workers in the labor force, the 1960s in the black community does roughly correspond to the 1930s in the development of ethnic settlement.

This parallel implies that one can interpret the racial conflicts that developed in the North in the 1960s as parallel to the Roosevelt electoral coalition and the industrial union movement of the 1930s. Such an interpretation was not prevalent at the time: People tended to see the riots in the northern urban ghettos as a reaction to the high rates of unemployment, welfare dependency, and the like, and these were in turn attributed to the difficulties of the poorly educated and ill-adapted southern rural migrants in the urban industrial North. The connection was generally drawn as well between the unorganized northern riots and the disciplined, organized black protest in the South, so that the former seemed to be a reaction to the latter.

In fact, however, more detailed studies of the economic indices in northern black communities suggest that the abnormally high levels of unemployment and welfare dependency are concentrated among people born and raised in the North, not among southern migrants. The latter often have lower incomes, but they derive these incomes from participation in productive economic activity.[38] The composition of arrests during riots also suggests that it is people reared in the North, not southern migrants, who were most active in those protests.[39] Riots, moreover, appear to have been only one form of protest mounted in the period, and unemployment, welfare dependency, and so on seem to be only partial indicators of the extent of the social pathology. Younger black workers also rebelled directly against the quality of existing employment opportunities. The revolt was not widely noted by the country at large. The press and the government made special efforts to suppress stories of racial conflict and violence on the job for fear of jeopardizing efforts to expand black employment opportunities and of encouraging other incidents, as the reporting in the media of riots while in progress was alleged to have promoted further disturbances: People sympathetic to black aspirations tended to discount interpretations that seemed to place the blame for the economic situation on the attributes of the workers. Nonetheless, numerous reports of resistance on the job circulated orally in the black community, among employers, and in white working-class neighborhoods. Black youth were known to have a high and rising turnover, to be insulting and insubordinate. There were many stories of sudden violence: A not atypical story, never reported by the press, concerned a black worker who took out a gun and shot his foreman. In a study of lower-wage jobs in Boston in 1972 it was found that every firm volunteered a series of incidents of this type: Many no longer hired blacks at all.[40] At the same time, in black neighborhoods in the late 1960s most people with contacts in the community were willing to admit that virtually anybody who wanted work could find it and attributed the high unemployment to a rejection of available jobs. All of this suggests that the concerns in the North were very different from the issues of voter registration and public accommodations upon which the southern protest focused, and that, although the protest in the South no doubt had a demonstration effect upon black workers in the North, the two may well have sprung from different causes.

To draw parallels between black migrants and foreign immigrants is not to deny that there were also differences between the black exodus from the rural South and the migration of European peasants. The black labor force is distinguished from the ethnic groups that preceded it in two important respects. First, second-generation blacks are seeking upward mobility in a labor market that is much more highly structured than the labor market for second-generation ethnic migrants. Earlier ethnic groups obtained upward mobility both by moving into jobs to which their parents had not previously had access *and* by changing the characteristics of the jobs in which they followed their parents. Both of these channels of mobility are now more restricted. These restrictions are in great measure the result of the organizational activities of the earlier immigrant groups. Because so much has already been done to separate out the stable portion of demand and to secure the employment opportunities that are involved in meeting it, there is much less opportunity to improve the characteristics of job opportunities within the existing economic system. It would now presumably be necessary to remove the underlying causes of instability itself. At the same time, as the demarcation between primary and secondary jobs has been much more clearly defined than it was for earlier groups, it has probably become correspondingly more difficult to cross.

A second major difference between the evolution of the two migration streams is that the black community never faced an event like World War I or the postwar legislative restrictions, which decisively cut off the possibility of return to the place of origin and forced even the first generation to reevaluate its relationship to urban industrial society. This quite possibly means that the settlement of the black community has been a longer, more drawn out process than was the case for earlier groups. And that may well have affected both the political organization of the community and the stability of the environment in which the second generation has grown up and developed its labor-market commitments. These two effects, it should be noted, are quite distinct from the issue of race, which constitutes a separate theme in American history, one which cannot have helped the upward economic mobility of blacks in the North. Thus, although the evolution of black migration does parallel that of the preceding ethnic groups and the 1960s was for blacks a phase in this evolution roughly comparable to the period of the late 1930s for the ethnic communities, it is not clear that its results have been nearly as successful in terms of economic mobility in either the short or the long run.

What the changes of the 1960s do seem to have done, and in a fairly forceful way, was to signal to employers that the black labor force is no longer a reliable source of labor for secondary jobs, and since the late 1960s, employers in the secondary labor market apear to have turned increasingly toward undocumented workers from the Caribbean and Latin America instead. We have, in this respect, begun a new chapter in the history of low-wage labor markets.

Undocumented workers: the newest wave

The latest wave of immigration is dominated by undocumented workers from Latin America and the Caribbean. Because this movement is clandestine, its precise character and dimensions are unknown, but 50 to 75 percent of the labor force is believed to be Mexican; the remainder is drawn largely from the Caribbean basin, and the two largest non-Mexican groups are probably from Santo Domingo and Haiti. There are a sizable number of Colombians and also some migrants from Southern Europe and the Orient.[41]

The roots of these migrations have a very long history. Large-scale migration of Mexicans can be traced to the Mexican Civil War: It was then extended by employer recruiting to meet the labor shortages engendered by World War I and the curtailment of European migration and promoted again during World War II, the Korean period, and to a lesser degree in the late 1950s. To a certain extent, this migration pattern follows that of the black migration from the South, and the development of the Chicano movement can be likened to the revolt in the black ghettos with which it coincides, but there are significant differences between the two patterns, which lead one to be very skeptical of placing too much weight upon whatever parallels can be drawn.

The most important difference is that the Mexican migration until most recently has been primarily into agriculture and within the agricultural sector has been largely confined to the Southwest. The institutional structure, involving special provisions in restrictive legislation for the western hemisphere, suspensions of regulations, contract-labor *(bracero)* programs, and the like, has been designed to promote a migration of this type. The migration has at certain times escaped these limits. The most prominent nonagricultural use of migrants was in the railroads, but in certain, apparently brief periods, Mexicans have been recruited in relatively large numbers for other industries, for example, the steel industry during World War I. These are as a result some urban industrial settlements of Mexicans. But the major settlements are in agricultural areas of the Southwest where the Mexican-American population today is not very different from the types of workers from underdeveloped agricultural regions that *contribute* to the migration streams we are examining.[42]

The second distinguishing feature of the Mexican migration in the past is that the communities have not been allowed to settle in the same way in which the black and earlier foreign communities have. They have experienced repeated waves of new migrants from Mexico itself, the latest of which promises to completely swamp whatever settlement exists. The Mexican population has also been subjected to forced repatriation. Since a significant portion of the population has always consisted of people without documents whose status has been ambiguous at best and who, when apprehended, are deported, one could say this has been almost continuous. But there have been two really massive repatriation efforts: one in 1929 and the second in the 1953–4 recession.[43] These have acted to disrupt existing settlement patterns and to discourage new migrants from settling permanently. Thus, although there has been considerable Mexican immigration since 1910 and a certain amount of urban, industrial penetration, the Mexican-American population and the locus of Mexican migration remained, even in the middle 1960s, basically rural and agricultural.

Much the same can be said of the other large component of current migrant flows, nationals from the countries of the Caribbean basin. There has always been some flow of migrants from the islands to the mainland. And in the case of the British West Indies, there are relatively large settled communities in New York, which date from World War II. But, again with certain limited exceptions, the islanders have been important only as a source of agricultural labor. And large-scale migration, especially from Spanish-speaking areas, is a product of the 1960s.[44]

The single exception to this pattern is the Puerto Rican migration to the New York City region and to Chicago. This pattern does resemble the black migration from the South, beginning however with World War II rather than World War I. This migration was concentrated in the decades of the 1940s and 1950s in response to war-generated labor shortages. In the 1960s it leveled off and in certain years has even reversed.[45] New York is now basically a second-generation Puerto Rican community. Puerto Rican youths, like black youths, generally refuse low-wage menial jobs, and such symptoms of second-generation rebellion as riots, welfare, and unemployment have been as pronounced in the New York Puerto Rican community as in the black community.

Elsewhere in the East and Midwest, however, the Puerto Rican migration follows a pattern resembling that of the other

Caribbean islands. Until the mid-1960s, extensive use was made of Puerto Rican migrants in agriculture, but there was little industrial penetration and little settlement. The latter, however, began to occur on a significant scale in the 1960s.[46]

The Caribbean and Mexican migrations into industry present the same basic mystery as the black exodus from the South: Why, given the rapidity and relative ease with which they developed in the late 1960s, didn't they occur earlier? The answer seems to be that much of the timing of the current migration is the result of the exhaustion of domestic labor reserves. The second-generation black workers who predominate in the labor force are no longer willing to perform secondary work, at least in a way that makes management comfortable in employing them. The social pressure that this generation generates within the community makes it difficult for even recent migrants to accept these jobs. In any case, labor reserves of the magnitude that prevailed in the 1940s and 1950s are no longer available in the South, and the reserves that do exist are by and large being absorbed in the industrial development of the South itself. The resulting shortage in the bottom of the labor market was filled by the new immigrants.

The characteristics of these newest migrants are essentially the same as the old. Several different studies of undocumented Mexican workers suggest the circular character of their migration, their basic attachment to Mexico, their basic motivation as an effort to accumulate funds for investment at home.[47] The newest Puerto Rican migrants exhibit precisely the same characteristics.[48] The undocumented aliens from elsewhere in the hemisphere seem to stay longer in the United States and to develop more permanent ties at a more rapid rate, but their underlying motivation appears similar and the difference in actual behavior seems to reflect, as will be discussed in the next chapter, the nature of the institutional arrangements that govern their migration. One must expect, given these other similarities, that the new migrants will eventually develop patterns of permanent settlement and pressures for upward mobility. Given the fact that the society seems unable to meet the demands of the offspring of the previous wave of black migration, this raises serious problems for our immigration policy. It is to that policy that we now turn.

7

The dilemmas of current U.S. immigration policy

The United States is not a closed economy. The country admits four hundred thousand permanent immigrants annually. But the immigration system has not been designed to meet the nation's manpower needs. The bulk of permanent immigrants are ostensibly coming for personal reasons, for example, to join family already here; many are not members of the labor force. The legal system operates to exclude a vast number of people who want to come to the United States to work and whom the economy is able to absorb. A large proportion of these excluded people enter and work, despite the law. Estimates of the number of these undocumented workers here at any one time imply that they are from four and a half to three times the resident alien population. The highest estimates would make them more than 10 percent of the labor force.[1] The presence of these people has become the central dilemma of U.S. immigration policy.

The goals of immigration policy

Understood in conventional terms, the dilemma is apparently insoluble and has a virtually unique capacity to divide people who on other issues are united by their concern for underprivileged and disadvantaged groups. It appears that one must choose between the migrants, who are seeking entry in order to escape the poverty of their own country, and native workers, who, however well off in comparison to the migrants with whom they must compete in the lower reaches of the labor market, feel themselves to be a disadvantaged and underprivileged class.

The terms in which this dilemma is posed, however, are largely irrelevant to the kind of perspective that we have sought to develop in the foregoing chapters. For native disadvantaged workers, trapped in the secondary market, the only real solution to their problem is escape through upward mobility or through the conversion of secondary into primary jobs. The restriction of immigration is an effective policy instrument from their point of view only if it operates to curtail the secondary labor market. To the extent that it fails to do this, employers will find other ways to fill secondary jobs. This may involve the search for other marginal workers who, within the existing social and institutional structure, find such work attractive: youth or women are, it would seem from our earlier analysis, to be the most likely candidates, given the social structures currently prevailing. But it may also involve, especially in the long run, an attempt to manipulate the context in which labor-market decisions are made so as to expand the supply of available labor. This might easily lead to restrictions upon the upward mobility of natives now in the secondary sector in an attempt to preserve them as a source of labor or upon the institutions that shape their labor-market decisions, such as welfare, unemployment insurance, retirement benefits, the period of compulsory school attendance, military service, and the like. As suggested earlier, the historical evolution of all of these things has been responsive to labor-market needs. Thus, it is clearly not sufficient to assume that restrictions upon the supply of alien workers will aid the disadvantaged: One must instead examine directly the problem of eliminating secondary jobs.

A second factor also argues against the conventional view that restrictions upon immigration will aid disadvantaged workers. It is extremely unlikely that the disadvantaged and underprivileged, who share the secondary sector with alien workers, will ever be in a position by themselves to impose immigration restrictions. Those restrictions arise only when other workers, much farther up the occupational hierarchy, better organized and more active politically, ally themselves with the disadvantaged and become their advocates in the political process. These other workers, as we have seen, have a very ambiguous relationship with foreign workers: In the early stages of migration, the foreigners tend to complement natives and their presence acts to preserve native jobs and the more advantageous job characteristics, especially those involving social status and security. It is only in the late stages of the process, when settlement occurs and the settled immigrants and their children begin to pressure for upward mobility, that the relationship between these more secure natives and the foreigners shifts from complementarity to competition. The distinction between the labor-market roles of the first and second generation is almost always absent from the policy debate. It is obscured by the way the problem is introduced in the political arena by the advocates of the disadvantaged with whom even the first generation seems to be in competition, and by the time the more privileged native workers join the debate, the issues have already been drawn in a way that precludes a recognition that competition and complementarity might possibly coexist. That possibility is also obscured by the inability of the natives to distinguish effectively between the two generations; whatever physical, cultural, or linguistic changes occur in the shift from the first to second generations, they are seldom sufficient to enable native workers to distinguish clearly between them. The real pressure for restriction upon immigration comes from people concerned about the second generation, and when it becomes clear that the major thrust of restrictions is upon the first generation who hold jobs complementary to their own, the enthusiasm for the legislation dissipates and they acquiesce to, and even actively support, a whole set of processes and procedures that circumvent it or undermine its intent. Thus, it is something of an illusion to see the contrast between the de jure and de facto immigration structure (which incidently exists in Europe as well as in the United States) as a hypocrisy that can be overcome by appeal to the instincts that led to the passage of the legislation in the first place. The political support for the impact that the legislation would have if fully enforced in the market shared by aliens with disadvantaged native workers was never there.

Although these considerations argue against preoccupation with the impact of immigration upon disadvantaged native

workers, which seems to motivate many of the advocates of restriction, the perspective out of which they emerge does not
validate either the preoccupations with the impact upon the
immigrants themselves, which motivates the adversaries, or the
other side, who favor open immigration. It tends to undermine
the rationale for this second position because of the emphasis
that it places on the changes in preferences and in expectations, which occur in the process of immigration itself, and in
the transition, after immigration, from the first to the second
generation. The concept of economic welfare has a clear, dis-
cernible meaning only so long as one assumes that the underlying wants and needs of people are the same, irrespective of the
particular social context in which they are manifest. The processes we are describing, however, are ones in which wants and
needs, and with them people's perceptions of their own well-
being, change systematically and in which those changes in
turn produce subsequent changes in welfare as *perceived* by
those who follow. Thus, even if it were true that the Mexican
peasant who gains access to the U.S. labor market through immigration is himself better off for that fact, it is not clear that
his children born in the United States, with access to the same
jobs there as their father, will be better off than if their father
had remained in Mexico. Nor is it clear that the people who
remain behind in Mexico, enjoying income that has been raised
by the departure of others but also with a set of expectations
generated by the immigration process, feel better off than if
the process had never been begun. The changes in needs and
wants need not necessarily mean that one must forgo any
normative evaluation of the process, but they do immensely
complicate the kinds of evaluations required to make those
judgments and clearly foreclose any presumption that the
immigrants, except possibly those isolated from the communities and the complex family structure composed of interlocking generations (a kind of individual isolation in terms of
which they clearly do not perceive themselves), are better off
because they are able to migrate.

This implies that one must judge the immigration process in
terms of the capacity of the society to meet the expectations it
generates. If we are correct in our analysis, for the first genera-

tion, at least in the early stages of a particular migration stream, the process pretty much takes care of this itself. Since the migrants come to accumulate funds to invest at home, they are unlikely to come, and most unlikely to stay, unless there are employment opportunities that are satisfactory from this point of view. The disjuncture between aspirations and opportunities is likely to occur, to the extent that it occurs, in settled migration communities and in the second generation, for the size of the latter is not responsive in any way to the available opportunities; it is governed by the parameters of the process in the first stages. This implies that the first stages of the process ought to be controlled, to the extent that they can be controlled by public policy, in the light of the opportunities for upward mobility.

If we had very powerful theories of the jobs structure and of the settlement process, we might be able to identify exactly what the opportunities for upward mobility were likely to be and, then, control the migration process in the first generation accordingly. The second and third chapters of this book make clear, however, that we have at best only a very general understanding. Recent historical experience suggests that the most likely outcome of the processes is a second generation that is larger than the number of jobs available to meet its aspiration. These considerations would seem to argue for a public-policy framework that sought to minimize the number of jobs that migrants were required to fill. Given such jobs, however, it implies a policy that would work in two directions. First, it would operate to maximize the temporary character of the migrant stay in the urban industrial country and capitalize upon the natural propensity of such populations to return home. In so doing, it would prolong the period in which the aspirations of the migrants were complementary to native workers, enhance the resources that the migrants contributed to the development process at home, and minimize the size of the second generation, reared in the destination with a set of labor-market aspirations competitive with those of native workers. Second, to the extent that it failed in its first goal – and we have emphasized repeatedly in the foregoing that virtually all migrant populations eventually develop permanent settlements so that, in the long run, failure is inevitable – it would encourage the second generation to acquire whatever traits (training, education, credentials, and the like) are requisite for upward mobility.

There is a certain degree of conflict inherent in these two goals. Any restriction that policy places on the first generation, in the attempt to control its access to jobs, is likly to affect the access of the second generation to channels of upward mobility. But it is nonetheless possible to go a fairly long way toward achieving both goals simultaneously.

Evaluated against these goals, the present U.S. immigration system does nowhere near as badly as it appears to in terms of the more conventional standards that have been applied in policy debate. To appreciate that fact, it is, first, necessary to understand how the present system operates and, in particular, not simply to recognize, but also to understand, the enormous gap between the de jure policy, which defines the ostensible system, and the system as it actually functions in practice.

The U.S. immigration system

The de jure policy appears to have the following goals: first, to admit a very limited number of permanent immigrants; second, to utilize immigration to overcome labor shortages in a select number of highly skilled jobs; third, to facilitate the reuniting of families; and fourth, to distribute the remainder of the immigration opportunities in an unbiased and equitable fashion among countries of the world and, within any given country, among individuals.[2]

Congress has never funded the agencies that administer our immigration policy at a level that would permit these goals to be realized. As a result, the de jure policy, and the philosophy that underlies it, is only very tangentially related to the immigration system that actually prevails.

The critical factor in determining the way in which the system operates is the underlying nature of the immigration flows and, in particular, the natural tendency of the immigrants themselves to return home. But the principal institutional feature that makes the system operate is ironically the very feature that makes it appear so irrational in terms of its announced goals, that is, the fact that it is "underfunded": The budget of the Immigration and Naturalization Service is so small in relation to the magnitude of the alien flows that it cannot possibly enforce the law as written. This underfunding, along with the fact that it has developed apparently by "default" with little congressional guidance as to priorities in the spending of the allocated funds, gives tremendous discretion to the Immigration Service in determining when and where the law is to be enforced. On the whole, the INS appears to utilize this discretion to minimize the competition between undocumented and other workers.

This is evinced in patterns of enforcement activity. Thus, for example, the INS appears to give priority to apprehending undocumented workers, as opposed to other undocumented persons, and among workers, to those in relatively high-paying, high-status jobs. The lowest level, most menial job category, private household help, receives virtually no attention at all. The INS concentrates its enforcement activities in the Southwest, ostensibly because of the heavy traffic from Mexico, but the effect is to encourage undocumented Mexicans to move quickly through this region, where they are in direct competition with Mexican-Americans, to the Middle West, where the native wage scales are much higher and there is a scarcity of low-wage labor. Some INS offices make a practice of varying enforcement activities seasonally so that alien workers are forced into a role that complements the seasonal work habits of native youth: When school lets out in June, various restaurant and hotel jobs are raided in order to open them for youth; when school resumes in the fall, such enforcement activities are relaxed. Enforcement activity also varies cyclically in some industries: In the 1974–5 recession, for example, the INS was active in pursuing Canadian workers in the construction industry; the entry of such workers, however, had been tolerated in the preceding boom when there had been a shortage of skilled natives.

One need not, however, rely solely upon inference from patterns of enforcement activity to determine the rationale underlying current practice. The power over individual lives involved in this area of policy is immense: Even when they are here temporarily and alone, the aliens see their stay in the United States as a unique opportunity for major economic and social advancement. And, although they may be a decided minority in the total picture, there is a sizable absolute number for whom apprehension means permanent separation from family and friends and return to a country of origin that has become quite foreign and, perhaps, economically and politically hostile, as well. The scenes played out daily in every INS office are tragic. Most agents are made to feel a little bit as if they were waking up each morning and picking from the literally hundreds of people known to be illegally present in the country three or four as candidates for that tragedy. While some people obviously enjoy this kind of power, and it lends itself to the worst kind of human and financial abuse, the burden of the decision weighs heavily and they are anxious to justify their actions to themselves, to each other, and to outsiders. Most agents can therefore be induced to discuss the rationale of practice in some detail.

Three policy factors seem most prominent in these discussions. As previously noted, the greatest weight appears to be the control of the labor market in the fashion described above. A second factor, it is evident from the discussions and from even cursory contact with INS in action, is that decisions are also tremendously sensitive to the personal rapport that develops, or fails to develop, between INS officials and the people, either individually or in groups, with whom they are dealing. To a certain extent, this will vary depending upon the individual agent and the particular case. But here also the patterns that emerge appear to be sufficiently widespread to classify as "unofficial" policy. Thus, for example, agents expect aliens to be respectful, submissive, even subservient, and those who do not have or refuse to adopt the proper attitude are more likely to be apprehended and more harshly treated once caught than those who do. This is especially evident on the Mexican border: There a kind of ritual is played out in which the fugitives are permitted to try every trick to get by but once tagged by an officer are expected to submit at once and assume a subservient attitude. Children reared in the border cities do not always play out this traditional game, and their refusal to do so infuriates the border patrolmen, sometimes provoking violent reactions of a kind completely absent in dealing with most of the aliens, who come (or affect to come) from a traditional rural background. INS agents also have beliefs about various ethnic groups and, in the case of Mexico, different regions–about which aliens, in the light of the economic and social conditions of their place of origin, are most "deserving"–that must affect the pattern of enforcement.[3]

The third major component of the de facto policy as evinced by the decision of INS officers is the maintenance of a labor force that from the employer's point of view is hardworking and docile. This aspect of policy is not explicit in the comments of agents. The values at stake, however, are essentially coincident with those at stake in the border patrols' distinction between good and bad Mexicans and the distinctions drawn in the East and Midwest among various ethnic groups. In addition, there are a variety of cases in which the INS has responded to employer requests to remove workers who appear to be distinguished from the many others not apprehended chiefly by a tendency to assert themselves in the shop. This could, as is often alleged, result from explicit collaboration between the INS and employers, apprehending workers before they are paid or because they are about to complain about substandard wages, engage in union activity, or the like. But it is evident from INS comments that an explicit collaboration would not be required to introduce into enforcement acitivity a bias of this kind.

How is it that the de facto system has come to express these particular values? A complete answer to this question would require an understanding of bureaucratic decision making in general and of the history of the INS in particular, which cannot be developed here. It will come as no surprise, in the light of the foregoing, that we believe that this policy expresses the basic economic interests at stake in the immigration process. The role of deliberate policy and the influence and decisions of individual administrators cannot be discounted completely. Most members of the Border Patrol, for example, are fluent in Spanish and have a sympathetic understanding of Mexican culture and of the motives of the Mexican migrants (or at least of the bulk of the migrants who come from the interior of the country), which is obviously acquired in the Border Patrol academy. The respect accorded a foreign culture and language in the INS is at variance with the values that predominate among Americans in general and with the prevailing ethos of most other U.S. government bureaucracies, and it is impossible to believe that it is in any sense spontaneous. On the other hand, the INS has not been noted for the forcefulness of its central administration in the late sixties and early seventies when patterns of response to the massive influx of aliens were established, and it would appear that those patterns are much more of a spontaneous and indirect expression of cultural values. The precise expression that those values have achieved in INS policy must have been importantly influenced, however, by the fact that, as noted above, the discretion the de facto policy places in the hands of individual agents is an enormous moral burden. It must also have been an administrative and political burden to bureaucratic officials, fearful that they would be blamed for the failure of the de jure policy that they are unable to enforce.

At both the top and at the bottom of the Immigration bureaucracy, therefore, officials have sought guidance in their administrative decisions. In the absence of explicit congressional guidelines, they have found that guidance in two other sources: first, in citizens' complaints, and second, in the pattern of political pressure as it is revealed in the history of immigration policy and in the day-to-day relationships with elected officials. Local offices appear to rely heavily upon the frequency and intensity of citizen complaints both in particular apprehension decisions and to establish the patterns upon which they base their overall enforcement strategy. They pretend sometimes that they do this because such complaints are their basic source of information, but, as one official explained, given the tendency of the aliens to live and work together, the INS is able to develop on the basis of a very limited number of specific cases a picture of the alien community that would permit virtually any enforcement strategy. Both the sensitivity to workers in competition with natives and the sensitivity to employers' needs, which we described earlier, can be traced to the dependence upon complaints.

The history of immigration policy, particularly in relationship to Mexico, reinforces these basic presumptions. As several scholars have now pointed out, our policy toward Mexican immigrants has varied in blatant fashion with U.S. business cycles and the requirements of particular American industries.[4] Thus, immigration was ignored in the twenties and during World War II and the postwar boom. But policy was reversed, often in a brutal and repressive fashion, in the 1930s and in the post-Korean recession. The reversal involved the repatriation of more than one million Mexicans but was accompanied by the introduction of the *bracero* program, which was designed to cushion the impact upon agricultural businesses. Thus, past history, like citizen complaints, carries the message that the country wants the INS to operate the system so as to minimize the competition in the first generation between undocumented foreign workers and the native labor force.

It would appear that, in terms of the labor-market requirements outlined, the present system is least effective in its handling of permanent settlement and the second generation. To the extent that the undocumented workers are indeed illegal, one would expect them to live at the margin of society in ways that minimize the exposure of their children to the kinds of institutions and experiences that would help them advance in the U.S. labor market. To a certain extent, these expectations are borne out. One can cite a variety of cases in which, for example, the parents have been afraid to send the children to school or to seek out medical attention for fear of making their presence in the country known to official authorities. Again, however, these effects are greatly mitigated by the way the law is enforced in practice. The mitigation occurs in part because the actual chances of getting caught are extremely small; the pattern in enforcement has basically to do with the role in the labor market and not the utilization of public services; and the INS already has so much more information about the undocumented population than it can possibly act upon that it need not rely upon the kinds of data that the aliens fear.

But the other mitigating factor is that the de jure immigration system has not been nearly as divorced from the prevailing de facto system as the term "illegal" suggests and has actually provided a variety of channels through which those who become permanent settlers and have children can regularize their status. Several mechanisms, which from another perspective are extremely invidious and inequitable, have been involved here. The most important of these is the system, termed in the business *equity*, whereby people with close relatives in the United States have been given priority in immigration visas. This, along with the fact that children born in the United States are automatically accorded citizenship, has in the past assured that anybody who had children in the United States and then returned to his or her home country and applied for legal entry was virtually assured of regularizing his status. A second procedure, which enhances the value of equity as a means of regularizing status, is *voluntary departure*. A record of illegal entry into the United States would normally act as a bar to subsequent entry through regular legal procedures. However, very few aliens apprehended by the INS pass through the kind of formal deportation procedures that are necessary to invoke this legal barrier. Most leave through voluntary departure, a kind of nolo contendere procedure in which the illegal character of their previous entry is never formally established. The INS prefers this procedure since it saves greatly in time and expense; but they also value it precisely because it preserves "equity," and I have seen immigration judges grant voluntary departure in place of formal deportation for no other reason than that the defendant had an American-born child. The fact that voluntary departure is so common means that an undocumented worker need not wait for his or her documents at home, a wait that is extremely long. It is apparently quite common for people to enter without documents, work, establish the relationships upon which equity is built, return home to file papers, reenter without documents and continue working until notified that the papers are ready, then return once again, pick up the papers, and reenter the United States, this time as a legal immigrant.[5]

While the combination of voluntary departure and equity appear to have been the most important factors in legitimizing the undocumented workers, other procedures worked toward the same end. It is, for example, relatively common for the INS to parole an undocumented worker whose papers are in process so that apprehended aliens whose status shows promise of being regularized need not even leave the country temporarily. Another common practice is to obtain work permits in "labor-scarce" occupations for jobs that were acquired as an undocumented worker and for which the main proof that an immigrant is required to fill the job is the fact that the applicant is already holding it.

What can one conclude about the operation of the current system? Evaluated in terms of its announced goals, it is obviously not very successful. Evaluated in terms of the goals in the introductory section of this chapter, however, it does not appear to work too badly. It works best with respect to Mexican migration on the West Coast. Most Mexicans appear to enter the country by crossing the border without inspection. Many are apprehended and are quickly returned to Mexico where, by all reports, they simply turn around and reenter, in most cases successfully, a second time. The process is temporary: The best available data suggest, as noted earlier, that the average Mexican returns home every six months; the total length of stay averages about two and a half years.[6] Family formation, which may be taken as both an indicator of permanent settlement and a measure of the size of the second generation, is also low. Only 11 percent of apprehended aliens had a spouse in the United States, although 50 percent were married. Similarly, although 50 percent had children, less than 10 percent had children in the United States.[7] Most Mexicans seem to work in the kind of secondary jobs that are complementary to those of native workers: Penetration into the higher-wage, presumably more attractive employments to which natives aspire has been slight.[8] At the same time, the system of equity works, as described, to provide a means of legitimation for people who do acquire permanent attachments to the United States and presumably operates in this way to facilitate the access of their children to the institutions that will provide them with means of upward mobility.

Judged by these same standards, the system operates somewhat less effectively for non-Mexican western-hemisphere workers. Most of these people appear to enter as visitors or tourists, with documents but without the right to work. They then violate the terms of their visas by taking a job; typically, they further violate the conditions of entry by staying in the States after their visas have expired. The migration of these workers also appears to be essentially temporary, with relatively low rates of family formation, and they are concentrated in the secondary sector of the labor market; but each of these characteristics is decidedly less pronounced than it is for the Mexicans. Migrants from elsewhere in the hemisphere go home less frequently than Mexicans (every twenty-two months);[9] a larger proportion have families in the United States (28 percent had spouses in the United States);[10] they send less money back to their place of origin and have advanced further up the occupational hierarchy into positions competitive with native workers.

Reform within the present system

Once the character of the present immigration system as it actually operates is recognized, it becomes clear that certain relatively minor changes in rather obscure characteristics of the system can produce substantial gains in terms of the goals that we outlined initially, whereas other proposals, which seem obviously beneficial, are likely to have quite negative results.

The most obvious defect of the present immigration system is the disparity between the experience of Mexican and other western-hemisphere aliens. It would be impossible, given available information, to confirm any particular explanation for the difference between the two populations, but discussions with the workers themselves suggest that a major factor is the relative difficulty of reentry. Mexican workers have very little difficulty moving back and forth across the border. Other workers who enter on regular documents have a very great difficulty in doing so. The documents are difficult to obtain in the first place: The State Department officials who issue them are extremely suspicious of the motives of would-be entrants. The migrants fear that, having violated the terms of entry once, they will be unable to gain entry again. Hence, because they cannot return, many feel obligated to stay on much longer than they had originally anticipated, and, in the process, develop attachments, often in the form of second families, that they never intended but which make it still more difficult to leave. This paradoxical effect of a tight entry policy upon the size and character of the migrant population is not unique to the population of visa violators in the United States. Western European countries experienced similar effects when they attempted to curtail immigration in the last several years by restricting entry: Workers already in the country, fearing that they could not reenter, delayed departure, often illegally, so that while the inflow did in fact decline, the outflow declined as well. The net effect may well have been an increase in the total alien population. There has certainly been an increase in the size of the second generation.

This suggests one obvious improvement in existing immigration policy: a change in the character of reentry for holders of tourist visas that would eliminate the current deterrence to return. Ideally, tourist visas should be issued for quite long periods of time and allow unlimited trips between the States and the place of origin. Such a change need have no effect upon the effort of the State Department to prescreen applicants in an attempt to exclude potential violators. It would only recognize the fact that a mistake in the screening process cannot be rectified ex post and that the attempt to do so simply aggravates the problem.

Similar dangers appear to be present in proposals that have been recently adopted, or seem about to be adopted, designed to make marginal changes or to improve the enforcement of what is believed to be the existing immigration system. The one that follows most directly from the difference in the character of the Mexican and the non-Mexican migration streams concerns increased efforts to patrol the Mexican border. The success of such efforts is problematic, but it should be clear from the foregoing that the implications of success, if it is to be had, are also problematic, and that it is quite possible that increased difficulty in crossing the border will simply cause those migrants who are successful to stay longer and in this way increase the rate of permanent settlement.

Four other changes that are particularly troublesome and are likely to create more problems than they solve are recent restrictions in the number of legal entrants, limitations upon the "equity" acquired through an American-born child, the denial of public services to undocumented laborers, and proposals to penalize employers for hiring aliens. The restrictions on legal entry were introduced by Congress recently as a part of a revision in the distribution of immigration quotas among countries.[11] The thrust of the reform was supposed to be a more equitable treatment of western-hemisphere countries relative to those of Europe. However, in the process, a limit of twenty thousand was placed upon the immigration from any single nation. This is substantially below the seventy thousand immigrants who were being admitted at the time from Mexico. Because legal immigration constitutes the principal channel through which permanent settlers can regularize their status and that of their children, this restriction may represent a major change in the capacity of the second generation to achieve its labor-market aspirations.

A second change introduced in 1976 amendments will work in a similar direction: It restricts the rights of parents of U.S.-born children to use that relationship to regularize their own status until the children are twenty-one years old. This may reduce the incentive for undocumented workers to have children in the United States, but it also increases the likelihood that those children will grow up at the margin of American society.

The trends inherent in these legislative amendments will be exacerbated by efforts, at the state and local levels, to limit the access of undocumented people to public services. The most subversive of these efforts is the movement in New York City to bar the children from the public education system. Given past difficulties even among second-generation children who have had access to public education, it would be difficult to exaggerate the potential damage of this policy in the long run to the individuals involved and to the social stability of the city itself. Education is a sine qua non for any kind of upward social mobility. One cannot argue that the denial of other services will have the same inevitable effect upon the future opportunities of the individuals involved. On a statistical basis, however, the denial of health, housing, food stamps, and the like will increase the size of the second generation with frustrated labor-market aspirations.

Against these effects must be weighed, it is true, the potential of such services to attract migrants and encourage permanent settlement. The argument developed above, however, implies that settlement, as opposed to migration, is the outgrowth of a process in which social variables predominate and in which conscious economic calculation plays a very subsidiary role.

These effects, which are, by and large, not being carefully monitored by either the policy makers or the general public, may be the most significant in terms of the long-run evolution of immigration policy. But the proposal that has received the greatest public attention is one that would make the employer liable for employing illegal aliens.

The issue of employer liability is really related to the broader question of the size of the secondary labor market and the possibility of controlling its size, and hence the demand for aliens, through public policy. We will explore this question in some detail shortly. Here, what seems important to emphasize, is that however large the secondary market currently is, its size appears to be limited by a network of legislative restrictions imposing minimal health and safety standards and mandating a minimum wage. By and large, that market also respects a series of other legal standards involving income, social security, and unemployment taxation. It is somewhat less effectively controlled by union organization, but it is not totally beyond that control either.

It is not exactly clear why the market for undocumented workers respects these standards. Such workers are an easily exploited group; they are afraid of being reported to authorities and are often willing to work below prevailing wages under substandard conditions. There is a lot of money to be made by forcing them to do so. One could easily imagine a market in which employers, by evading taxation and letting working conditions deteriorate, were able to make a higher profit while paying their workers substantially what they take home now. It is possible that the market is already drifting in this direction: We have no good data about alien job characteristics over time, and it is quite possible that the limited violations found in the one-shot studies are the first signs of a long-run deterioration.

A chief factor in limiting the abuse that is taking place, however, must be the particular legal situation of employers. They risk nothing in employing the aliens; they risk substantial financial and criminal penalties in tax evasion and in violations of labor and work-standard laws. Were penalities to be imposed for the employment of aliens, they might as well take full advantage of the profits to be made. In many industries where aliens work, only a few employers need make this calculation to place the remainder under irresistibly competitive pressure to follow suit.

Toward a different system

To argue, as we have, that the present migration system has been misrepresented in the public debate, that it is more effective than is generally recognized in meeting society's *real* goals, and that many proposals to reform the system are misguided, unlikely to work as intended and most likely to aggravate the social problems surrounding the migration process, is not to argue that the present system is ideal. In terms of the goals outlined initially, three major reforms seem desirable: first, restrictions on the now legal entry of high-level manpower; second, a concerted effort to reduce the size of what we have called the secondary sector; and third, the legitimization of the migrant labor force required to fill the jobs that remain.

Restrictions upon high-level manpower

In terms of the current immigration system, this is probably the most radical proposal, but it follows directly from our earlier analysis. If labor shortages in industrial society are concentrated in low-level occupations, if the problem with migration as a solution to those low-level shortages is a lack of opportunity in higher-level positions for the offspring of the migrants, and if the society already has an accumulated obligation to black workers that it is unable to meet, then obviously we cannot affort to allocate the few high-level positions that we do have to foreigners. And, indeed, it appears that in a number of areas, most especially in the medical industry, immigration has been used to avoid social pressures to expand domestic employment opportunities for nationals.

Reduction in the size of the secondary sector

Many of the advocates of restricting immigration see such restrictions as a way of reducing the size of the secondary sector. As suggested earlier, however, this cannot be assumed, and the argument developed earlier suggests that it is, in fact, a dangerous way to approach the policy goal.

The basic dangers are twofold: The first danger is that if the restrictions are successful but the work cannot be dispensed with, the society will attempt to create a labor force by restricting the upward mobility of nationals. The extreme of this process would be the reimposition of the type of racial caste system that prevailed in the South. The second danger is that if the restrictions are successful—and history is extremely discouraging on this score—the immigration will become clandestine: It is then likely to escape legal restrictions upon the size of the secondary sector. To the extent that these restrictions actually set the limits upon the employment in that sector, the sector will then begin to expand beyond its present limits. Eventually, social forces will presumably react to check the expansion. but by that time we may have become accustomed to the expanded standard of living that immigration permits, making it difficult or impossible to reverse the process. Efforts to curtail the secondary sector by curtailing the supply of labor are, thus, likely to have exactly the opposite effect.

The wiser course of action appears to be to approach the problem directly by attempting to tighten the legal standards that act to limit the sector. At the current time, this implies four types of reform: (1) increases in the minimum wage; (2) more stringent health and safety standards, particularly for low-paying jobs; (3) greater encouragement and protection for union organization (in this sense, current proposals to repeal 14b of the National Labor Relations Act, to extend to agricultural workers the right to organize and bargain collectively, to restrict employers' unfair labor practices, to index the minimum wage, and the like, are tightly bound up with immigration policy and ought to be considered in combination with it); and (4) finally, to make all of these laws more effective, the INS should be prohibited from responding to employer complaints about undocumented workers in their establishments once a union organizing campaign is in progress and whenever that employer is found in violation of a labor statute.

The legitimacy of the present alien labor supply

The arguments against attempts to curtail the secondary sector by restricting the supply of labor also argue in favor of regularizing the status of the existing labor supply. As we have repeatedly emphasized, so long as the labor supply is extralegal, there is a danger that the market will escape its present legal limits and, once it does so, begin to expand. Available data suggest that this has not yet happened at least on a large scale,[12] but the data do not permit us to analyze the evolution of this phenomenon over time, and the violations of statutory restrictions, which the data do reveal, although in themselves trivial, would be disturbing if read as the beginnings of a long-run trend.

Proposals for legitimizing the existing migrant labor force have recently been outlined by the Carter administration. The basic thrust of these proposals seems reasonable, but their success will very much depend on how a number of specific practical problems are resolved in their implementation.

In evaluating the proposals, I would distinguish, at least conceptually, between more or less permanent settlers, on the one hand, and temporary workers, on the other. The object with permanent settlers should be to legitimize their status and that of their children as completely as possible so as to maximize access to channels of upward social mobility. For temporary workers, on the other hand, one wants to provide legitimation without encouraging any form of permanent attachment. In addition, because some temporary workers are likely to develop permanent attachment in any case, and because any administrative process is likely to make mistakes in its initial classification, there must be some mechanism through which temporary workers can convert to permanent status.

The proposals presently being discussed appear to be attempting to handle the problem through a two-tier amnesty. One tier covers people who have been in the country for more than seven years and would give them immigrant status, which would enable them to bring their families from abroad or to regularize the status of family members already here. The second tier would cover workers in the country as of January 1977 and would give them a legitimate status in the country but would provide no rights for their families abroad. The distinction could be more or less construed as corresponding to the conceptual distinction between permanent and temporary migrants. The correspondence is quite imperfect, because some permanent settlers will have been here fewer than seven years and a number of temporary migrants will be legitimized as relatives of people who fall within the seven-year amnesty. However, it is not obvious what would constitute a more perfect division. The chief problem is that no provision is made whereby the currently temporary migrants could convert their status.

The conversion might be handled easily by giving temporary migrants priority in the allocation of existing immigration quotas, with the order of priority based upon length of stay in the United States. People should be able to exercise this priority at any time in the future in order to minimize the incentive for immediate conversion. It may also be desirable to expand the existing immigration quotas to accommodate these adjustments in status or to create a special quota for this purpose. At a minimum, it would seem advisable to raise the Mexican quota, either permanently or as a special quota for conversion from temporary to permanent status, to the rate of sixty thousand to seventy thousand, which prevailed before the twenty thousand per country limit was established in 1976.

There is a presumption in current proposals that if the present alien population can be legitimized, further entry can be handled by more effective law enforcement. Indeed, the amnesty problem has been justified on essentially humanitarian grounds. If the program is supported instead, as we have to argue here, as a means of bringing an essentially irreversible process within the law and under some form of control, one is forced to face as a distinct possibility that illegal entry will continue after the amnesty. The tenor of the preceding analysis is that such entry will initially be limited; that the secondary labor market is a contained one, and that so long as sufficient legal labor is available to meet its needs any tendencies to draw upon illegal labor can be controlled. Over time, however, one would expect the pool of legal labor to decline, hopefully in large measure, through upward mobility. It would be desirable, then, to have some means of expanding the available labor pool. One such measure, which would introduce a safety valve in the system without creating the open-ended immigration system that the electorate seems to fear, would be to provide a special temporary work permit for those people who, because of their status as relatives of resident aliens, would eventually become eligible for permanent immigration but are now barred by the quota and by administrative delays from immediate entry: This valve might be activated by the Secretary of Labor. Over the long run, this proposal would not expand the number with immigration rights but would enable us to adjust the time at which those rights are exercised in accord with the requirements of the economy.

It should be noted that if a regular labor supply large enough to fill existing jobs was created in this way, the force of the objections to employer liability expressed above would be substantially weakened.

Other related issues

Two other issues arise repeatedly in discussions of immigration policy: the linkage between migration and underdevelopment in the place of origin and the impact of immigration on unemployment among nationals at the destination. Both issues have been addressed in earlier chapters, but because of their prominence in the public-policy debate, it appears useful to repeat the conclusions here.

Development abroad

It is sometimes proposed that the immigration policy in the United States should be linked to development aid to the donor countries.[13] Such a proposal is, for example, one of the components of the Carter administration program. Generally, such proposals derive from the notion that the migration is propelled by economic deprivation abroad. The notion runs contrary to the tenor of the argument we have sought to develop here. Economic development in particular donor countries cannot solve the "migration problem" of a country like the United States because the migration is generated by industrialization, not underdevelopment. If the supply of labor from one country was to be cut off by its own economic development, the United States would simply turn, as it has turned historically, to some other nation.

A very different case can, however, be made for linking immigration policy to development aid: Economic development in the donor country tends to foster return migration. The migrants are motivated by a desire to invest in business and agricultural projects in their home communities and such projects are more likely to be viable in an expanding, rapidly developing country. As noted in Chapter 5, however, the projects involved are of a kind that are not readily "planned" or easily fostered by the large and distant bureaucracies through which development aid is generally funneled, and the rationale for linking such aid to immigration policy must be that the kinds of projects that are fostered by such aid and the general economic expansion they produce will indirectly expand the opportunities for the kinds of small businesses in which the migrants desire to invest.

Unemployment among nationals

The analytical framework we have sought to develop in the preceding pages suggests that long-distance migrants compete with secondary workers, such as youth and housewives, and not with the primary labor force, and to the extent that migration aggravates unemployment, it is the unemployment of these groups. Because of the tight geographic restraints upon the employment opportunities that youth and housewives will accept and their peculiar requirements with respect to working hours, there is considerable doubt about how extensive even that competition actually is. That doubt cannot be resolved a priori and, indeed, the nature of the competition may vary seasonally and over time, as the migration stream ages and the preferences of women and youth change. The Immigration Service, exercising its discretion within the terms of its current understanding of its job, acts to minimize the actual competition to the extent that its budget permits, and the most promising approach would appear to be experimentation with increased resources allocated to particular labor markets and geographic areas, rather than a radical change in institutional procedures.

Such a policy must be conceived and understood within the broader framework of macroeconomic policy. It is not possible to develop such a framework in a book of this kind. But it is important to note that unemployment could be reduced even without an attempt to cut back migration through a general economic expansion. The immediate restraint upon such an expansion in a country like the United States is the fear of the inflation that it is thought likely to produce. Several reasons have been advanced in earlier chapters to suggest that any attempt to curtail immigration will itself aggravate these inflationary pressures. Conventional economic theory does not necessarily accept those particular arguments, but neither does it suggest that reductions in unemployment accomplished by curtailing immigration and substituting unemployed nationals for migrants will be any less inflationary than a comparable reduction in unemployment accomplished in other ways. Indeed, to the extent that unemployment acts to curtail inflation by moderating wage demands, such a policy will definitely *not* be less inflationary.

Equity and due process

The final issue that arises in a consideration of immigration policy is the issue of equity and due process in its administration. The present policy is not equitable. It lends itself to corruption and abuse. But even at best, when government officials and foreign petitioners are operating within the letter of the law, it is extremely inequitable and personalistic. Because it places tremendous discretion in the hands of the Immigration Service, it gives great advantage to people with the skills and inclination to "play" the system through institutional manipulation, personal appeal, and persistence. It makes the immigrants moreover vulnerable not just to the official system but to the professional manipulators that the system encourages. The proposals contained in this chapter will not materially change this, and to the extent that they rely heavily upon discretionary action by the INS to control the labor market, they hinge upon those very aspects of the system that seem to generate the abuse. I am not unmindful of this or untroubled by it.

One must ask, however, whether the standards of equity and due process sometimes applied to this law-enforcement system are in any sense realistic. They are certainly unrealistic in terms of the budgets that have been allocated to their pursuit, and if, as we have argued, the budgetary shortfall is not accidental but systematic, they may be unrealistic in terms of the underlying politicoeconomic system. And they may be unrealistic in another sense as well. They derive from an ideal of impersonal rules, impersonally administered. There is a certain parallel here between the notions of a blind, impartial justice and the idea of impersonal market forces governing the behavior of economic man. And what appears to be undermining our ideals of justice and governing in their stead are the very forces that undermine and replace the impersonal forces of the labor market: man's tendency to form communal ties and to relate one to one directly and personally in a social setting. One need not entirely abandon one's commitment to equity and due process to argue that "justice" in the present system could be improved if, instead of referring continually to an ideal we have not achieved in the administration of the law, we sought also to understand in a deeper and more analytical way how the social system and the personal ties that develop within it arise and govern the decisions that are actually made. Surely, the system is not uninfluenced by the fact that the INS is forced to administer, and the migrants to live within, a structure that fundamentally contradicts official policy and haute rhetoric. It is hard to believe that the community of Immigration officials, which sanctions its members' behavior, would not come closer to embodying and accepting the standards of honesty and compassion of the community at large, and weighing them accurately against the values of due process and equity, if the nation was willing to accept explicit responsibility for its own ambivalence, if, in other words, we lifted from the INS the burden of bearing our own hypocrisy. But about this, as in so much of immigration policy, we can only guess. The main reason we can only guess is because we have failed to look at administrative law, as we have failed to look at the labor market, as a social process. Clearly, migration will not wait for us to do so. But the basic message of this volume is not the specific policy proposals: It is rather the importance of an analysis that roots human behavior in general and migration in particular in the social context out of which it springs.

Notes

1. Introduction

1 *The Economist,* Vol. 264, No. 6990 (August 20, 1977), pp. 60–3. The current country-by-country data are collected in *SOPEMI, Continuous Reporting System on Migration,* Annual Reports, Organization for Economic Cooperation and Development, Directorate for Social Affairs, Manpower and Education. This document does not always report data as a percent of the labor force, however.

2 *Population Bulletin,* Vol. 32, No. 4 (September 1977), p. 22.

3 These particular figures are taken from David S. North and Marion F. Houstoun, *The Characteristics and Role of Illegal Aliens in the U.S. Labor Market: An Exploratory Study* (Washington, D.C.; Linton, 1976), p. 27. Most figures quoted in the press fall within this range.

4 Because we return to these points in the body of the text, extensive documentation is not included in this chapter. For a general review of the issues surrounding international migration as they have been perceived in Europe see: Stephen Castles and Godula Kosack, *Immigrant Workers and Class Structure in Western Europe* (London: Oxford University Press, 1973), and Georges Tapinos, *L'economie des migrations internationales* (Paris: Librairie Armand Colin et Presses de la fondation nationale des sciences politiques, 1974). For a shorter summary see Kurt B. Mayer, "Intra-European Migration During the Past Twenty Years," *International Migration Review,* Vol. 9, No. 4 (Winter 1975), pp. 441–7; for the most recent experience, see Bernard Kayser, "L'echange inegal des ressources humaines: migration, croissance, et crise en Europe," *Revue Tier-Monde,* Vol. 17, No. 69 (January–March 1977), pp. 7–18. The most comprehensive discussion of undocumented workers in the United States is North and Houstoun, ibid.

5 Martin Slater, "Migration and Workers' Conflicts in Western Europe," unpublished doctoral dissertation, MIT, Department of Political Science, 1977.

6 Tapinos, op. cit., pp. 186–96. See, more specifically, the reports of the Inwood-Nuffic, Molenstraat 27 Den Haag-2003, on their project, "The Contribution of Returning Migrant Workers to the Development Process in Their Home Countries."

7 Michael J. Piore, "Jobs and Training," in Samuel Beer and Richard Barringer, *The State and the Poor* (Cambridge, Mass.: Winthrop Publishers, 1970), pp. 53–83; Peter B. Doeringer and Michael J. Piore, "Equal Employment Opportunity in Boston," *Industrial Relations,* Vol. 10, No. 3 (May 1970), pp. 324–39; Michael J. Piore, "Racial Negotiations: The Massachusetts Welfare Confrontation," prepared for the Institute of Industrial Relations, University of Michigan-Wayne State University Study of the "Negotiations in Racial Confrontations"; "On-the-Job Training in a Dual Labor Market: Public and Private Responsibilities in On-the-Job Training of Disadvantaged Workers," in Arnold Weber, et al. (eds.), *Public-Private Manpower Policies* (Madison, Wis.: Industrial Relations Research Association, 1969), pp. 101–32; "Changes in the Mississippi Agricultural Economy and the Problems of Displaced Negro Farm Workers," *American Journal of Psychotherapy,* Vol. 22, No. 4 (October 1968), pp. 592–601; "Negro Workers in the Mississippi Delta: Problems of Displacement and Adjustment," *Proceedings,* Industrial Relations Research Association (Winter 1967), pp. 366–74.

8 Michael J. Piore, "Immigration, Work Experience and Labor Market Structure," in Pastora San Juan Cafferty and Leon Chestang (eds.), *The Diverse Society: Implications for Social Policy* (Washington, D.C.: National Association of Social Workers, 1976), pp. 109–28; and "The Role of Immigration in Industrial Growth: A Case Study of the Origins and Character of Puerto Rican Migration to Boston," MIT, Department of Economics, Working Paper No. 112 (May 1973).

9 Michael J. Piore, "Undocumented Workers and United States Immigration Policy," MIT, Center for International Studies, Migrations and Development Study Group, Working Paper C/77-18 (December 1977); "The 'Illegal Aliens' Debate Misses the Boat," MIT, Working Papers (March–April 1978), pp. 60–69; "Illegal Immigration in the United States: Some Observations and Policy Suggestions," in *Illegal Aliens: An Assessment of the Issues* (Washington, D.C.: National Council on Employment Policy,

1976), pp. 25–34; "The 'New Immigration' and the Presumptions of Social Policy," in *Proceeding of 27th Annual Meeting*, Industrial Relations Research Association, 1975, pp. 350–8.

10 Michael J. Piore, "Alcune note sul dualismo ne mercato de lavoro," *Revista di Economia e Politica Industriale*, Vol. 3, No. 2 (1977), pp. 185–210; and "Dualism in the Labor Market: A Response to Uncertainty and Flux; the Case of France," *Revue economique*, Vol. 19, No. 1 (January 1978), pp. 26–48.

11 This material appears in Chapter 6.

2. The jobs

1 Report on *The State of the Irish Poor in Great Britain*, pp. ix, xxx–i, quoted in E. P. Thompson, *The Making of the English Working Class* (London: Victor Gollanz, Ltd., 1963), p. 435.

2 David Brody, *Steelworkers in America* (Cambridge, Mass: Harvard University Press, 1960), pp. 96–111, especially p. 97.

3 Sterling D. Spero and Abram L. Harris, *The Black Worker: The Negro and the Labor Movement* (New York: Atheneum, 1968), pp. 149–82, especially pp. 152, 155.

4 Stephen Castles and Godula Kosack, *Immigrant Workers and Class Structure in Western Europe* (London: Oxford University Press, 1973), p. 112.

5 David S. North and Marion F. Houstoun, *The Characteristics and Role of Illegal Aliens in the U.S. Labor Market: An Exploratory Study* (Washington, D.C.: Linton, 1976), pp. 152–3.

6 Cf. W. R. Bohning, *Mediterranean Workers in Western Europe: Effects on Home Countries and Countries of Employment*, World Employment Project, International Labour Office, Geneva, July 1975, WEP 2-26/WP. 2.

7 Castles and Kosack, op. cit., pp. 28–45.

8 Charlotte Erickson, *American Industry and the European Immigrant, 1860–1885* (Cambridge, Mass.: Harvard University Press, 1957), Chapters 1–6; Gird Korman, *Industrialization, Immigrants and Americanizers: The View From Milwaukee, 1860–1921* (Madison, Wis.: The State Historical Society of Wisconsin, 1967), pp. 15–40.

9 Brody, op. cit.; Spero and Harris, op. cit.

10 Michael J. Piore, "Immigration, Work Experience and Labor Market Structure," in Pastora San Juan Cafferty and Leon Chestang (eds), *The Diverse Society: Implications for Social Policy* (Washington, D.C.: National Association of Social Workers, 1976), pp. 109–28.

11 Michael J. Piore, "The 'New Immigration' and the Presumptions of Social Policy," in *Proceedings of the 27th Annual Meeting,* Industrial Relations Research Association, 1975, pp. 350–8.

12 Castles and Kosack, op. cit., pp. 25–45. For more recent trends in Western Europe see Bundesanstalt für Arbeit der Präsident, *Trends in the Use of External Sources of Labour in France, Germany and Great Britain: An Essay on Behalf of the European Communities,* Directorate-General for Social Affairs, Nuremberg, December 1974, and *SOPEMI, Continuous Reporting System on Migration,* Annual Report 1977, Organization for Economic Cooperation and Development, Directorate for Social Affairs, Manpower and Education.

13 See Chapter 5.

14 See note 3, Chapter 1.

15 Castles and Kosack, op. cit., p. 42.

16 Ibid., p. 34.

17 The leading example of this way of thinking about the problem is, Charles P. Kindleberger, *Europe's Postwar Growth: The Role of Labor Supply* (Cambridge, Mass.: Harvard University Press, 1967). See also Georges Tapinos, *L'economie des migrations internationales* (Paris: Librairie Armand Colin et Presses de la fondation nationale des sciences politiques, 1974), pp. 68–73.

18 Lester C. Thurow, *Generating Inequality: Mechanisms of Distribution in the U.S. Economy* (New York: Basic Books, 1975), pp. 75–97.

19 Ibid.; Castles and Kosack, op. cit., pp. 374–430.

20 See, for example, the comparison between different migrant streams in the contemporary United States, in North and Houstoun, op. cit., pp. 105–11. Also Charles B. Keely, et al., "Profiles of Undocumented Aliens in New York City: Haitians and Dominicans," paper presented to the Latin American Studies Association, Houston, Texas, November 1977, Table 15. See also the comparison between Jewish and Italian immigrants in Thomas Kessner, *The Golden Door: Italian and Jewish Immigrant Mobility in New York City, 1880–1915* (New York: Oxford University Press, 1977).

21 See, for example, Barbara Wootton, *The Social Foundations of Wage Policy* (New York: W. W. Norton, 1955), pp. 316–19; John M. Keynes, *The General Theory of Employment, Interest and Money* (New York: Harcourt Brace, 1958), pp. 12–21, 252–3, 267; George W. Taylor and Frank C. Pierson (eds.), *New Concepts of Wage Determination* (New York: McGraw-Hill, 1957), pp. 117–72; Michael J. Piore, "Labor Market Stratication and Wage Deter-

mination," MIT (October 1974), mimeo, and "Fragments of a Sociological Theory of Wages," *American Economic Review,* Vol. 63, No. 2 (May 1973), pp. 377–84.

22 Exemplary of theorizing along these lines are: Stephen Marglin, "What Do Bosses Do?" *The Review of Radical Political Economics,* Vol. 6, No. 2 (Summer 1974), pp. 33–60; and Katherine Stone, "The Origins of Job Structure in the Steel Industry," in Richard C. Edwards, Michael Reich, and David M. Gordon (eds.), *Labor Market Segmentation* (Lexington, Mass.: D. C. Heath, 1975), pp. 27–84.

23 See Peter L. Berger, *The Sacred Canopy: Elements of a Sociological Theory of Religion* (Garden City, N.Y.: Anchor-Doubleday, 1967), Part I.

24 The argument that follows is developed in detail in Michael J. Piore, "The Political and Economic Origins of Dualistic Structures in Labor Markets," MIT mimeo, to appear in a volume of essays with Suzanne Berger, Lisa Peattie, and Martin Rein, tentatively titled *Dualism and Discontinuity in Industrial Society.* The argument is also developed, in part, in the essays cited in note 10 of Chapter 1.

25 See Alfred D. Chandler, Jr., *The Visible Hand: The Managerial Revolution in American Business* (Cambridge, Mass.: Harvard University Press, 1977).

26 Rose Mary Stevens, Louis Wolf Goodman, and Stephen S. Mick, *The Alien Doctors: Foreign Medical Graduates in American Hospitals* (New York: John Wiley and Sons, 1978).

27 Clinton Bourdon and Raymond E. Levitt, "A Comparison of Wages and Labor Management Practices in Union and Nonunion Construction," Research Report R-78-3, MIT, Department of Civil Engineering, March 30, 1977.

28 United States Department of Housing and Urban Development, *Action Against Seasonal Unemployment in the Construction Industry, Lessons from Foreign Experience* (Washington, D.C.: U.S. Government Printing Office, 1971).

29 Bourdon and Levitt, op. cit.

30 J. Bouteiller, J. P. Daubigney, and J. J. Silvestre, *Comparison de hierarchie des salaires entre l'Allemagne et la France,* Laboratoire d'economic et de sociologie du travail, Aix-en-Provence, December 31, 1972.

31 Ronald Dore, *British Factory-Japanese Factory: The Origin of National Diversity in Industrial Relations* (Berkeley, Calif.: University of California Press, 1973).

3. The migrants

1 Stephen Castles and Godula Kosack, *Immigrant Workers and Class Structure in Western Europe* (London: Oxford University Press, 1973), pp. 39–43 and passim.

2 David S. North and Marion F. Houstoun, *The Characteristics and Role of Illegal Aliens in the U.S. Labor Market: An Exploratory Study* (Washington, D.C.: Linton, 1976), pp. 84–6.

3 Michael J. Piore, "The Role of Immigration in Industrial Growth: A Case Study of the Origins and Character of Puerto Rican Migration to Boston," MIT, Department of Economics, Working Paper No. 112 (May 1973), p. 15.

4 Castles and Kosack, op. cit., p. 54.

5 Immigration Commission (The Dillingham Commission), *Abstract of Reports of the Immigration Commission,* U.S. Senate, 61st Congress, 3rd Session, Document No. 747 (Washington, D.C.: U.S. Government Printing Office, 1911), Vol. I, pp. 179–84.

6 Joan M. Nelson, "Temporary Versus Permanent Cityward Migration: Causes and Consequences," MIT, Center for International Studies, Working Paper C/76-14, Migration and Development Study Group.

7 Julie da Vanzo, "Differences Between Return and Nonreturn Migration: An Econometric Analysis," *International Migration Review,* Vol. 10, No. 1 (Spring 1976), pp. 13–25. For parallel findings in other studies and a discussion of the variety of explanations that have been offered for them see Michael J. Greenwood, "Research on Internal Migration in the United States: A Survey," *Journal of Economic Literature,* Vol. 13, No. 2 (June 1975), pp. 412–14.

8 Bernard Kayser, "L'echange ineqal des ressources humaines: migration, croissance, et crise en Europe," *Revue Tier-Monde,* Vol. 17, No. 69 (January–March 1977), pp. 7–18.

9 Peter L. Berger, "Some General Observations on the Problem of Work," in Peter L. Berger et al., *The Human Shape of Work* (London: Macmillan, 1964), pp. 211–41.

10 This and the following quotations in this chapter are taken from my own interviews in Massachusetts, New York, Puerto Rico, and California over the last four years.

11 A similar attitude is implicit in a commentary on Spanish workers in France, which notes that they often accept work in France that they would have refused at home. Juiliette Minces, *Les travailleurs étrangers en France* (Paris: Editions du Seuil, 1973), p. 202.

12 The living arrangements and the attitude of migrants toward them were remarkably similar for European migrants to the

United States at the turn of the century. See David Brody, *Steelworkers in America* (Cambridge, Mass.: Harvard University Press, 1960), pp. 102–3; Thomas Kessner, *The Golden Door: Italian and Jewish Immigrant Mobility in New York City, 1880–1915* (New York: Oxford University Press, 1977); *Immigration Commission Report*, op. cit., Vol. I, pp. 727–72. For contemporary France, see Minces, ibid.

13   North and Houstoun, op. cit., p. 80.

14   Castles and Kosack, op. cit., p. 97.

15   See Brody, op. cit., pp. 95–100; *Immigration Commission Report*, op. cit., Vol. I, pp. 103–79; Vol. II, pp. 425–7.

16   Georges Tapinos, *L'economie des migrations internationales* (Paris: Librairie Armand Colin et Presses de la fondation nationale des sciences politiques, 1974), p. 188.

17   See, for example, the comparison of the Italian and the Jewish experience in Kessner, op. cit.

18   See Piore, op. cit.; Tapinos, op. cit., p. 104.

19   See, for example, Orde Coombs, "Illegal Immigrants in New York: The Invisible Subculture," *New York*, Vol. 9, No. 11 (March 15, 1976), pp. 33–41.

20   For a review of many of these see Charles A. Valentine, *Culture and Poverty* (Chicago, Ill.: University of Chicago Press, 1968).

21   For some further suggestions toward this end, however, see S. N. Eisenstadt, *The Absorption of Immigrants* (London: Routledge & Paul, 1954); also Joseph J. Barton, *Peasants and Strangers: Italians, Rumanians and Slovaks in an American City, 1890–1950* (Cambridge, Mass.: Harvard University Press, 1975), and Manike Maykovich, "To Stay or Not to Stay: Dimensions of Ethnic Assimilation," *International Migration Review*, Vol. 10, No. 3 (Fall 1976), pp. 372–87.

22   Oscar Lewis, *La Vida* (New York: Random House, 1966).

23   Eliot Liebow, *Tally's Corner* (Boston, Mass.: Little, Brown, 1967).

24   The most extreme statement of this view is probably that of Edward C. Banfield, *The Unheavenly City* (Boston, Mass.: Little, Brown, 1968), p. 126: "Lower-class poverty . . . is 'inwardly' caused (by psychological inability to provide for the future, and all that this inability implies)."

25   See Herbert J. Gans, *The Urban Villagers* (New York: The Free Press, 1962), pp. 229–62. The following discussion draws heavily upon this view of the working-class culture.

26   See, for example, Piri Thomas, *Down These Mean Streets* (New York: Knopf, 1967).

27   Gans, op. cit.

4. Particular characteristics of the migrant labor market

1 See, for example, Leonard F. Chapman, Jr., "Silent Invasion That Takes Millions of American Jobs," *U.S. News & World Report,* Vol. 80, No. 49 (December 9, 1974), pp. 77–8.

2 For example, Phillip Bernoux, "L'O.S. face a l'organisation industrielle," *Sociologie du Travail,* Vol. 14, No. 4. (October–December 1972), pp. 410–36. Also Charles Sabel, "Industrial Conflicts and the Sociology of the Labor Market," unpublished doctoral dissertation, Harvard University, June 1978, Chapter 3.

3 For example, Jan de Vries, *The Economy of Europe in an Age of Crisis, 1600–1750* (Cambridge: Cambridge University Press, 1976), pp. 85–6; T. S. Ashton, *The Industrial Revolution* (London: Oxford University Press, 1964), pp. 34–5.

4 Massimo Paci, *Mercato del lavoro e classi sociali in Italia* (Bologna: il Molino, 1973), pp. 192–201. Also "Il lavoro a domicilio," *Rassegna Sindacale Quaderni,* Vol. 11, No. 44–45 (September–December 1973).

5 See Ray Marshall, *Rural Workers in Rural Labor Markets* (Salt Lake City: Olympas, 1974), pp. 23–7. For example, Marshall reports that in 1970 "U.S. farm operators got 52% of their income off the farm." In 1969 58 percent of all farmers had off-farm income.

6 For an expression of this view of female motivation from a managerial point of view, see Ray A. Kilian, *The Working Woman: A Male Manager's View* (New York: American Management Association, 1971), especially pp. 22–31.

7 Paul S. Osterman, "The Labor Market for Young Men," unpublished doctoral dissertation, MIT, Department of Economics and Urban Studies, 1976.

8 Bennett Harrison, "Institutions on the Periphery," in David M. Gordon (ed.), *Problems in Political Economy: An Urban Perspective* (Lexington, Mass.: D. C. Heath, 1977), pp. 102–7.

9 Robert Berrier, "The Politics of Economic Survival: The French Textile Industry in the Postwar Period," unpublished doctoral dissertation, MIT, Department of Political Science, 1978.

10 Reported in Twentieth Century Fund, Task Force on Working Women, Exploitation from 9 to 5 (Lexington, Mass.: D. C. Heath, 1975), pp. 96–8.

11 For example see Chester W. Gregory, *Women in Defense Work During World War II* (New York: Exposition Press, 1974), pp. 192–4. See also François Eymard-Duvernay and Robert Salais, "Une analyse des liens entre l'emploi et le chomage," *Economie et Statis-*

tique, No. 69 (July–August 1975), p. 23; Claude Thelot, "Le fonctionnement du marche de l'emploi: l'example des pays de la Loire" *Economie et Statistique,* No. 69. (July–August 1975), pp. 51–8.

12 Such a view, for example, underlies Martin Feldstein's argument in *Lowering the Permanent Rate of Unemployment,* a study prepared for the use of the Joint Economic Committee, U.S. Congress, 93rd Congress, 1st session, September 18, 1973.

13 See Barbara Wootton, *The Social Foundations of Wage Policy* (New York: A. W. Norton, 1955). These views are neatly summarized in Neil W. Chamberlain, *The Labor Sector* (New York: McGraw-Hill, 1965), pp. 404–6, See also pp. 459–60 on the social minimum wage.

14 See, for example, Lloyd Reynolds, *The Structure of Labor Markets* (New York: Harper, 1951).

15 Charlotte Erickson, *American Industry and the European Immigrant, 1860–1885* (Cambridge, Mass.: Harvard University Press, 1957).

16 Juan Diez-Canedo, "Migration, Return and Development in Mexico," doctoral dissertation in progress, MIT, Department of Economics, expected date of completion, 1979.

17 This second type of migration would seem to be too well known to require documentation, appearing, for example, in virtually all historical studies of U.S. immigration cited in Chapter 6.

18 One Dominican in New York in 1975 commented, "If you can't find at least two jobs, it doesn't pay to stay." Parallel phenomena occur in Europe; see, for example, Stephen Castles and Godula Kosack, *Immigrant Workers and Class Structure in Western Europe* (London: Oxford University Press, 1973), p. 189.

19 For evidence of the impact of migration on the country of origin see Steven Zell, "A Comparative Study of the Labor Market Characteristics of Return Migrants and Non-migrants in Puerto Rico," Commonwealth of Puerto Rico, Office of the Governor, Planning Board, Area of Economics and Social Planning, Bureau of Social Planning, July 1973. While Zell's work makes clear that return migrants have a higher rate of unemployment than non-migrants, it does not permit a distinction among alternative causes for these differences.

20 This seems to be a large part of the explanation for the high unemployment among black youth. For example, Osterman finds that black youth tend to quit more often and spend a longer time before taking another job than do white youth in similar economic climates. Paul Osterman, "Racial Differentials in Male

Youth Unemployment," paper prepared for U.S. Department of Labor, Office of the Assistant Secretary for Policy, Evaluation and Research, Conference on Employment Statistics and Youth, Los Angeles, Calif., 1978.

21 The complexity of the relationship between migration and unemployment, along with the way in which it changes as migration streams age, is probably a major reason why unemployment has proved such an elusive variable in economic studies of migration. For example, one review of the literature concludes: "One of the most perplexing problems confronting migration scholars is the lack of significance of local unemployment rates in explaining migration." Michael J. Greenwood, "Research on Internal Migration in the United States: A Survey," *Journal of Economic Literature,* Vol. 13, No. 2 (June 1975), p. 411.

22 Michael P. Todaro, "A Model of Labor Migration and Urban Unemployment in Less Developed Countries," *American Economic Review,* Vol. 58, No. 1 (March 1968), pp. 138–48, and John R. Harris and Michael P. Todaro, "Migration, Unemployment and Development: A Two Sector Analysis," *American Economic Review,* Vol. 60, No. 1 (March 1970), pp. 126–42.

23 Myron Weiner, *Political Demography: An Inquiry into the Political Consequences of Population Change* (Cambridge, Mass.: Center for International Studies, MIT, 1969). Wayne Cornelius, "Urbanization and Political Demand Making: Political Participation Among the Migrant Poor in Latin American Cities," *American Political Science Review,* Vol. 68, No. 3 (September 1974), pp. 1125–46; W. H. Wriggins and J. F. Gugot (eds.), *Population Politics and the Future of Southern Asia* (New York: Columbia University Press, 1973). See also Joan M. Nelson, "Temporary Versus Permanent Cityward Migration: Causes and Consequences," MIT, Center for International Studies, Working Paper C/76-14, Migration and Development Study Group, especially pp. 68–83.

24 Martin Slater, "Migration and Workers' Conflicts in Western Europe," unpublished doctoral dissertation, MIT, Department of Political Science, 1977.

25 For example, Gerald Rosenblum, *Immigrant Workers: Their Impact on American Labor Radicalism* (New York: Basic Books, 1973).

26 Erickson, op. cit., p. 114.

5. The impact of migration on place of origin

1 See, for example, W. R. Bohning, "Return Migrants' Contribution to the Development Process–The Issues Involved," pp.

28–32, and John B. Sacchetti, "Premises for the Re-integration of the Migrant Worker in the Country of Origin," pp. 74–80, in Ayse Kudats and Yilmaz Ozkan (eds.), *International Conference on Migrant Workers* (Berlin, West Germany: International Institute for Comparative Social Studies of the Social Science Center, 1975.) See also, Georges Tapinos, *L'economie des migrations internationales* (Paris: Librairie Armand Colin et Presses de la fondation nationale des sciences politiques, 1974), pp. 172–91, for a summary of much of the literature.

2 Tapinos, ibid., p. 188, summarizes the experience of return migrants from Europe. "Dans ces societes, le signe le moins equivoque de la mobilite sociale c'est l'independence, qui se traduit sur le plan personnel par l'acquisition d'une maison et, sur le plan professionel, par le preference pour les metier nonagricoles et nonsalaries."

3 Herbert J. Gans, *The Urban Villagers* (New York: The Free Press, 1962), p. 244. To the considerable extent that the working-class subculture upon which Gans focused in Boston derived from the migration of southern Italian peasants, it is obviously very difficult to distinguish class from peasant origins as an explanation of the phenomenon.

4 The interaction between social integration and skill training is demonstrated most clearly in the longitudinal study of the training of black workers in an all-white plant by Leonard M. Davidson, "The Process of Employing the Disadvantaged," unpublished doctoral dissertation, MIT, June 1973.

5 See, for example, Clark Kerr, John T. Dunlop, Frederick H. Harbison, and Charles A. Myers, *Industrialism and Industrial Man* (Cambridge, Mass.: Harvard University Press, 1960); also see and compare Howard R. Bowen and Garth L. Magnum (eds.), *Automation and Economic Progress: A Summary of the Report of the National Commission on Technology and Economic Progress* (Englewood Cliffs, N.J.: Prentice-Hall, 1966). This also seems to be the model implicit in John Kenneth Galbraith's *The Affluent Society* (Cambridge, Mass.: Riverside Press, 1958).

6 See, for example, International Labour Office, *Small Enterprise Development: Policies and Programmes* (Geneva, Switzerland: International Labour Office, 1977), or Paulo R. Souza and Victor E. Tokman, "The Informal Urban Sector in Latin America," *International Labour Review*, Vol. 114, No. 3 (November–December 1976), pp. 355–65.

7 Suzanne Berger, "The Uses of Traditional Classes," MIT mimeo, 1975.

8   Michael J. Piore, "On the Technological Foundations of Economic Dualism," MIT, Department of Economics, Working Paper No. 110 (1973), p. 16.

9   The importance of this sector, however, is evident in other developing countries. For example, Leo Van Uclzen, *Peripheral Production in Kayseri Turkey: A Study of Prospects for Industrialization Arising from Small and Middle Scale Enterprises in a Peripheral Growth Pole* (Ankara, Turkey: Ajans-Turk Press, 1977), p. 59.

10 Juan Diez-Canedo, "Migration, Return and Development in Mexico," doctoral dissertation in progress, MIT, Department of Economics, expected date of completion, 1979.

11 Wayne Cornelius and Juan Diez-Canedo, "Mexican Migration to the United States: The View From Rural Sending Communities," MIT, Center for International Studies, 1976.

12 Joan M. Nelson, "Temporary Versus Permanent Cityward Migration: Causes and Consequences," MIT, Center for International Studies, Working Paper C/7614, Migration and Development Study Group, 1976, pp. 34–44.

13 Several of these studies are summarized in Joseph J. Barton, *Peasants and Strangers: Italians, Rumanians and Slovaks in an American City, 1890–1950* (Cambridge, Mass.: Harvard University Press, 1975), pp. 27–47. See also Takenori Inoki, "Aspects of German Peasant Emigration to the United States, 1815–1914: A Reexamination of Some Behavioral Hypotheses in Migration Theory," unpublished doctoral dissertation, MIT, 1974, pp. 101–50.

14 Piore, op. cit.

15 For example, Vernon Briggs, "Mexican Workers in the United States Labour Market," *International Labour Review*, Vol. 112, No. 5 (November 1975), pp. 351–68.

16 See, generally, Charles E. Silberman, *Crisis in Black and White* (New York: Random House, 1966), especially pp. 168–223; and, more specifically, Howard Zinn, *SNCC, The New Abolitionists* (Boston, Mass.: Beacon Press, 1964); Robert H. Brisbane, *The Black Vanguard* (Valley Forge, Pa.: Judson Press, 1970); and Nic Kotz and Mary Lynn Kotz, *A Passion for Equality, George Wiley and The Movement* (New York: W. W. Norton, 1977).

17 Joseph P. Fitzpatrick, *Puerto Rican Americans: The Meaning of Migration to the Mainland* (Englewood Cliffs, N.J.: Prentice-Hall, 1971), pp. 71–2, 144, 179.

18 Oscar Handlin, *The Uprooted* (Boston, Mass.: Little, Brown, 1951), pp. 145–95; also Nathan Glazer and Daniel Patrick Moynihan,

Beyond the Melting Pot (Cambridge, Mass.: M.I.T. Press, 1963), pp. 241–4.

19 Michael J. Piore, "Immigration, Work Experience and Labor Market Structure," in Pastora San Juan Cafferty and Leon Chestang (eds.), *The Diverse Society: Implications for Social Policy* (Washington, D.C.: National Association of Social Workers, 1976), pp. 109–28.

20 Ellie Glaessel-Brown, "Migration Policy: The Case of a Two Nation Caribbean Island," unpublished paper, Harvard University, May 1975, mimeo. See also, André Corten, "La migration des travailleurs Haitiens vers les centrales cusieres dominicaines," in *Culture et Development,* Vol. 2, No. 3 (Autumn 1970), pp. 713–31.

21 Tapinos, op. cit., p. 184.

22 Inoki, op. cit., pp. 188–202.

23 However, foreign migration clearly played a *much* larger role in early European industrialization than is generally thought. See, for example, Stephen Castles and Godula Kosack, *Immigrant Workers and Class Structure in Western Europe* (London: Oxford University Press, 1973), pp. 19–25.

24 Michael J. Piore, "Negro Workers in the Mississippi Delta: Problems of Displacement and Adjustment," *Proceedings,* Industrial Relations Research Association, Winter 1967, pp. 366–74.

25 Caribbean countries also drew upon foreign labor after the end of slavery.

26 D. Maillat, *Recherche sur les consequences economiques de l'emploi des travailleurs etrangers: Le cas de la Suisse,* Document de Travail, O.C.D.E., Direction de la main-d'oeuvre et des affaires sociales, MS/M/404/392 (March 1972).

27 Inoki, op. cit.

28 Exemplary of this is the following quotation taken from a study of undocumented Dominican workers in New York City: "The majority of incoming immigrants, as immediate participants in on-going social networks, rely heavily upon other participants as mediators between themselves and whatever aspect of the new environment they are unable to cope with. However, even the established resident Dominican is seldom so acculturated that he can provide all the assistance that is necessary in this highly technical and specialized American society. Both because of the actual need for specialized culture-broker roles as well as their existence in the form of *tributarios* in Dominican culture, it is to be expected that such structural roles will be replicated in New York. The travel agent catering to a clientele of Hispanos has undergone a

process of syncretism and become the culture broker for large segments of Hispanic society. While overtly such an office appears to be primarily involved in selling tickets and tours, actually it encompasses a whole host of activities, that seem unrelated to the travel business: translations, notary public, income tax preparation, driving instruction, real estate and rental information, and, most importantly, help in the preparation of immigration forms." Glenn L. Hendricks, "The Phenomenon of Migrant Illegality: The Case of Dominicans in New York," unpublished paper submitted for presentation at the Society for Applied Anthropology Congress, Amsterdam, The Netherlands, March 19–22, 1975, pp. 11–12.

6. The historical evolution of long-distance migration in the United States

1 Alan Dawley, *Class and Community: The Industrial Revolution in Lynn* (Cambridge, Mass.: Harvard University Press, 1976), pp. 42–73. Also Alfred D. Chandler, Jr., *The Visible Hand: The Managerial Revolution in American Business* (Cambridge, Mass.: Harvard University Press, 1977), pp. 50–78.

2 Dawley, ibid., p. 52.

3 Ibid., pp. 3–76; also Chandler, op. cit., Chapter 2.

4 Alexander Keyssar, "Men Out of Work: A Social History of Unemployment in Massachusetts 1870–1916," unpublished doctoral dissertation, Harvard University, 1977.

5 See Dawley's discussion of the development of the floating labor force in Lynn, Mass., Dawley, op cit., pp. 139–42.

6 Chandler, op. cit.

7 Michael J. Piore, "On the Technological Foundations of Economic Dualism," MIT, Department of Economics, Working Paper No. 110 (1973); Robert T. Averitt, *The Dual Economy: The Dynamics of American Industrial Structure* (New York: W. W. Norton, 1968).

8 Chandler, op. cit., p. 442.

9 U.S. Bureau of Labor Statistics, "Labor Union and Employee Association Membership 1976," news release, September 1977.

10 See Michael J. Piore, "The Political and Economic Origins of Dualistic Structures in the Labor Markets," MIT mimeo, 1978.

11 Immigration Commission (The Dillingham Commission), *Abstract of Reports of the Immigration Commission*, U.S. Senate, 61st Congress, 3rd Session, Document No. 747 (Washington, D.C.: U.S. Government Printing Office, 1911), Vol. I, p. 24.

12 Simon Kuznets and Ernest Rubin, *Immigration and the Foreign Born* (New York: National Bureau of Economic Research, 1954), Occasional Paper No. 46.

13 Charlotte Erickson, *Invisible Immigrants: The Adaptation of English and Scottish Immigrants in 19th Century America* (Coral Gables, Fla.: University of Miami Press, 1972), p. 31.

14 See John Bodnar, *Immigration and Industrialization, Ethnicity in an American Mill Town, 1870–1940* (Pittsburgh, Pa.: University of Pittsburgh Press, 1977), pp. 29–34, for an especially detailed contrast between this and subsequent migration.

15 Gerald Rosenblum, *Immigrant Workers: Their Impact on American Labor Radicalism* (New York: Basic Books, 1973), p. 51.

16 *Immigration Commission Report,* op. cit., Vol. III, p. 12.

17 Ibid., Vol. I, p. 24.

18 Ibid., Vol. I, p. 182, Table 16.

19 Ibid., Vol. I, p. 183, Table 18.

20 Kuznets and Rubin, op. cit., pp. 19–37.

21 David Brody, *Steelworkers in America* (Cambridge, Mass.: Harvard University Press, 1960), pp. 97–98.

22 For example, *Immigration Commission Report,* op. cit., "Dictionary of Races," Vol. 5, pp. 15–40.

23 Charlotte Erickson, *American Industry and the European Immigrant, 1860–1885* (Cambridge, Mass.: Harvard University Press, 1957), pp. 67–105; Gird Korman, *Industrialization, Immigrants and Americanizers: The View From Milwaukee, 1866–1921* (Madison, Wis.: The State Historical Society of Wisconsin, 1967), pp. 15–40; Bodnar, op. cit., pp. 24–8.

24 Erickson, ibid., pp. 72–6; *Immigration Commission Reports,* "The Floating Immigrant Labor Supply," Vol. 18, part 22, pp. 347–85.

25 *Immigration Commission Reports,* op. cit., Vol. I, Table 19, p. 183.

26 Erickson (1972), op. cit., p. 236, see also pp. 247–54.

27 Rosenblum, op. cit., p. 51.

28 Thomas Kessner, *The Golden Door: Italian and Jewish Immigrant Mobility in New York City, 1880–1915* (New York: Oxford University Press, 1977), p. 27; see also Erickson (1957), op. cit., p. 227, note 103.

29 Stanley Lebergott, *Manpower in Economic Growth* (New York: McGraw-Hill, 1964), p. 541.

30 Kuznets and Rubin, op. cit.

31 Edgar Robinson, *They Voted for Roosevelt: The Presidential Vote, 1932–1944* (Stanford, Calif.: Stanford University Press, 1947).

32 Peter Friedlander, *The Emergence of a U.A.W. Local, 1936–1939*

(Pittsburgh, Pa.: University of Pittsburgh Press, 1975); see also Bodnar, op. cit., pp. 138–49, 153–5.

33 Sterling D. Spero and Abram L. Harris, *The Black Worker: The Negro and the Labor Movement* (New York: Atheneum, 1968); see also Brody, op. cit., pp. 268–9.

34 See especially Bodnar, op. cit.

35 Gunnar Myrdal, *An American Dilemma* (New York: Harper & Row, 1962), pp. 185–91.

36 Spero and Harris, op. cit., in general, pp. 140–82, and "Garments," pp. 337–8; "Stockyards," pp. 264–7; "Steel," p. 257.

37 Ibid., pp. 178–9.

38 See, for example, subemployment surveys conducted for the U.S. Department of Labor in November 1966. The results of these surveys are summarized in the U.S. Department of Labor, *Manpower Report of the President,* (Washington, D.C.: U.S. Government Printing Office, 1967); pp. 74–5. Note especially the comparison of Harlem and Bedford-Stuyvesant.

39 National Advisory Commission on Civil Disorder (The Kerner Commission), *Report* (New York: Bantam Books, 1968), pp. 172–8.

40 Michael J. Piore, "Immigration, Work Experience and Labor Market Structure," in Pastora San Juan Cafferty and Leon Chestang (eds.), *The Diverse Society: Implications for Social Policy* (Washington, D.C.: National Association of Social Workers, 1976), pp. 109–28.

41 David S. North and Marion F. Houstoun, *The Characteristics and Role of Illegal Aliens in the U.S. Labor Market: An Exploratory Study* (Washington, D.C.: Linton, 1976).

42 See especially, John Martinez, *Mexican Immigration to the U.S., 1910–1930* (San Francisco, Calif.: R. and E. Research Associates, 1971). Also Leo Grebler, Ralph C. Guzman, and Joan W. Moore, *The Mexican-American People* (New York: The Free Press, 1970), pp. 61–81.

43 Grebler, et al., ibid., pp. 523–6.

44 Roy S. Bryce-Laporte and Delores M. Mortimer (eds.), *Caribbean Immigration to the United States* (Washington, D.C.: Smithsonian Institution, Research Institute on Immigration and Ethnic Studies, 1976), Occasional Papers No. 1.

45 Stanley Friedlander, *Labor Migration and Economic Growth: A Case Study of Puerto Rico* (Cambridge, Mass.: M.I.T. Press, 1965). Steven Zell, "A Comparative Study of the Labor Market Characteristics of Return Migrants and Non-migrants in Puerto Rico,"

Commonwealth of Puerto Rico, Office of the Governor, Planning Board, July 1973.
46 Piore (1976), op. cit.
47 North and Houstoun, op. cit.; Wayne Cornelius, "Urbanization and Political Demand Making: Political Participation Among the Migrant Poor in Latin American Cities," *American Political Science Review*, Vol. 68, No. 3 (September 1974), pp. 1125–46; Juan Diez-Canedo, "Migration, Return and Development in Mexico," doctoral dissertation in progress, MIT, Department of Economics; Julian Samora, *Los Mojados: The Wetback Story* (Notre Dame, Ind.: University of Notre Dame Press, 1971).
48 Piore (1976), op. cit.

7. The dilemmas of current U.S. immigration policy

1 For undocumented migration see David S. North and Marion F. Houstoun, *The Characteristics and Role of Illegal Aliens in the U.S. Labor Market: An Exploratory Study* (Washington, D.C.: Linton, 1976). For documented migration see the *Annual Reports* of the Immigration and Naturalization Service.
2 For a brief background on current legislation see Abba P. Schwartz, *The Open Society* (New York: Simon & Schuster, 1968), pp. 99–138.
3 These, as much else in this business, do not always conform to conventional expectations about American racism. Immigration agents with whom I have talked are most sympathetic to undocumented workers from the poorest countries. They are quite bitter about those from wealthier nations. Usually this means they favor the racial groups "least white" (to use their terms). As one officer put it, "The Dominican I understand. But what is wrong with the Brazilians? The country is booming, and there is plenty of opportunity. Especially if you are white." This man left little doubt about whom he was interested in apprehending.
4 For example, Jorge A. Bustamante, "The Silent Invasion Issue," paper presented to the Annual Meeting of the Population Association of America in Montreal, Canada, 1976.
5 "Twenty-five to 35% of all Western Hemisphere immigration results from exceptions from labor certification for parents of minor U.S. citizen children." Austin T. Fragomen, Jr., "1976 Amendments to the Immigration and Nationality Act," *International Migration Review*, Vol. 11, No. 1 (Spring 1973), pp. 95–100.
6 North and Houstoun, op. cit., pp. 85–6.
7 Ibid., pp. 76–9, p. 82.

8   Ibid.
9   Ibid., p. 85. Cf. Charles B. Keely, et al., "Profiles of Un-
    documented Aliens in New York City: Haitians and Dominicans,"
    paper presented to the Latin American Studies Association,
    Houston, Texas, November 1977.
10 North and Houstoun, ibid., pp. 76–9, 82.
11 For a review of the amendment, see Fragomen, op. cit.
12 North and Houstoun, op. cit., pp. 128–32. Edward M. Gramlich,
    "Impact of Minimum Wages on Other Wages, Employment and
    Family Incomes," *Brookings Papers on Economic Activity* Vol. 2
    (1976), pp. 409–51; and Orley Ashenfelter and Robert Smith,
    Compliance with the Minimum Wage Law, U.S. Department of
    Labor, Technical Analysis Paper No. 19A (Washington, D.C.: Of-
    fice of the Assistant Secretary for Policy Evaluation and Research,
    1974).
13 Domestic Council on Illegal Aliens, *Preliminary Report,* U.S. De-
    partment of Justice, Office of Policy and Planning, December
    1976, p. 243.

Bibliography

Banfield, Edward C. (1968), *The Unheavenly City* (Boston, Mass.: Little, Brown).

Barton, Josef J. (1975), *Peasants and Strangers: Italians, Rumanians and Slovaks in an American City, 1890–1950* (Cambridge, Mass.: Harvard University Press).

Berger, John, and Jean Mohr (1975), *The Seventh Man, Migrant Workers in Europe* (New York: Viking Press).

Berger, Peter L. (1967), *The Sacred Canopy: Elements of a Sociological Theory of Religion* (Garden City, N.Y.: Anchor-Doubleday).

Berger, Suzanne (1975), "The Uses of Traditional Classes," MIT mimeo.

Berrier, Robert (1978), "The Politics of Economic Survival: The French Textile Industry in the Postwar Period," unpublished doctoral dissertation, MIT, Department of Political Science.

Bodnar, John (1977), *Immigration and Industrialization, Ethnicity in an American Mill Town, 1870–1940* (Pittsburgh, Pa.: University of Pittsburgh Press).

Bohning, W. R. (1975), *Mediterranean Workers in Western Europe: Effects on Home Countries and Countries of Employment*, World Employment Project, International Labour Office, Geneva, WEP 2–26/WP. 2.

Bourdon, Clinton, and Raymond E. Levitt (1977), "A Comparison of Wages and Labor Management Practices in Union and Nonunion Construction," Research Report R-78-3, MIT, Department of Civil Engineering.

Bouteiller, J., J. P. Daubigney, and J. J. Silvestre (1972), *Comparison de hierarchie des salaires entre l'Allemagne et la France*, Laboratoire d'economie et de sociologie du travail, Aix-en-Provence.

Briggs, Vernon (1975), "Mexican Workers in the United States Labour Markets," *International Labour Review*, Vol. 112, No. 5, pp. 351–68.

Brody, David (1960), *Steelworkers in America* (Cambridge, Mass.: Harvard University Press).

Bryce-Laporte, Roy S., and Delores M. Mortimer (1976), *Caribbean Immigration to the United States,* Smithsonian Institution, Research Institute on Immigration and Ethnic Studies, Occasional Papers No. 1.

Bundesanstalt für Arbeit der Präsident (1974), *Trends in the Use of External Sources of Labour in France, Germany and Great Britain: An Essay on Behalf of the European Community,* Directorate-General for Social Affairs, Nuremberg.

Bustamante, Jorge A. (1976), "The Silent Invasion Issue," paper presented to the Annual Meeting of the Population Association of America in Montreal, Canada.

Castles, Stephen, and Godula Kosack (1973), *Immigrant Workers and Class Structure in Western Europe* (London: Oxford University Press).

Chandler, Alfred D., Jr. (1977), *The Visible Hand: The Managerial Revolution in American Business* (Cambridge, Mass.: Harvard University Press).

Coombs, Orde (1976), "Illegal Immigrants in New York: The Invisible Subculture," *New York,* Vol. 9, No. 11, pp. 33–41.

Cornelius, Wayne (1974), "Urbanization and Political Demand Making: Political Participation Among the Migrant Poor in Latin American Cities," *American Political Science Review,* Vol. 68, No. 3 (September 1974), pp. 1125–46.

and Juan Diez-Canedo (1976), "Mexican Migration to the United States: The View From Rural Sending Communities," MIT, Center for International Studies.

Dawley, Alan (1976), *Class and Community: The Industrial Revolution in Lynn* (Cambridge, Mass.: Harvard University Press).

Diez-Canedo, Juan, "Migration, Return and Development in Mexico," MIT, doctoral dissertation in progress, Department of Economics.

Doeringer, Peter B., and Michael J. Piore, *Internal Labor Markets and Manpower Adjustment* (Lexington, Mass.: D. C. Heath, 1971).

(1970), "Equal Employment Opportunity in Boston," *Industrial Relations,* Vol. 10, No. 3, pp. 324–39.

Dore, Ronald (1973), *British Factory-Japanese Factory: The Origin of National Diversity in Industrial Relations* (Berkeley, Calif.: University of California Press).

Eisenstadt, Shmuel Noah (1954), *The Absorption of Immigrants* (London: Routledge & Paul).

Erickson, Charlotte (1972), *Invisible Immigrants: The Adaptation of English and Scottish Immigrants in 19th Century America* (Coral Gables, Fla.: University of Miami Press).

(1957), *American Industry and the European Immigrant, 1860–1885* (Cambridge, Mass.: Harvard University Press).

Fitzpatrick, Joseph P. (1971), *Puerto Rican Americans: The Meaning of Migration to the Mainland* (Englewood Cliffs, N.J.: Prentice-Hall).

Fragomen, Austin T., Jr. (1977), "1976 Amendments to the Immigration and Nationality Act," *International Migration Review*, Vol. 11, No. 1 (Spring 1973), pp. 95–100.

Friedlander, Peter (1975), *The Emergence of a U.A.W. Local, 1936–1939* (Pittsburgh, Pa.: University of Pittsburgh Press).

Friedlander, Stanley L. (1965), *Labor Migration and Economic Growth: A Case Study of Puerto Rico* (Cambridge, Mass.: M.I.T. Press).

Gamio, Manuel (1969), *Mexican Immigration to the United States* (New York: Arno Press).

Gans, Herbert J. (1967), *The Levittowners* (New York: Pantheon Books).

(1962), *The Urban Villagers* (New York: The Free Press).

Glazer, Nathan, and Daniel Patrick Moynihan (1963), *Beyond the Melting Pot* (Cambridge, Mass.: M.I.T. Press).

Grebler, Leo, Ralph C. Guzman, and Joan W. Moore (1970), *The Mexican-American People* (New York: The Free Press).

Greenwood, Michael J. (1975), "Research on Internal Migration in the United States: A Survey," *Journal of Economic Literature*, Vol. 13, No. 2, pp. 397–433.

Handlin, Oscar (1951), *The Uprooted* (Boston, Mass.: Little, Brown).

Harris, John R., and Michael P. Todaro (1970), "Migration, Unemployment and Development: A Two Sector Analysis," *American Economic Review*, Vol. 60, No. 1 (March 1970), pp. 126–42.

Hicks, J. R. (1963), *The Theory of Wages* (London: Macmillan).

Inoki, Takenori (1974), "Aspects of German Peasant Emigration to the United States, 1815–1914: A Reexamination of Some Behavioral Hypotheses in Migration Theory," MIT, unpublished doctoral dissertation.

Kayser, Bernard (1977), "L' echange inegal des ressources humaines: migration, croissance, et crise en Europe," *Revue Tier-Monde*, Vol. 17, No. 69, pp. 7–18.

(1971), *Manpower Movements and Labour Markets* (Paris: OECD).

Keely, Charles B., Patricia J. Elwell, Austin Fragomen, Jr., and Silvan M. Tomasi (1977), "Profiles of Undocumented Aliens in New York City: Haitians and Dominicans," paper presented to the Latin American Studies Association, Houston, Texas.

Kessner, Thomas (1977), *The Golden Door: Italian and Jewish Immigrant Mobility in New York City, 1880–1915* (New York: Oxford University Press).

Keynes, John M. (1958), *The General Theory of Employment, Interest and Money* (New York: Harcourt Brace).

Kindleberger, Charles P. (1967), *Europe's Postwar Growth: The Role of Labor Supply* (Cambridge, Mass.: Harvard University Press).

Korman, Gird (1967), *Industrialization, Immigrants and Americanizers: The View From Milwaukee, 1866–1921* (Madison, Wis.: The State Historical Society of Wisconsin).

Kuznets, Simon, and Ernest Rubin (1954), *Immigration and the Foreign Born* (New York: National Bureau of Economic Research), Occasional Paper No. 46.

Lebergott, Stanley (1964), *Manpower in Economic Growth* (New York: McGraw-Hill).

Lewis, Oscar (1966), *La Vida* (New York: Random House).

Liebow, Eliot (1967), *Tally's Corner* (Boston: Little, Brown).

Marglin, Stephen (1974), "What Do Bosses Do?" *The Review of Radical Political Economics,* Vol. 6, No. 2 (Summer 1974), pp. 33 – 60.

Martinez, John (1971), *Mexican Immigration to the U.S., 1910–1930* (San Francisco, Calif.: R. and E. Research Associates).

Maykovich, Manike (1976), "To Stay or Not to Stay: Dimensions of Ethnic Assimilation," *International Migration Review,* Vol. 10, No. 3, pp. 372–87.

Minces, Juiliette (1973), *Les travailleurs étrangers en France* (Paris: Editions du Seuil).

Moore, Joan W. (1976), *Mexican Americans* (Englewood Cliffs, N.J.: Prentice-Hall).

Myrdal, Gunnar (1962), *An American Dilemma* (New York: Harper & Row).

Nelson, Joan M. (1976), "Temporary Versus Permanent Cityward Migration: Causes and Consequences," MIT, Center for International Studies, Working Paper C/76-14, Migration and Development Study Group. A slightly different version of this paper appears under the same title in *Economic Development and Cultural Change,* Vol. 24, No. 4 (July 1976), pp. 721–57.

North, David S., and Marion F. Houstoun (1976), *The Characteristics and Role of Illegal Aliens in the U.S. Labor Market: An Exploratory Study* (Washington, D.C.: Linton)

Organization for Economic Cooperation and Development, Directorate for Social Affairs, Manpower and Education, *SOPEMI, Continuous Reporting System on Migration,* Annual Report, 1973, 1974, 1975, 1976, and 1977.

Osterman, Paul S. (1976), "The Labor Market for Young Men," unpublished doctoral dissertation, MIT, Department of Economics and Urban Studies.

Paci, Massimo (1973), *Mercato del lavoro e classi sociali in Italia* (Bologna: il Molino).

Piore, Michael J. (1978), "The Political and Economic Origins of Dualistic Structures in Labor Markets," MIT mimeo.

(1978), "Dualism in the Labor Market: A Response to Uncertainty and Flux, the Case of France," *Revue economique,* Vol. 19, No. 1, pp. 26–48.

(1976), "Immigration, Work Experience and Labor Market Structure," in Pastora San Juan Cafferty and Leon Chestang (eds.), *The Diverse Society: Implications for Social Policy* (Washington, D.C.: National Association of Social Workers).

(1976) "Notes for a Theory of Labor Market Stratification," in David Gordon et al. (eds.), *Labor Market Segmentation* (Lexington, Mass.: D. C. Heath).

(1975), "On the Technological Foundations of Economic Dualism," in Roberto Artioli (ed.), *Il dualismo nelle economie industriali* (Turino: Editoriale Valentino). Also appears as MIT, Department of Economics, Working Paper No. 110 (1973).

(1975), "The 'New Immigration' and the Presumptions of Social Policy," *Proceedings,* Industrial Relations Research Association, Madison, Wis.

(1974), "Labor Market Stratification and Wage Inflation," report prepared for Assistant Secretary for Policy Evaluation and Research, U.S. Department of Labor.

"Notes on Welfare Reform and the Design of Income Maintenance Systems," prepared for the Secretary's Committee on Work in America, Department of Health, Education and Welfare.

(1973), "Fragments of a Sociological Theory of Wages," *American Economic Review,* Vol. 63, No. 2, pp. 337–84.

and David P. Taylor (1971), "Federal Training Programs for Dispersed Employment Occupations," in Stanley M. Jacks (ed.), *Issues in Labor Policy; Papers in Honor of Douglas V. Brown* (Cambridge, Mass.: M.I.T. Press).

(1970), "Jobs and Training," in Samuel Beer and Richard Barringer, *The State and the Poor* (Cambridge, Mass.: Winthrop Publishers).

(1969), "On-the-Job Training in a Dual Labor Market: Public and Private Responsibilities in On-the-Job Training of Disadvantaged Workers," in Arnold Weber et al. (eds.), *Public-Private Manpower Policies* (Madison, Wis.: Industrial Relations Research Association).

(1968), "Changes in the Mississippi Agricultural Economy and the Problems of Displaced Negro Farm Workers," *American Journal of Psychotherapy*, Vol. 22, No. 4, pp. 592–601.

(1967), "Negro Workers in the Mississippi Delta: Problems of Displacement and Adjustment," *Proceedings,* Industrial Relations Research Association, Winter 1967, pp. 366–74.

Rosenblum, Gerald (1973), *Immigrant Workers: Their Impact on American Labor Radicalism* (New York: Basic Books).

Sabel, Charles (1978), "Industrial Conflicts and the Sociology of the Labor Market," unpublished doctoral dissertation, Harvard University.

Samora, Julian (1971), *Los Mojados: The Wetback Story* (Notre Dame, Ind.: University of Notre Dame Press).

Schneider, Jane, and Peter Schneider (1976), *Culture and Political Economy in Western Sicily* (New York: Academic Press).

Schwartz, Abba P. (1968), *The Open Society* (New York: Simon & Schuster).

Sennett, Richard, and Jonathan Cobb (1972), *The Hidden Inquiries of Class* (New York: Knopf).

Slater, Martin (1977), "Migration and Workers Conflicts in Western Europe," unpublished doctoral dissertation, MIT, Department of Political Science.

Spero, Sterling D., and Abram L. Harris (1968), *The Black Worker: The Negro and the Labor Movement* (New York: Atheneum).

Stevens, Rosemary, Louis Wolf Goodman, and Stephen S. Mick (1978), *The Alien Doctors: Foreign Medical Graduates in American Hospitals* (New York: John Wiley & Sons).

Stone, Katherine (1975), "The Origins of Job Structure in the Steel Industry," in Richard C. Edwards, Michael Reich, and David M. Gordon (eds.), *Labor Market Segmentation* (Lexington, Mass.: D. C. Heath).

Tapinos, Georges (1974), *L'economie des migrations internationales* (Paris: Librairie Armand Colin et Presses de la fondation nationale des sciences politiques).

Taylor, George W., and Frank C. Pierson (eds.) (1957), *New Concepts of Wage Determination* (New York: McGraw-Hill).

Thompson, E. P. (1963), *The Making of the English Working Class* (London: Victor Gollanez Ltd.).

Todaro, Michael P. (1968), "A Model of Labor Migration and Urban Unemployment in Less Developed Countries," *American Economic Review*, Vol. 58, pp. 138–48.

U.S. Congress, Immigration Commission (The Dillingham Commission) (1911), *Reports*, 42 Volumes (Washington, D.C.: U.S. Government Printing Office).

U.S. Department of Justice, Domestic Council on Illegal Aliens (1976), *Preliminary Report*, December.

U.S. Senate (1911), *Abstracts of Reports of the Immigration Commission*, 61st Congress, 3rd Session, Document No. 743, Immigration Commission (The Dillingham Commission) (Washington, D.C.: U.S. Government Printing Office).

Valentine, Charles A. (1968), *Culture and Poverty* (Chicago, Ill.: University of Chicago Press).

Weiner, Myron (1969), *Political Demography: An Inquiry into the Political Consequences of Population Change*, (Cambridge, Mass.: MIT Center for International Studies).

Wootton, Barbara (1955), *The Social Foundations of Wage Policy* (New York: W. W. Norton).

Zell, Steven (1973), "A Comparative Study of the Labor Market Characteristics of Return Migrants and Non-migrants in Puerto Rico," Commonwealth of Puerto Rico, Office of the Governor, Planning Board.

Index

absenteeism, 107
accounting for unemployment,
    106–7
adolescents, 66, 89
    in U.S. working class, 74
    see also children; youth in labor
        market
advancement
    of aliens, 174
    in jobs, 17
Africa, 116
    North Africa, 25, 133
aggregates, economic, 45–6
agricultural labor, 2, 41, 117, 153
    aspirations, 130
    collective, 124
    devaluation of, 131
    industrialization, 142–3
    job hierarchy, 58
    "old" immigration, 149
    peasant workers, 87, 91
    small-scale enterprises, 123, 125
    undocumented workers, 164–5
    unionization, 185
    variability, 46
    workers, 12, 20, 129
Aid to Families With Dependent
    Children (AFDC), 89–90
Algerian migration to France, 13, 56
America, *see* United States
amnesty for undocumented workers,
    187–8
apprentices, 142
Armenian migration to U.S., 151
aspirations, 125–6, 129
    second generation, 171
    settlement, 82

assembly-line jobs, 18
assimilation, 82–5, 129
    cultural, 116, 119
    settlement versus, 76–81
authority, 48
automobile-related jobs, 18, 41, 123

backward-bending supply curve, 27,
    95–8
balance of payments, 28
birth
    place of, 65
    in U.S. working class, 74
black Americans, 70, 130, 157
    education, 109, 118
    entrepreneurial activity, 117–18,
        126
    high-level jobs, 184
    migration in U.S., 5, 12, 15, 25,
        106, 147, 158–63, 164, 165
    organization of, 110
    recruitment of, 23, 159
    return migration, 140
    unionization, 112
    upward mobility, 101, 162
Bohemian migration to U.S., 151
Border Patrol, 175–6
Bosnian migration to U.S., 151
Boston, 67
    Italians in West End, 77
    Puerto Rican migration to, 5, 23–4,
        51, 68, 137
Bourdon, Clinton, 48
bracero program, 164, 177
Britain, 48–9
    migration to, 15
    "old" immigration, 148

British West Indies, 165
Brody, David, 152
Bulgarian migration to U.S., 151
bureaucracy, 175
buses, 123

Canadian migration to U.S., 173
capitalism, 36–37, 42–3
career, 53
  decisions, 71, 72
  settlement, 64–5
Caribbean basin, 132
  migration to U.S., 5–6, 12, 14, 134, 137, 148
  secondary labor market, 163
  undocumented workers, 163–6
caste, 27
Chandler, Alfred, 144
change
  institutional, 49
  resistance to, 31, 35
Chicano movement, 164
children, 72, 87
  education, 108–9
  immigration regulation, 182
  job values, 79–80
  "new" immigration, 155, 156
  turnover and, 107
  in U.S. working class, 74
civil rights movement, 130, 134
civil-service regulations, 109
Civil War, 148, 149
clandestine migration to U.S., 1, 3, 5–6, 163–6
  see also undocumented workers in U.S.
class struggle, 43
clerical jobs, 21
collective agriculture, 124
collective bargaining, 100
Colombia, 132, 133, 135
  undocumented migration to U.S., 164
commerce, 125, 126
communication jobs, 18
  in underdeveloped countries, 123
community, 68–81, 84
  alternate labor force, 90
  assimilation, 77
  first and second generation, 66
  home, 54, 63, 67, 130

settlement and development, 61–5
U.S. working class, 75–6
wage determination, 94
competition
  migrant-alternate labor forces, 86–93, 190
  migrant-native, 13, 81, 82, 86, 99, 167–9, 177
competitive market, 127
complaints, citizen, and immigration policy, 176
complementarity, migrant-native, 169
consciousness, political, 109
conscription, 93
consolidation, industrial, 144–6
construction jobs, 18, 20, 41
  in Europe, 121
  "new" immigration, 153
  unionization, 147
  undocumented Canadian workers, 173
  in U.S., 47, 48
  variability in, 46
consumer
  durable goods, 123
  environment, 117
consumption, 2, 29
  patterns of, 35, 56, 128, 129, 130
contract-labor program, 164
control of work force, 90, 92
Cornelius, Wayne, 125
corruption, 190–1
crafts, 142, 143
  associations, 111
  craftsmen, 53, 145
crime, 70
Croatian migration to U.S., 149, 150, 151, 152
Cuba, 132
  migration to U.S., 3, 56
culture
  industrial, 77
  of poverty, 69–76
currency, 104
curtailment of migrant labor, 17, 26, 28, 29, 32, 154, 157–8, 163, 164

Dalmatian migration to U.S., 151
dead-end jobs ,33, 89
decision-making model, 72

de jure–de facto immigration
  structure, 169, 172, 177
delayed gratification, 71
demand for migrants, 13, 16, 44, 141
  small-scale enterprises, 122
  variability of, 37, 45
departure, voluntary, 178
deportation of aliens, 178
devaluation of traditional
  occupations, 131
developed countries, 4–5, 140
  job hierarchies, 57–68
  migration from underdeveloped,
    16, 25
developing countries, 51
development
  external migration, 136
  migration, 115–27, 139, 140
  U.S. aid and immigration
    regulation, 189
Diez-Canedo, Juan, 103, 123–6, 130,
  136
disadvantaged groups, 167–9
discharge, 38, 39, 41, 105
  unions and, 146
distaste for available work, 107
division of labor, 10–11
documentation, 137, 138
  immigration regulation, 179, 180
domestic work, 19, 20, 173
Dominican Republic, 132
donor countries, impact of
  migration, 59, 133–40
dualism, 36, 121–2
dual labor-market structure, 35–43,
  44–5, 47
  in Italy, 88
  settlement and, 78
due process, 190–2
durability of work force, 90, 92
Dutch migration to U.S., 151

Eastern Europe
  migration to U.S., 12, 15, 147
  recruitment by France, 25
East Germany, 13, 56
East Prussia, 133
economic aggregates, 45–6
economics
  Marxian analysis, 9–11
  profession of, 6–7
economistic view of wages, 93

education, 4, 93, 108, 139
  black Americans, 109, 118
  middle-class migration, 139
  settlement and, 80–3
  upward mobility, 111, 172
efficiency, 122
ejidos, 124, 136
elasticity of labor supply, 98
employee-initiated turnover, 104
  see also labor
employers, 92, 175
  backward-bending supply curve,
    96–7, 98
  complaints by, 186
  liability for undocumented
    workers, 182, 183, 184, 188
  Marxian economics, 9
  recruitment by, 17, 19–24, 30
  supply of labor, 98–9
employment, 9
enforcement of U.S. immigration
  regulations, 173
English migration to U.S., 151
entrepreneurial status, 117, 125, 126
entry restrictions, 106, 109 180–1
equal employment opportunity, 91
equilibrium, 108
equity
  due process, 190–2
  immigration policy, 178, 179, 182
Erickson, Charlotte, 148, 153, 154
ethnic communities, 68, 70
  traits of, 106
Europe, 3, 12, 121, 133, 135
  dual labor-market hypothesis, 41
  labor markets, 6, 18, 133
  job security, 47
  U.S. recruitment in, 24
  see also Eastern Europe; Northern
    Europe; Southern Europe,
    migration to U.S.; Western
    Europe
expansion, 27, 143–4
expectations, 125–6
  immigration process, 170–1
external migration, 133–40

factory production, 142, 143–4
failure and migration, 50, 60–1
family, 1–2, 71
  community development, 63
  culture of poverty, 69

first and second generation, 66–7
public assistance system, 89–90
settlement, 77–81
U.S. immigration regulations, 172,
179, 180, 187
U.S. working class, 73–6
farmers, 21, 88
see also agricultural labor
fatalism, 94
father, 74
Finnish migration to U.S., 151
first-generation migrants, 65–8, 92
job turnover, 107
union organization, 114
see also second-generation migrants
fishing jobs, 20
fixed-duration contracts, 84
Flemish migration to U.S., 151
flexibility, 122
flux in economic activity, 39, 43, 45
foreign-born in U.S., 156
foreign exchange, 1, 2, 116
forestry jobs, 20
France, 1, 48
dual labor-market hypothesis, 38,
39, 41
immigration to, 15, 18, 19, 20, 21,
26
migration to U.S., 151
permanent migrant settlement in,
56
recruitment by, 24, 25
substitution of migrants for
women, 91
free-floaters, 103
French Antilles, 132
French Guiana, 132
"frictional" unemployment, 103
friends, 73
see also peer group
fugitives, 174

Gans, Herbert, 77, 78, 80, 81
garment industry, 100
unions in, 112
Germany, 1, 48, 55, 135
dual labor-market hypothesis, 41
immigration to, 15, 18, 20, 23, 26,
152
migration to U.S., 148, 151
recruitment of migrants by, 24, 25

West Germany, 1, 13, 24, 51, 56,
83–4
ghetto, 70
government
jobs, 18, 20
market management, 46
recruitment of migrants by, 23
regulation of wages, 99
see also United States
grandfather, 74
Great Depression, 157
Greek-Americans, 130
Greek migration to U.S., 149, 151
growth, economic, 4, 44

Haiti, 132, 135, 137
undocumented migration to U.S.,
164
Harris, John R., 108
health
services, 83
standards, 5, 185
Hebrew immigration to U.S., 151
Herzegovinian migration to U.S., 151
hierarchy, 33–5
development and, 57–8
immigration policy, 168
migration and, 33–5, 44
wage determination, 93
higher education, 93
Hispanic migrants, 112
see also Puerto Rican migration
home community, 54, 130
settlement, 63, 67
household
help, 173
units, 142, 149
workers, 21
housewives in labor market, 87,
88–9, 91, 92, 189–90
housing, 2, 84
human-capital theory, 108
husband, 74

illegal aliens, 51
illiteracy, 57
immigration, 167–72
limiting, 26
"new," 147, 148, 149–57
"old," 147, 148–9, 153
reform of U.S. system, 180–4
see also migration

Immigration and Naturalization
  Service (INS), 173–6, 178, 186,
  190, 191, 192
Immigration Commission, 148, 149,
  150, 152
imports, 116
incipient industrialization, 142–3
income, 7–8, 52–3
  differential, 4–5, 8, 25, 57
  settlement and, 78
  success, 61
  temporary migration, 54
  unionization, 113
independence, 117
Independentista movement, 130
individualism, 62
industrial countries, 113
  migration to, 3, 12, 128, 139
  settlement and assimilation, 81, 82
  unemployment in, 102, 108
industrialization, 87, 120–2, 125
  consolidation, 144–6
  incipient, 142–3
  industrial culture, 77
  Marxian economic analysis, 10–11
  migration characteristics, 4–5
  "new" immigration, 153
  oligopolistic, 84
  in underdeveloped nations, 59
inertia, 53
  of economic structure, 31, 35
inflation, 190
  structural, 31–3
informal sector of economy, 102,
  108, 122
information, 58
insecurity, job, 17
instability
  cyclical, 45
  unemployment, 105
institutions, 47, 48, 49
insubordination, 107
integration, social, 116
internal migration, 51, 133–40
  in developing countries, 51
  in U.S., 147–8, 157–63
International Labor Organization,
  122
Ireland, 130
  migration to Boston, 67
  migration to Britain, 15, 151
  migration to U.S., 56, 148, 151

Iron Curtain, 25
Israeli state, 130
Italy, 38, 39, 130
  dual labor-market structure, 88
  internal migration, 136, 140
  Italians in Boston, 77, 80, 81
  labor surplus, 133
  migration to U.S., 149, 150, 151,
    152, 155, 156, 160
  recruitment of Italians, 24, 25
  unionization, 122

Jalisco, Mexico, 123–5, 126, 130
Japan, 48–9
Jews, 70, 79
  migration to U.S., 13, 56
  unions, 112
  Zionist movement, 130
jobs, 2, 15–49, 58, 78, 141
  dead-end, 33
  description of, 7
  hierarchy, 33–5
  security, 39, 47, 48–9, 59, 64–5,
    105, 146;
  social roles, 52–3
  stability in U.S. working class, 74
  see also primary job sector;
    secondary job sector
"job shop," 37–8
journeymen, 142
justice, 191

Keynesian economics, 45–6
Kuznets, Simon, 148, 150, 154

labor
  agents, 152–3
  capitalism, 36–7, 42–3
  demand for migrants, 13, 16, 44,
    141
  division of, 10–11
  dual labor-market hypothesis,
    35–43, 44–5, 47, 78, 88
  immigration regulation, 175
  -intensive technique, 36–7
  migration characteristics, 4–15
  shortages, 26–31, 32, 96, 97, 131,
    172
  specialization, 142, 144
  substitute supply, 44
  supply of, 25–6, 44, 95, 98–9
  in U.S., 6
  wage determination, 100

Labor Department, 47
labor market, 7, 174, 192
  characteristics of migrant, 86
  culture of poverty, 71
  settled communities, 67
  social roles, 53
  structure in U.S., 141–7
  unemployment, 102–8
  U.S. immigration policy, 168–9
  U.S. working class, 74–6
labor movement, *see* union
    organization
land-tenure systems, 126, 136
large-scale production, 142, 145
latecomers in community, 67
Latin American migrants, 54–5, 62,
    79
  middle-class migration to U.S.,
    137, 138
  secondary job sector, 163
  undocumented, 163–6
La Vida, 69, 70
law, 123
  enforcement, 187–8, 191
layoff, 38, 39, 41, 105
  by seniority, 49
  unionization, 146
leadership, 110–11
legal status of immigrants, 27
legislation restricting immigration,
    154, 157–8, 163, 164
legitimization of undocumented
    workers, 184, 186–8
leisure time, 89
Lewis, Oscar, 69
licensing requirements, 109
Liebow, Eliot, 69
Lithuanian migration to U.S., 151
living standards, 29
long-distance migration, 12
  in U.S., 141, 189
longshoring, 147
low-income communities,
    unemployment in, 102
low-wage sector, 141

macroeconomic theory, 45, 190
  wage structure, 32
Magyar migration to U.S., 150, 151,
    152
managerial workers, 9, 21, 118
manipulation of work force, 90, 92

manpower programs, 88
manual jobs, 18, 21
manufacturing
  hierarchy, 58
  jobs, 18, 20, 23
  "old" immigration, 149
  return migration, 117
  trusts, 142
marginal workers, 168
market
  competitive, 127
  control, 144
  mechanism in Keynesian formula, 45
  see also labor market
marriage, 74
Marxian economic analysis, 9–11, 42
mass production, 37
matriarchal families, 69
maturation, 72, 74
mechanization, 134
medical care system, 123, 185
  dual labor-market hypothesis, 40
  national, 101
melting pot, 76
men
  in community development, 63
  culture of poverty, 69
  U.S. working class, 73
Mexico, 135, 157, 170
  immigration regulation, 173,
    174–6, 177, 179, 180–2
  migration to U.S., 6, 8–9, 12, 14,
    25, 47, 147–8
  quota, 187
  temporary migration, 51, 54, 55
  two-stage migration, 136
  undocumented migration to U.S.,
    164–5, 166
microeconomics, 32
middle class
  adolescents, 75
  migration to U.S., 137–40
Middle East, 116
migrants
  demand for, 13, 16, 44, 141
  ethnic groups, 150
  leadership, 110–11
  length of stay, 99
  organization of, 13, 86, 108–14
  recruitment of, 17, 19–24, 28, 30,
    85, 152–3
  U.S. working class, 75

migration
  characteristics, 3–14, 16–26
  curtailment, 17, 26, 28, 29, 32, 154,
    157–8, 163, 164
  development process, 119–20
  disruptive effects, 71–2
  external, 133–40
  goals of immigration policy,
    167–72
  image of, 50
  internal, 51, 133–40, 147–8,
    157–63
  labor shortages, 26–31
  long-distance, 12, 141, 189
  middle-class, 137–9
  reform of U.S. system, 180–4
  as safety valve, 115, 127–33
  size of labor market, 30
  social context, 8
  spontaneous, 25–6
  temporary patterns, 50, 52
  two-stage, 136
  unemployment, 102–8
  U.S. working class, 75–6
  see also return migration
military service, 93, 168
minimum wage, 5, 42, 93–5
  immigration reform, 185, 186
  in permanent communities,
    99–101
  "social," 5
  statutory, 94, 97
mining jobs, 20
mobility in labor market, 90, 91
money, 55–6
moneylenders, 124
monopoly, 144, 145
Montenegrin migration to U.S., 151
moratorium, 89
Moravian migration to U.S., 151
mothers, 88, 92
motivation, 34, 44
  economic development, 119
Moxhamn, Arthur, 144
Myrdal, Gunnar, 158

nationality, 28
National Labor Relations Act, 185
National Labor Relations Board, 100
nation-states, 135–6
native workers, 3
  aspirations of, 171

children of migrants as natives, 60
competition with migrants, 13, 81,
  82, 86, 99, 167–9, 177
disadvantaged, 168
dual labor-market hypothesis, 35,
  41
undesirable work, 107
unionization, 112, 113, 157
unskilled jobs, 120
Negroes, *see* black Americans
New Deal, 157
"new" immigration, 147, 148,
  149–57
"new" new immigration, 148
New York (city)
  denial of public services to
    migrants, 182
  Puerto Rican migration to, 68, 137,
    165
night shifts, 91
North Africa, 25, 133
Northern Europe, 1
  "new" immigration, 149
  "old" immigration, 148
Northwestern Europe, 147

occupational structure, 131, 139
"old" immigration, 147, 148–9, 153
oligopolistic industries, 84
opportunities, 171
organization of migrant workers, 13,
  86, 108–14
Orient, undocumented migration to
  U.S., 164
Osterman, Paul, 89
out-migration, 115
  political impact of, 125

parents, 90
  see also family
parole of undocumented workers,
  178
passports, 137
patriarch, 74
peasant-workers, 129
  in labor marekt, 87–8, 91, 92
  tradition, 117
peer group, 73–6, 77
pension programs, 112
period of moratorium, 89
permanent migrant settlements, 3,
  50, 52, 56, 76, 81, 167, 186
  black American, 158

culture of poverty, 70
length of stay, 99
minimum wage determination,
    99–100
"old" immigration, 148
organization of migrants, 109–10
undocumented workers, 166
U.S. immigration policy, 171, 172,
    177
personal relationships in culture of
    poverty, 69
personal services, 19
pioneers, 128
place of origin, 54, 115
planning, 126, 127
plasticity of work force, 90
Poland, 133, 135
    migration to U.S., 149, 150, 151,
        152, 155, 156, 160
    recruitment of migrants by France,
        25
policy affecting migration, 6, 81–5,
    115, 171, 172, 177
politics
    black community, 163
    consciousness, 109
    participation of ethnic
        communities, 110
    power, 111
    pressure and immigration, 176
    second generation, 129
    worker organization, 42
poor communities, 68
population, 115–16
    flows
        (developed–
            underdeveloped), 58
    migration as safety valves, 127–8
    pressure, 1
Portugal
    migration to U.S., 151
    recruitment of migrants in, 25, 133
poverty, 68
    culture of, 69–73, 76
power, political, 111
preindustrial work organization,
    142
preschooling, 93
prestige in wage structure, 31–2
primary job sector, 35–43
    black Americans, 163
    native disadvantaged workers, 168

permanent migrant settlement, 67
    see also secondary job sector
production, 10–11
    elimination of migrants, 29
    large-scale, 144
    technology of, 36
professionals, 53, 123
    associations of, 94, 111
    black American, 118
promiscuity, 71
promotion, 59
public assistance system, 89–90
public services, denial of, 182
Puerto Rican migration, 57, 83–4,
    131–2, 147, 165–6
    to Boston, 5, 23–4, 51, 68, 137
    Independentista movement, 130
    to New York City, 68, 137
    political participation, 110
    return migration, 140
    temporary patterns of migration,
        54
putting-out system, 142–3

quota system, 154, 187

race
    conflict, 161–3
    prejudice, 2
    traits, 106
racism in Immigration Commission,
    152
railroads, 144, 164
recruitment of migrants, 17, 19–24,
    28, 30, 85, 152–3
    of black American workers, 23, 24,
        159
    return migration, 116
reentry of migrants, 180, 181
reform of U.S. immigration system,
    180–4
relatives, 178
religion, 118
remittances, migrant, 116, 123–4,
    126, 130
repatriation of undocumented
    workers, 165, 167
resources, immigrant, 125
restrictions on migration, 168, 182,
    185
    high-level manpower, 184–5
    legislation, 154, 157–8, 163, 164
retirement benefits, 168

return migration, 2, 115–19, 125, 150, 153
  economic development, 189
  Puerto Rican, 140
  U.S. immigration system, 172
revolution, 10, 11
riots, 161, 165
roles, 71, 72
  alternate labor force groups, 90
  U.S. working class, 73
  work and family, 77
Roumanian migration to U.S., 149, 151
Rubin, Ernest, 148, 150, 154
rural migration, 28, 56, 138, 139
Russian migration to U.S., 149, 150, 151
Ruthenian migration to U.S., 151

sabotage, 32
safety standards, 5, 185
safety valve, migration as, 115, 127–33
sail, 149
sales jobs, 21
Santo Domingo, 132, 135, 137
  undocumented migration to U.S., 164
Sardinia, 133
Scandinavian migration to U.S., 151
school, 109
  compulsory attendance, 168
  settlement and, 80
  youth in labor market, 89, 91
  see also education
Scotch migration to U.S., 151
seasonal industry, 37
secondary job sector, 35–43, 141
  black Americans, 163, 166
  culture of poverty, 69
  native disadvantaged workers, 168
  permanent migrants, 56, 67
  reduction in size, 184, 185–6
  settlement and, 78
  undocumented workers, 179, 180, 183
  unemployment, 189–90
second-generation migrants, 65–8, 87, 92, 129
  competition with natives, 82
  denial of public services, 182
  distaste for types of work, 107, 131

immigration policy, 169, 171–2, 177
  "new" immigration, 156
  return migration, 118
  unionization, 113, 157
  upward mobility, 11, 162
  unemployment, 106
  U.S. working class, 76
security, job, 39, 47, 48–9, 59, 64–5, 105, 146
self-employment, 20, 138
self-perception, 54
seniority, 41
  layoff by, 49
Servian migration to U.S., 151, 152
service workers, 21, 121
  and job hierarchy, 58
settlement process, 59–65, 75–6, 87, 106–7, 169, 171, 185
  assimilation, 76–81
  culture of poverty as model, 76
  public policy, 82–5
  upward mobility, 154–7
sewing machines, 117
Sicily, 133
skill
  dual labor-market hypothesis, 37, 38, 40
  industrial, 116, 119, 120
  in labor, 4, 10
  requirement of jobs, 37
  turnover, 97
Slovak migration to U.S., 149, 150, 151, 152
Slovenians, 150, 151
slowdowns, 32
small-scale enterprises
  industrial consolidation, 145
  return migration, 117, 122–3, 126
Smith, Adam, 37, 143, 144
social context of migration, 8, 52–4
  labor market, 94
  in workplace, 105
socialism, 10, 11
socialization of production, 10
"social minimum" wage, 95, 101
social security system, 101
social services, 83
  denial of, 182
social-welfare reforms, 142
Southern Europe, migration to U.S., 12, 15, 147

undocumented, 164
Spain
    internal migration, 136, 140
    labor surplus, 133
    migration to U.S., 150, 151
    recruitment of migrants in, 25
Spanish-speaking Americans, 147–8
specialization of labor, 142, 144
standard of living, 185
State Department, 180, 181
status, 17, 80, 89
    consciousness, 65
    hierarchy, 33
    migration, 27, 59
    settlement, 64–5, 78
    wage structure, 31–2
statutory minimum wage, 94, 97
steelworkers, 152
"streetwise" children, 66
strikes, 32, 113
    strikebreakers, 113
success in migrants, 60–1
supplemental income, 88
supply of labor, 25–6, 44, 95, 98–9
    curve, 27, 95–8
    migrant, 17, 95, 141, 147–8
    wage determination, 93
Sweden, 148
Switzerland, 134–5
    migration to, 15
Syrian migration to U.S., 151

Tally's Corner, 69, 70
target earning, 27, 61, 95–8, 99,
    123
taxis, 123
technology, 4, 58
    development and, 36
    new industry, 153
    production, 36
telegraphy, 144
temporary patterns of migration, 3,
    50, 52, 54, 56, 59–60, 186
    organization of migrants, 109–10
    settlement and community, 76
textile industry, 100
    in Jalisco, Mexico, 123–5
time horizon, 59
    culture of poverty, 71
    in permanent settlements, 64
    unionization, 113, 114
Todero, Michael P., 108

tourists, 179
    visas, 181
trade jobs, 18, 20
trade union, *see* union organization
trainee, 119
training, 108–9
    institutions, 83
    on-the-job, 119
    upward mobility, 172
traits, 82, 83
transatlantic crossing, 154
transient migrants, 103
    culture of poverty, 70, 71, 76
    incipient industrialization, 145
    old and new immigration, 150–2
    permanent migrant settlements, 81
    unemployment, 107, 108
transportation jobs, 18, 20, 84
    migration and, 137, 138
    in underdeveloped countries, 123
trusts movement, 144–6
Turkey
    migration to U.S., 151
    recruitment in, 24, 25
turnover, 27
    culture of poverty, 69, 70, 71
    employee-initiated, 104
    natives' work attitudes, 107
    unemployment, 102, 105
    unionization, 100–1, 112
    unskilled labor, 97
two-stage migration, 136

uncertainty in economic activity, 39,
    43, 45
underdeveloped regions, 3, 4–5, 115,
    120, 139, 188
    migration to developed regions,
    16, 25
    temporary migration, 57
    unemployment in, 102
underground labor market, 104
underprivileged groups, 167–8
undocumented workers in U.S., 5, 8,
    14, 148, 163–6
    U.S. immigration policy, 173, 177,
    183
unemployment, 1, 3, 13, 86, 94
    community settlement, 64
    "frictional," 103
    immigration policy, 168, 188,
    189–90

unemployment *(cont.)*
  insurance, 168
  low-status jobs, 58
  migrant labor markets, 102–8
  racial conflicts, 161, 162, 165
  rural, in Puerto Rico, 131
  unionization, 147
union organization, 109, 111–14,
  146–7, 161, 183, 185, 186
  immigrants and, 27
  in U.S., 18, 41, 48, 156, 157
  wage determination, 94, 100
United States
  dual labor-market hypothesis, 38,
    39, 40, 41
  education, 109
  external and internal migration,
    133–40, 147–8, 157–63
  farmer-workers, 80
  history of migration in, 14
  immigration policy, 167, 172–80, 189
  inflation, 190
  job characteristics, 16
  labor market, 6
  long-distance migration, 141
  migration to, 1, 3, 12, 20, 21, 26,
    151, 155, 156
  Mexican migration to, 6, 8–9, 12,
    14, 25, 47, 147–8
  political leadership, 110
  public assistance system, 89–90
  unionization, 112, 113
  working class in, 73–6
  see also black Americans,
    undocumented workers in U.S.
unskilled work, 3, 17, 105
  dual labor-market hypothesis, 41
  labor shortages, 97
upward mobility, 111
  black Americans, 101, 162
  education, 111
  legitimizing aliens, 186, 188
  middle-class migration, 138, 140
  public policy, 168, 169, 171
  reducing secondary job sector, 185
  rural versus urban, 58
  settlement, 154–7
  undocumented workers, 166, 179
urban migrants, 56
urban regions and job hierarchies, 58
urban renewal, 81
Urban Village, The, 77, 79

value structure, and assimilation, 77,
  79, 82
variability of demand, 37, 41, 45, 46,
  84
Venezuela, 133, 135
violence, 161, 162, 175
visas, 137
visitors, 179
voluntary departure, 178
voting behavior, 157
voyage, 149

wages, 2
  determination of, 13, 86, 93–101
  differential, 100
  labor shortage, 96, 132
  settlement, 64
  structure of, 31–3
  subsidy, 131
  unemployment, 108
  see also minimum wage
welfare, 89–90
  immigration policy, 168
  race conflict, 161, 165
  services, 83
Welsh migration to U.S., 151
Western Europe, 1, 115–16
  "new" immigration, 149
  permanent migrants, 56
  unionization, 112
West Germany, 1
  migration from East Germany, 13,
    56
  organization of migration process,
    83–4
  recruitment of migrants by, 24, 51
wife, 88
women, 88, 90–91, 92, 101, 168, 189
  black, 15
  in community development, 63
  culture of poverty, 69
  rights of, 92
  target earning, 95–6
  in U.S. working class, 73
work, 17
  conditions, 2, 17
  permits, 179, 188
  roles, 77–8
  see also jobs; labor
workers, 7
  consolidation of, 146–7
  former, 88

marginal, 168
in Marxian economics, 9
organization of, 86, 108–14
peasant-, 87–8, 91, 92, 117, 129
politics of organization, 42
working class, 73–6, 117
World War I, 163, 164
  migration and, 154
  internal migration and, 157

World War II, 158

Young Lords, 130
youth in labor market, 87, 89, 90–1,
  92, 93, 101, 168, 189–90
  target earning, 96
Yugoslavia, 25, 130

Zionist movement, 130